Praise for The Last Madam

"In this world there are great characters who have no idea that they are great characters, and great characters who are fully aware of their greatness. [Norma] Wallace must be counted among the latter. She had the wit of Dorothy Parker and the instinct for self-dramatization of Tallulah Bankhead."

Michael Lewis, *New York Times Book Review*

"Christine Wiltz has done a remarkable and rare thing: she has captured perfectly the essential, earthy complexity of the most fascinating city on this continent. *The Last Madam* is an exhilarating mardi gras of a book."

Robert Olen Butler

"The arresting story of a domineering, conflicted American businesswoman and a vivid social study ᵣᶠ ᵗᵇᵉ ᶦᵗᵢᵐᵃᵗₑ ᵣₒₕₐᵦᵢₜₐₜᵢₒₙ ₒᶠ politics and vice in the Crescent City."

Minneapolis Star-Tribune

"Juicy, jaunty."

D1124785

Entertainment Weekly

"Affecting . . . Wiltz elevates a sometimes impeccably assembled historical narrative above its elementary bawdy elements into something more elegant and fragile: the resurrection of a secret world like those uncovered by Luc Sante and James Ellroy."

Publishers Weekly

"In New Orleans the water table is so high the underworld is never far beneath the surface. *The Last Madam* is a fascinating study of the unrivaled Mistress of that world, delightful and serious by turns, an insider's look at an insider's life in a city both know and love."

Valerie Martin, author of *Mary Reilly*

"Wiltz . . . roams beyond Wallace's professional and romantic affairs to spotlight her state's infamously crooked politics, the licensed depravities of the French Quarter, and Wallace's humorous attempt to realize a pastoral ideal in the backwoods amid a community of righteous citizens."

Kirkus Reviews

"In telling [Wallace's] remarkable story, Christine Wiltz has vividly re-created the New Orleans underworld in the first half of the 20th century. It is hardly pretty, but it is never less than absorbing. . . . A journey of revelation, the discovery of a secret world."

The State (Columbia, SC)

"The book takes the reader by the hand just as Norma's girls did when they took a customer into one of her upstairs rooms. It's always reassuring to be in the hands of a pro, and *The Last Madam* gives the reader this feeling right from the get-go. It provides as good an experience in its way as Wallace must have in hers."

David Cuthbert, *Times-Picayune*

Glass House (1994)
The Emerald Lizard (1991)
A Diamond Before You Die (1987)
The Killing Circle (1981)

The Last Madam

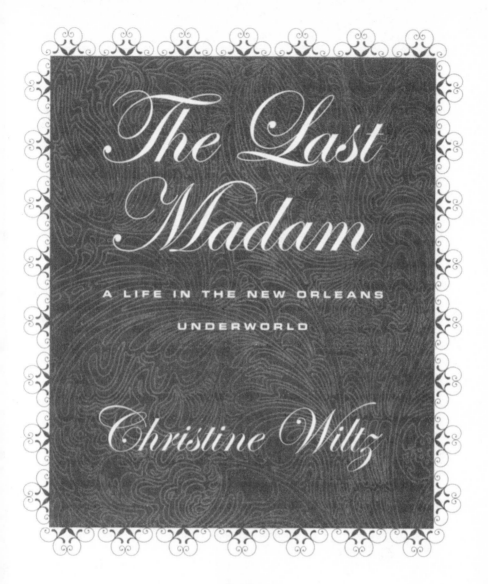

The Last Madam

A LIFE IN THE NEW ORLEANS

UNDERWORLD

Christine Wiltz

DA CAPO PRESS

Grateful acknowledgment is made to the following for permission to reproduce photographs in this book: *The New Orleans Times-Picayune* for photographs of Norma Wallace in the 1930s and at her grand jury appearance; the Vieux Carré Commission for photographs of 1026 Conti Street and of Pete's Ringside Bar; the Historic New Orleans Collection for the photograph of Canal Street in the 1950s; the New Orleans Public Library Louisiana Division for photographs of Frederick Soulé and Jim Garrison; Charles Gennaro for Randy Moses' photographs of Norma's nudes, painted by Pâl Fried; Louis E. Darré for his photograph of Norma that appeared in *New Orleans* magazine; and John Datri and Paul Nazar for photographs of themselves. All other photographs appear courtesy of Wayne Bernard.

Designed by Jonathan D. Lippincott

CIP information for this book is available from the Library of Congress.

First Da Capo Press Edition 2001
ISBN-13 978-0-306-81012-1   ISBN-10 0-306-81012-3

Published by Da Capo Press
A Member of the Perseus Books Group
http://www.dacapopress.com

20 19

To the girls

Contents

The Last Madam

CHAPTER ONE

Lemon Pie

Norma Wallace stood on a bed of pine needles deep in the Mississippi woods, dressed in a smart red pantsuit and low-vamp leather pumps; she spread her feet apart, sighted down the barrel of her .410 shotgun, and blew the head off the rattlesnake in front of her. There had been a time, not so long ago, when shooting a rattler made Norma feel like a cowgirl. Now the very sight of one made her jumpy as an old maid. The isolation of the place was getting to her. Her Irish setter, Rusty, ran ahead as she walked to the cedar-shingled house. He seemed to be her only company lately.

Norma's hands shook slightly as she put the gun on the rack. Settling herself on the plush-velvet contour sofa facing the brick fireplace, she listened for the sound of a car on the two-and-a-half-mile road to the house. Her white hair glowed in the firelight.

Norma's young husband, Wayne Bernard, didn't always make it home these days. Sometimes he called, but it was getting dark now, and she'd heard nothing from him. She could feel a long night stretching out before her.

The clock on the mantel softly chimed seven. Norma got a rush of the old excitement and anticipation—what was this night going to bring? She'd had that feeling at nightfall for over forty years, when she ran her business in the French Quarter. Tonight it passed quickly, because now her life was all about waiting, worrying, and remembering. To pass the time she started dictating into the tape recorder beside her. Her hope was that she'd come up with a best-selling book about her life and times as the last madam of New Orleans to run an elegant French Quarter parlor house.

"How do you write a book about forty years of intrigue, fools, deals, and propositions—that panorama so peculiar to New Orleans?" she mused. Her voice was deep and raspy, though not the whiskey voice given to madams in the movies. She had a trace of an accent, not Southern but New Orleans, that slow way of talking associated with downtown, an accent that sounds like Manhattan in a tropical heat wave.

More to the point, she wondered how she'd gotten from a life of adventure and intrigue to this one, that of the disappointed wife waiting at home. That word—*disappointed*—triggered her memory, and she began telling her tape recorder a story about her childhood, the only story she chose to tell about her early years.

"The greatest disappointment of my life happened when I was eight. We were so poor that we used to move instead of pay the rent. An old colored man with a horse and wagon would move us for two bucks, which was cheaper than paying eight dollars for the house."

Many people were poor in 1909, as revealed by the number of empty houses on New Orleans's streets. "People would all hole up in the same place because it took four or five of them to make a living and pay the rent. But we were just my parents, my brother, Elmo, and me. So we would move about every three months, after the landlord knew he was beat and put us out. We finally got so hot in one neighborhood that we had to move to another section of town."

The family found a small place with no gas or electricity on Salcedo Street in what Norma called the back part of town, now Mid-City. The amenities were a coal-burning stove and an outhouse.

Eight-year-old Norma would have liked to have had a new dress, something pretty and frilly, but mostly she wanted something to eat. There wasn't much to cook on that old stove, and Norma was hungry all the time. The worst of it was that on the corner was a bakery. They baked little lemon pies, and Norma could smell them, their mouthwatering aroma filling the neighborhood, the house, even her dreams. What she wouldn't have given for one of those pies! They sold for ten cents each, as out of reach as a party dress—or the moon. But that didn't keep Norma from nagging her mother about them.

Then one evening her father brought home a boarder, Mr. McCann. "How was he going to board with us? We didn't have anything to eat! I don't even know where he slept because I don't remember but two beds. But he came to live with us. He was an alcoholic, and he used to drink Four Roses. I've remembered Mr. McCann with his Four Roses all my life. He stayed pretty drunk, but we needed the help bad so we would take a chance on anything.

"Every day I smelled those lemon pies and I was dying for one. Lemon pie became the big thing in my life. I would needle my mother—I have to have one!"

Norma's mother finally said, "When Mr. McCann pays next time, I'll get you a lemon pie." His rent was due in three weeks. Norma was counting the days.

"So here it was three weeks later, and I'm figuring the next day I'll be eating lemon pie. That evening Mr. McCann went out to the toilet in the yard and he didn't come back. After a long time my mother decided she better go check on him. She came back pretty shook up. Mr. McCann had drunk carbolic acid and he was dead, dead.

"And that was the end of lemon pie for me." Norma laughed.

"That was the first great disappointment of my life."

Four years after the suicide of Mr. McCann, Norma began to figure out how to get what she wanted. Before that her life was all about deprivation, and her earliest memories were of poverty.

When Norma Lenore Badon was only three months old, her parents moved from McComb, Mississippi, where she was born, to New Orleans. Her father, John Gauley Badon, had come from Covington, Louisiana, on the north shore of Lake Pontchartrain across from New Orleans. Her mother, Amanda Easley Badon, was the daughter of Warren Easley, the first mayor of McComb.

In 1972, when the writer Clint Bolton profiled Norma for *New Orleans* magazine, she told him that both her parents had come from good families, that her mother was college educated at Bowling Green, Kentucky, and played the piano. She told Bolton that all her mother had ever wanted was to get to New Orleans. She didn't tell him why, though, or what happened after the family got there. Nor did she confide to her tape recorder the horror of her first twelve years, except to tell about the suicide of Mr. McCann, a pivotal episode in her young life, to be sure, but one that she told in a spirit of self-mockery.

Years later Norma told her sister-in-law Helen Moran, the wife of her half brother, J. G. Badon, that her mother had wanted to come to New Orleans to live the wild life, and that her own mother had put her out on the streets as a prostitute. To other confidantes she recalled how her mother had left her and Elmo, who was five years younger than Norma, alone in the French Quarter for weeks at a time after Gauley Badon abandoned the family because he caught Amanda in bed with another man. The children were left with no money and no food, in a house with no electricity or heat. Elmo stole food to keep them alive, until the black families who were their neighbors realized that the children were starving and uncared for and took them in. When Norma became wealthy she made it possible for those people to own their homes.

She said to Helen, "I'll tell you what kind of mother I had. I can remember her bathing Elmo, and she'd take his little penis and say, 'Boy, this is going to make some women happy!' "

But that was confidential information, not for public consumption in either Bolton's profile or Norma's memoirs. Norma held her family's secrets close, not because she was ashamed but because she had great family loyalty. In spite of Amanda's irresponsibility, Norma bought her a house and took care of her until she died. She resented that Gauley had abandoned her and Elmo, and that he later moved to Slidell, a town about forty miles from New Orleans, where he started a lumber business with his brothers, one of whom, Eugene, became the town sheriff and the other, Alonzo, the mayor. Gauley also started another family, a respectable family. But he did not fare as well as his two brothers. He had drinking problems and money problems, and somewhere along the line Norma bought him a piece of property called Shady Pond, on the Pearl River, which she then said she'd inherited after Gauley died.

Gauley also had a sister, Carrie Badon, who had a wild streak like Norma's mother, Amanda. Alonzo and Eugene wouldn't let their daughters speak to Carrie, but Norma was close to her aunt until Carrie died, even taking care of her during a long illness. Amanda and Carrie operated as prostitutes in the French Quarter for a time, but eventually they both found husbands.

In her memoirs Norma said she didn't have much education, that if you didn't go to school, nobody cared, so she didn't go more than a year or two, which she regretted. But she matured early. A small girl, never weighing over eighty-five or ninety pounds, she menstruated at eleven and developed young. Innately intelligent and street smart, Norma developed two personas early in her life: one that operated in the respectable world of family and another that was equally comfortable in the underworld.

Her nature was to put a positive spin on events, but her parents' actions had set her on a life course from which there would be no return. Norma's parents had split up by the time she was twelve; the year was 1913. Storyville was still going strong just across Basin Street from the Quarter, but a shoot-out that year between two bar owners erupted into what was called the Tenderloin War. Bars and cabarets were closed. Many musicians left for Chicago then. The Tenderloin War also may have caused or accelerated an illegal, clandestine movement of prostitutes into the Quarter. These women and the characters they associated with were a rough crowd. Living with her mother in the French Quarter and being something of a street urchin with her brother, Norma could have had her initiation as a prostitute with the Storyville migrants, but it is also possible that Amanda Badon sent her daughter to Memphis, because the story that Norma chose to tell for her autobiography leaves her mother out of the picture and sets her first experience as a streetwalker there.

·   ·   ·

When Norma was twelve years old in Memphis, she met a bootlegger, an older man who had been a lifelong friend of her family. This man took one look at her and said, "Norma, darling, you know it's going to be rough, but one hair on that thing is stronger than a cable under the ocean."

"*That thing* is what he called it," Norma said. "So that stuck in my mind."

Norma had gone first to stay with her grandmother in McComb, then to visit some cousins in Memphis who took her out and walked her past the ritzy Gayoso Hotel. Memphis was wide open then, with big-time gambling and bootlegging. At the Gayoso, Norma saw her first hustling girls ("spectacular ladies" she called them). Immediately she was fascinated.

Within the next couple of years, she decided to become a streetwalker. Petite, well-developed Norma, with her slightly too high forehead, a bit of a hook to her nose, and her thin lips, may not have been an eye-catching beauty. But she was attractive with her thick, chestnut hair and soft, brown eyes under full lids. She had something, though, that made up for anything lacking in her looks—a strong sense of self, an irrepressible personality. And something more—chutzpah.

"I was still young, but I came up with an idea I thought would work. I got some schoolbooks—they weren't my books—I put them under my arm, put on my big black Milan hat, and I said, 'I'm going to turn out.'"

The first man to pick her up was Dr. Silvester, a veterinarian. She judged him to be at least sixty. He asked Norma if he could take her to dinner. She told him he could take her to the posh Gayoso Hotel.

As they ate their way through the first course, Dr. Silvester said, "You're awfully young."

Norma pulled her shoulders back and said haughtily, "I'm seventeen years old." She was fourteen.

Dr. Silvester decided to believe that Norma was seventeen and fall in love with her. She knew what he wanted from her, and she wanted clothes from him. But Norma hadn't been to bed with a man yet. "I figured I'm too smart to go to bed with this old man, but I'm going to make him think I'm going to bed so I can take him. So I strung him along and he dressed me up, bought me a black velvet dress, with thirty-five-dollar long white kid gloves. That was my first present. We went on the excursion boats together, and I drug him around town. He kept thinking he was going to make me. This lasted about six weeks." Then the doctor got tired of waiting.

Soon Norma met a dashing young bootlegger named Andy Wallace. "Call it love at first sight," she said.

Wallace had money and looks. He set her up in an apartment. "Naturally, he said we were Mr. and Mrs. Wallace. I don't know why we didn't marry, I married so many, but I ended up keeping the name the rest of my life. No way I was going to call myself Norma Badon and live this kind of life, anyway. I just wouldn't do that to my family.

"I kept the name, Andy kept me, and I was fine with the situation. But a man like that, in a dangerous life, running with a dangerous crowd, who knows when's your last day? And then to have looks like that? Andy Wallace was deadly good-looking, and every woman in Memphis and within a gunshot beyond knew it. They lusted after him and he couldn't resist them. For him, the grass was always going to be greener across the road. I wasn't fifteen years old. Imagine me trying to tame *that*. I would have had better luck with a rattlesnake.

"I kicked up something of a fuss, you might say, and I'll tell you what I got for my trouble. I got shot. Well, I also got a seven-carat diamond ring."

When Norma told Dr. Silvester she was seventeen years old, her lie began a lifelong preoccupation with age, but it was the last time she lied to make herself older. When Clint Bolton, for his *New Orleans* profile, asked her when she was born, she said, "Don't ask me what year because I lied so much about that I don't even know anymore. My mother caught me lying about my age once. Then she started lying about her age, and I wound up older than my mother!"

Her obituary in *The Times-Picayune* in 1974 reported that she was sixty-eight years old, but that was based on the age she'd given at the time of her 1953 arrest—she'd shaved off six years.

After she reached her twenties, the only math Norma did was subtraction, the difference between truth and appearances becoming bolder as she aged. She married Wayne Bernard, her fifth husband, on February 18, 1965. He was two months away from his twenty-fifth birthday. She had just turned sixty-four. On the marriage certificate, she gave her birth date as January 24, 1916, and fifteen years disappeared.

Less than two years before this marriage, her lucrative career as a French Quarter madam came to an end less by choice than by circumstance. Norma Wallace's was the longest continuous operation on record in the history of the city, beginning around 1920 at 328 Burgundy Street, moving to 410 Dauphine in 1928, then to 1026 Conti Street in 1938. After her 1962 bust and her first jail term in forty-two years, Norma continued to run her high-class bordello on Conti Street for another ten months, but gradually she shifted the operation to Waggaman, twenty minutes from New Orleans across the Mississippi River, where she had bought the old Cedar Grove Plantation in 1954. She ran a sporting house there for another year, until April 1964; then, in the same house, she and Wayne opened the Tchoupitoulas Plantation Restaurant, and Norma made another fortune.

They sold the restaurant in 1968 and moved to Poplarville, Mississippi, where Wayne had been building a house for them. They lived in a trailer until he finished it. But Norma had tried a permanent move to the country once before. It hadn't worked then, and it didn't work this time.

Norma's photograph was on the cover of *New Orleans* magazine in June 1972. The piece inside told her story. Her white hair shone, and she wore her trademark dark glasses. She held a bird in her hand, a baby chick. She seemed to have the whole town in her hand. She was presented with a key to the city at the Press Club. Reporters, politicians, former clients, and the curious waited in line for her autograph. The piece was so popular that the magazine ran it again in an anniversary issue four years later.

For years Norma Wallace had money, power, and influence. From her Poplarville retreat—her exile, as she called it in the magazine—she now achieved something more: recognition from the establishment, respectability. She seemed to have it all, except she was on the verge of losing her young husband.

Twenty-five years later Wayne sat in the kitchen at his Bush, Louisiana, house, a country house dressed with dormer windows and carriage lamps at the door, where he and Norma moved three months before her death, and recalled their last days together.

He'd met Jean, the woman he eventually married, while he and Norma were still in Poplarville. "Norma knew I was fooling around," Wayne said, "but then, I wasn't trying to keep it much of a secret. She told me she wasn't staying out in the country all by herself anymore, that she had decided to sell the Poplarville property. I was against it— I loved the place—so I put what I thought was an outrageous price on it and told her if we could get that, then okay. It sold almost immediately. We moved here to Bush. Well, I moved my things here, but I wasn't really living here. I took the trailer we'd lived in while I was building the house in Poplarville and went to Bogalusa. I was going to stay there until I could figure out what I was doing."

Bush, Louisiana, is a sleepy little town across Lake Pontchartrain from New Orleans. A far remove from the life of a French Quarter madam, it has more in common with the Bible Belt than with Sin City to the south. Norma's motives for moving to Bush were puzzling. If she was lonely or afraid of being out in the woods in Poplarville without Wayne, Bush wasn't much of an improvement. Its only advantage was a shorter drive to New Orleans, about an hour door to door.

Two months before the move to Bush, Howard Jacobs of *The Times-Picayune* wrote a two-part profile of Norma from Poplarville, which ran June 30 and July 1, 1974. Jacobs quoted Norma: "When Wayne and I first moved here, the settlers living within twenty miles were consumed with curiosity about our relationship, and one of 'em tried to wheedle a little matrimonial information out of me. She said, 'A lot of people are asking me what was a woman of your age doing with this young man.' I said, 'You tell 'em I'm a rich old lady and I'm supportin' 'im.' This shook her up so much that she dropped the subject like a hot potato."

But Wayne was supporting himself by that time, collecting his paycheck and keeping it, something he'd never done at the restaurant;

he'd signed all his checks there back over to Norma. Now his pay-checks gave him something he had not had for almost ten years—independence.

"After I went to work and Norma found out I was seeing a woman my own age, she told me the only thing that would come of it was that I'd have a bunch of kids and have to work like a dog until I was sixty.

"The funny thing is, Jean and I had been on again, off again; when Norma died we hadn't been together for a couple of months. But I didn't tell Norma that. I came over here the Thursday before it happened, and I ended up spending the night on the living room sofa. I fell asleep with my head in her lap. I woke up a number of times, and every time I did, she was still sitting there, wide awake. She'd stroke my head and I'd fall asleep again. We stayed like that all night." Wayne paused before he said, "She always knew it couldn't last forever."

After Norma's death, Wayne moved into the Bush house. He and Jean married the following year, 1975. Many of Norma's things are still there—a copper kettle on the hearth, a ship's lantern beside the door, both from the restaurant; and her furniture—tables, lamps, chairs, and most notably the sofa that was in her private apartment on Conti Street. It dominates one end of the dark-paneled living room. It's a sexy sofa, a broad contour, a wide bench seat with one continu-ous cushion that curves into two sharp, pointed ends, hard, stylized lines that were ultramodern in the 1950s, and brass-tipped stiletto legs. The sofa once was covered with plush, sensual, siren red velvet. Now it's covered in white Naugahyde; it has about as much bounce as a silicone job.

And the bullet hole is still visible in the ceiling of the Bush kitchen, a small, almost unnoticeable depression in the textured acoustic tile.

"Norma used to tell me she was never going to get old," Wayne said. "She used to say she hoped her death would be that her husband caught her in bed with a sixteen-year-old and shot her." Her vision of her death was violent, romanticized, but in that vision she was still sexy and powerful enough to command a sixteen-year-old's attention.

Norma's life revolved around sex, money, and power; her scan-dalous escapades made front-page headlines. In her autobiography she wanted to be perceived as a smart, classy, glamorous, and generous woman who was independent yet always had a powerful, sexy, and usually younger man in tow. But the reality was much more complicated, an ambitious, domineering, yet vulnerable woman who was glamorous, yes, but also vain and afraid of growing old. She proudly attached herself to a man thirty-nine years younger, saw herself through his eyes as sexy and seductive and through the public eye as outrageous and exciting, but she did not see that her pride was leading her into the dark embrace of obsessive love.

Norma Wallace made a fortune selling the art of seduction. She practiced that art in her personal life and was herself seduced by a young and beautiful man, largely because she had no vision of growing old as a privilege and an achievement. In her work life Norma's power rose from knowledge and experience; in her personal life she relinquished her power to an obsession.

CHAPTER TWO

The Tango Belt

 When Norma returned to New Orleans from Memphis in 1916, she found that the French Quarter was considerably more populated than she remembered. There were throngs of exotic people, most of them residents, since the Quarter was not the tourist mecca it is today. There were European Creoles, as well as the Creoles of Caribbean and African ancestry who plied their trades in the streets, from the vegetable vendors to the musicians, from the bricklayers to the chimney sweeps carrying the palmetto fronds they used to clean the chimneys. Norma found that life for French Quarter residents had improved in some ways, but in other ways it remained unchanged.

By 1910 sewage systems were completed in the Quarter, and over the next few years people began to use indoor plumbing. Gone were the horse-drawn wagons that collected the contents of the courtyard privies. The familiar streets Norma walked were cleaner than before, but wagons carrying coal, kerosene, ice, and wood still rumbled over the Belgian blocks that paved some of them (ballast from European ships), and the horses made their scatological contributions to the remaining filth.

The stark contrasts that visually define New Orleans were nowhere more in evidence than in the French Quarter, from the diverse population to the residents' abodes. The softly colored façades of the shuttered, stucco row houses were laced with wrought- and cast-iron balconies, intricate and beautiful, which identified the Vieux Carré, the old town, with the Old World, with wealth and the master crafts-manship of European artisans (though some of the iron was wrought by African Americans). But these ornate, airy structures overhung streets full of foul-smelling garbage that fed alarming populations of rats. Luckily, Norma had been in Memphis in 1914, when these con-ditions had caused an outbreak of bubonic plague.

From the time Norma was born (in 1901) until the time she left for Memphis, she'd seen the French Quarter courtyards as the center of family life, functional areas for hanging the wash and housing chickens, even cows and mules. Though she found many of them still being used this way, she also saw that some people were turning their courtyards into lush tropical havens, where they could escape the squalor of the streets. In contrast, the only way to access these hidden, verdant places of refuge was through narrow, dank alleyways.

At fifteen years old Norma saw this dirty, crowded old city through very different eyes than when she'd been living on the streets with Elmo. Then she had an eye only for survival; now she had a vision of what she wanted. She was drawn through the chaos of the French Quarter to the place where she hoped to find it. The Cosmopolitan Hotel, a half block off Canal Street, had addresses on both Bourbon and Royal Streets—its lobby ran straight through the entire block. The Cosmopolitan catered to the affluent—for a time it was called the Hotel Astor. It had a reputation as a family hotel. The ladies' entrance was on Royal Street, but, as Norma observed, not all the women who used it were ladies—except of the night. Attracted as she had been to the Gayoso in Memphis for its wealthy clientele and its class, Norma was drawn to the Cosmopolitan to try her hustling act.

"I could see all these girls decked out in diamonds and beautiful clothes. They were eating sumptuous meals in the dining room, hav-ing drinks, having a ball. I was ready to turn out. Those girls spotted me before I walked across the lobby the first time. They told me I was too young. They said a lot of people were afraid to fool with you when you're young. They weren't about to let me hustle on their ter-ritory, and it seemed a pretty good idea not to find out how they would stop me. They said, 'Why don't you go to this or that fine house, learn how to do it?'"

Norma returned to New Orleans, determined to learn every trick of the trade, just as Storyville was being dismantled in 1917. One of the earliest experiments to confine prostitution to a limited area, Story-ville ended with an order from the Department of the Navy, which banned open prostitution within five miles of a military installation. Politicians traveled to Washington armed with statistics proving the success of the experiment. The New Orleans red-light district (such districts were named for the red lanterns trainmen left outside the doors of brothels they visited) now had only a quarter as many prosti-tutes as it had had in 1898.

From the girls at the Cosmopolitan, Norma heard that Bertha Anderson's house had the best reputation, so she went there. Bertha had worked in Storyville, as the protégée of one of the district's most famous madams, Josie Arlington. Bertha had the foresight to get out of Storyville before it was officially shut down; she was part of the clandestine movement into the French Quarter, which began around 1913.

Bertha set herself up in a house at 335 Dauphine Street, and by the time Norma arrived she already had a thriving business there.

Bertha liked Norma. The first thing she did was try to talk Norma out of the life. But Norma told her that her family needed her support.

Neither Norma's mother, an alcoholic without resources and well past the age that she could have made much money as a prostitute, nor her brother could fend for themselves. Through Aunt Carrie Norma stayed in contact with her father, and the same year she arrived at Bertha's, Norma's half brother, J. G., was born. His mother, a woman of American Indian descent, died in childbirth, and Norma could have thought this baby would need her help as well.

Bertha Anderson saw the girl's determination and took her in. Norma celebrated her sixteenth birthday at Bertha's house.

During the two years she stayed there, Norma learned two critical lessons. "Bertha told me about dope—how it affected people, to stay away from it and save my money. She also got me to understand that when you hit your late twenties, you were old in the prostitution racket." So Norma started a program of self-education. "I read good books, looking up every word I didn't know in the dictionary, learning everything I could because I was pushing eighteen. I had to get a move on."

By her eighteenth birthday, she had decided that she wasn't going to be a streetwalker. "I was going to be a big landlady on my own." (The madams all called themselves landladies, never madams, a term only squares used.) This desire to be the "top dog," as Norma called it, became a consuming ambition.

Norma had left Andy Wallace because he had shot her; she walked away with only a grazed ankle. Even so, she admitted that she returned to Memphis over the next few years to see him because he was so good-looking she couldn't help herself. She left Bertha's for Memphis to begin her new career. She said, "I got in the mind that I could take on Memphis." She didn't say if that meant taking on Andy too.

With the help of a Memphis friend, Norma found an apartment and called girls in for two or three men a day. Her clientele was hustlers and bootleggers. "The bootleggers were generous with their money. The gamblers liked to throw their money around, and the crooks were particularly loose. I don't know whether it's because they are lonesome and hunting company or they're just damn fools.

"A couple of years up there and the apartment bega. .o get hot, but I wanted to go back to New Orleans by then anyway. You can do very well other places, and I didn't know so many people in New Orleans anymore, but I still wanted to come back. This damn place down here just draws you like crazy."

The largest city in the South at the time, this is the New Orleans, circa 1920, that drew Norma like crazy: "The French Quarter was full of hookers, nightspots like the old Cadillac and La Vida Club, and dance halls. The Quarter runs ten blocks across and thirteen down, from Canal Street to Esplanade. From the river to Rampart I can't tell you how many whores there were. Between Iberville and St. Louis

Streets and from Bourbon to Rampart, every door had a girl hustling in it. I didn't start it; they were there when I got there."

The corner of the Quarter that Norma gave the street boundaries for was known as the Tango Belt, after the dance that had become an international craze by the summer of 1913. The area was thick with dance halls and cabarets, restaurants and cafés where women could wear their "tango bustles" and couples could indulge their obsession with the stylish, sensual dance—vulgar and immoral to many— twenty-four hours a day.

Jack Stewart, a New Orleans musician who founded the New Leviathan Oriental Foxtrot Orchestra and is also a writer and music historian, has been reconstructing the street and music scene of the Tango Belt in the 1920s. He says, "The Tango Belt was interesting because, unlike Storyville, it didn't have the spotlight on it. It was in a section of the Quarter that was most marginal. The area was seedy."

During the 1920s artists and writers—people like William Spratling, Sherwood Anderson, and William Faulkner—gravitated to New Orleans. So many congregated around Jackson Square that the section was called Little Bohemia or Little Greenwich Village, though John Magill, curator at the Historic New Orleans Collection, says, "Greenwich Village was part of America, and Paris was part of the twentieth century. The French Quarter was unto itself, not American, not twentieth century."

The Quarter attracted writers and artists because it was an inexpensive place to live. It had been left in a state of decay in the latter half of the nineteenth century as many citizens fled to Esplanade Avenue or even to the opposite side of Canal Street, to the American Sector, where the wealthier ones built what is now known as the Garden District. For years some Creoles refused to cross Canal Street into the American Sector, and the median on it became known as the neutral ground, a term New Orleanians still use for the grass or concrete divisions on the wider streets and avenues around town.

The artists liked the bohemian aspect of the Vieux Carré, its exotic appearance and kinship with the Old World. They didn't mind its shabbiness. They liked the life on the streets that couldn't be found Uptown, a sense of community, a looseness that defied the staid Uptowners' preoccupation with money and tradition. Life in the French Quarter was antibourgeois, adventurous, risqué.

So in the twenties, when the Quarter was experiencing some revitalization after years of being neglected, the artists were afraid that it was losing its flavor. The area they populated around the square was becoming more commercial, less shabby and cleaner. But their idea of flavor was naïve compared with what was going on in the Tango Belt. In fact, they didn't seem to have any idea what was going on there; it was rarely written about, and it certainly wasn't the romantic French Quarter scene most artists were painting.

The tango, by 1914, had been officially declared immoral, and dancers went through its showy steps under threat of being dragged off the floor to jail unless light was visible between the partners and they refrained from doing any demoralizing dance steps, like "snake-wiggling" at the shoulders. But the tango had started a craze for dancing, and it had helped identify a section of the French Quarter as the place to go for a good time. Little cabarets sprang up in storefronts or in the front rooms of buildings; the lewder programs, like the "freak shows," kinky displays of eroticism, were relegated to the back rooms. Small-time local dance bands played tangos and foxtrots around the clock; hot, sexy jazz could be heard all night. From the theaters and the jazz clubs to the brothels, the Tango Belt was racially integrated, which sharpened the edge of excitement and fear associated with it. If the blacks wanted vaudeville, they could have it in the Tango Belt—it wasn't wanted anywhere else in the city.

"You could say it was an easygoing kind of place," says Jack Stewart, a figure from another era with his muttonchops and soft, courtly speech, "or you could say it was the armpit of the French Quarter."

The Uptown ladies dismissed the Tango Belt as Frenchtown; others called it Shuttertown. The action in the Tango Belt was sub rosa, as Stewart says, but some of that action, according to Norma's description, wasn't taking place behind shutters. Girls worked the streets aggressively because competition was keen and prices were cheap. They'd take men back to their cribs—grimy, sordid, one-room hovels, furnished with little more than a chair and a bed—for as little as twenty-five cents. Travelers compared the place with similar districts in Marseilles, Honolulu, and Singapore.

Yet when Norma returned to New Orleans, she did not return to Bertha Anderson's, which was in the heart of this action. Instead she went to work for a friend she'd met at Bertha's, Louise Jackson, who had started her own house at 144 South Rampart, across Canal Street, outside the French Quarter altogether. It may be that Norma no longer had the contacts to put herself in the heart of the action.

But Louise had a good business going on South Rampart. She also had epilepsy and a man with itchy fingers. After a bad seizure that left her hospitalized, Louise asked Norma to run her house while she recovered. "Imagine me running a large house, three or four maids, and keeping her man out of the money at my age," Norma said. She was barely twenty.

One evening a man died in the house. "The night before Louise was getting out of the hospital, a date went in the front bedroom with one of the girls. They weren't there long when the girl ran out in the hall screaming. It seemed the man had had his pleasure and conked out. There was nothing we could do—we had to call the police. It was a good thing the girl had managed to get out from under him. After I handled the police and a dead man *and* kept Louise's man out of the till as well as all of us out of jail, I figured I'd better go get my own place if I could do that good a job."

Getting her own place might not have been so easy for Norma at that point in her life, young as she was and without much money, except that one Sunday night she met a man who would become her lover and her business partner, then her husband, and then a lifelong friend. Around New Orleans he was known as the Champ. When Norma met Pete Herman, he had won the title of world bantam-weight champion twice. He was Peter Gulotta, a bootblack and bellhop, until he read about a flashy lightweight named Kid Herman and changed his name.

Early in his career Pete had been thumbed in the eye during a fight. From that time on he had problems with his eyes. Yet he continued boxing. Rapidly losing his sight, he lost his title too, but regained it with a feint-and-touch system that the New Orleans sportswriter Marty Mulé called "boxing by Braille." When Norma met Pete, he was nearly blind.

Norma and Pete, both five feet two, stood eyeball to eyeball on the dance floor at a juke joint in Bucktown, clear across town from the French Quarter, on Lake Pontchartrain. Bucktown is not a town, merely a few clubs and restaurants and some shrimp boats tied to rickety docks around the Seventeenth Street Canal, a large drainage ditch that empties into the lake a few hundred yards away. "It's where all the characters used to go on Sunday nights," Norma explained. "Pete was out there with some other fighters, and I was with my boyfriend Louis Giacona. Louie introduced me to Pete and we all sat together. After a while, Pete asked me to dance, and we liked each other immediately."

Pete had left boxing with nearly half a million dollars. He decided to invest some of it in a nightclub and bought a place on the corner of Conti and Burgundy. "He asked me to come down when he opened his club," Norma said. "I did, and that's when I fell in love with Pete, and I'm sure he fell in love with me. He asked me if I wanted to move upstairs and operate over his nightclub, said that he would fix it up for me. I went to Maestri's on the corner of Rampart and Iberville and bought all my furniture." Robert Maestri would eventually become mayor of New Orleans.

Norma left Louise's and moved in above Pete's at 938 Conti, bringing three girls with her. All three were younger than Norma. One was Dora Russo, who became a notorious madam in her own right.

Pete Herman's Ringside Bar and Lounge became a hub of nightlife in the Tango Belt. Its entrance was set catty-corner to the intersection of Conti and Burgundy. Above it was a huge neon sign featuring Pete in boxing regalia. Norma and her girls did so well there that she removed the partitions and expanded onto the entire second floor of the building. She now had an address on Conti and at 328 Burgundy. "I was quite a swinger. I worked the doorways, stood out on the street and did the Charleston—anything to attract attention."

•   •   •

Norma had arrived in the Tango Belt, but the reformers were at it again. A roar would go up from the Lions Club, or the Kiwanians would emerge from one of their powwows crying for prostitution reform. The mayor would jump all over the superintendent of police, who would then order a crackdown, and the Tango Belt would come under siege. Captain Theodore Ray, a dignified, stodgy man, an upholder of discipline and law and order, had been given the charge to eradicate prostitution from the French Quarter, and he was arresting prostitutes all over the Tango Belt.

"I had to get around Ray somehow," Norma said. "There were two adjacent entrances to Pete's building on Burgundy Street. Inside one, I opened a bar. The other entrance bypassed the bar for the stairway. This gave us a great escape route. Behind the bar we put a peephole in the door. If the police came in, we could get out on both Burgundy and Conti. This arrangement gave me liberty and peace of mind.

"But the part I liked the best about it—outwitting Captain Ray had caused me to run a more discreet operation. With discretion, I got a better class of clientele. I always did say, Without the police, I'd never have made it for forty years."

On New Year's Eve 1923, Norma put on her long-waisted dress with its short, pleated skirt, her stylish brown cloche, and a string of fake pearls good for twirling. The stars looked frozen in the sky above the French Quarter, but she wouldn't have to be out long to gather a few dates and take them upstairs for some holiday cheer and auld lang syne.

She strolled along the sidewalk in front of 938 Conti. The street was still noisy with celebration, but people would be clearing out soon, finding a place to be at midnight. Norma spotted Nellie Jolie, a tall, well-groomed brunette who made a great deal of money, coming from the direction of the Cadillac Club, on the corner of Conti and North Rampart Streets. She had a man on each arm, the three of them in high spirits. They disappeared behind an iron gate in a seven-foot red-brick wall. Across the street the Chinaman was open, but no one was interested in chow mein or coffee on New Year's Eve. Another girl, Edna, passed the café and waved at Norma. Edna's sweetheart was Eddie, an ex-fighter and friend of Pete's. But she wasn't with Eddie. She and a date were undoubtedly going to rent a room somewhere. Norma saw Bobbi Hackett too. She was tipsy, tripping along the brick sidewalk, her date loud and raucous, Bobbi laughing boisterously with him, but Norma knew that she was still broken-hearted over losing her lover. A few weeks earlier he'd been murdered at the corner of Tulane and Jeff Davis Parkway, out from the French Quarter.

Norma hustled a few men upstairs and was about to call it quits so that she and Pete, after they saw in the new year at their establishments, could rendezvous for a little celebration of their own. Besides, she was cold.

She saw the two men walking toward her and waited. Two more and she'd have a full house. One of them walked with a swagger—the kind of man Norma liked, full of himself and ready to unload a roll of money on one of her girls. The men walked purposefully, straight for her. As they got closer, she noticed that they seemed awfully sober.

Norma was arrested for the first time that night, December 31, 1923. The charge was soliciting for prostitution, and the arresting officer, the one with the swagger, was Detective George Reyer, a policeman known for being as colorful as some of the characters he collared. Reyer would eventually become chief of police, and Norma would come to respect him and like him, mostly because of the hands-off attitude he developed toward prostitution. But that night Norma, along with a score of other girls caught in Reyer's roundup, saw in the new year at night court, where sleazy lawyers grubbed for clients among the drunk and disorderly benchwarmers and heavily rouged, scantily clad women. Then she went home to business as usual.

CHAPTER THREE

Vidalias and
the Good Men

Congress passed the Volstead Act in 1919, and Prohibition began the following year. Norma opened one illegitimate business, a house of prostitution; then, because of Captain Ray's crackdown on the Tango Belt prostitutes, she opened a second illegal business, a bar, to cover the first one. Ray's determination to eradicate prostitution went against custom. Historically, the city's attitude toward both prostitution and gambling had been tolerant.

For most of three centuries gambling had been carried out openly and behind closed doors. Cockfighting was one of the earliest, most ubiquitous forms of gambling, with pits located all over the French Quarter. Predating Comus, New Orleans's oldest carnival krewe, which appeared in 1857, the first Mardi Gras float in 1838 depicted a giant fighting cock. (Today Louisiana is one of only five states in the country where cockfighting is legal, and in 1999 the legislature struck down yet another effort to do away with it.) The Creole millionaire Bernard de Marigny, whose estate was directly below the French Quarter and is known now as the Faubourg Marigny, introduced a somewhat more elegant form of gambling than cockfights. Heavily in debt from his losses, he introduced New Orleans to the game of craps (after *crapaud*, French for "toad," or in New Orleans, "toad-frog," the slang commonly applied to Frenchmen). The game caught on; de Marigny lost his fortune.

By the time Norma was operating in the Tango Belt, round-the-clock gambling houses had sprung up all over the city, some catering to the low life, others more sophisticated. These places enjoyed complete police protection. Once when the legislature enacted a Sunday blue law, the state attorney general struck it down in New Orleans only—no explanation forthcoming.

Gambling operations proliferated in the expected nightlife locations—saloons, poolrooms, and clubs—then spilled over into daylight businesses such as groceries and barbershops. Everybody was doing it, twenty-four hours a day, including prostitutes who took bets at the soft-drink stands they operated, once for the sole purpose of soliciting men.

Prohibition was no different from anything else illegal in the city—the law was flagrantly disregarded. Good liquor was easy to get citywide, from the elite men's clubs like the Boston Club to the cabarets of the Tango Belt and saloons like LaMothe's (now Tavern on the Park), where Pete Herman, his brother Gaspar Gulotta, his fighting buddies and fans liked to meet. Speakeasies went to elaborate lengths to carry out their clandestine activities and convince their patrons they were safe. One called the Bat had a one-ton steel door installed to keep out federal agents.

Norma's bar helped her attract a more affluent and influential clientele. Early in the 1920s she established her characteristic pattern of using the very worst circumstances to improve her own. Her business acumen seemed impervious to federal agents and the local law; it certainly helped her keep well ahead of the competition and their low prices. The more she charged her customers, the more customers flocked in to hand over their money. Business was so good that one of the girls who'd left Louise Jackson's with Norma, Dora Russo, decided to strike out on her own.

Dora had gotten into the business almost by accident. One day she had visited Norma at Louise's, and that afternoon a ship's captain came by looking for some company. He liked women of substance, preferably in the form of lots of soft, cushioned flesh. He took one look at Dora and knew he'd found what he wanted. Dora turned her first trick that day and never looked back.

"Dora wasn't anybody's fool," Norma said. "She was with me for about a year when she got smart." Dora had been kept by a rich Jewish man from Uptown, she dressed well, and she knew how to talk. She decided that Norma had the right idea, not to turn tricks but to find them—and to hire the girls who would keep them coming back. She left Norma and opened her own house right across the street, at 335 Burgundy. From pre-Storyville days this block, between Bienville and Conti, was the worst in the Tango Belt. It had been known as Smoky Row in the latter half of the nineteenth century. Even after the turn of the century, residents were still finding bloodstained wallets and articles of male clothing buried in their courtyards. It was rumored that the men's corpses had been buried too.

In no time Dora had ten or fifteen girls living with her. Some of them were legendary, like Teeny, who had killed her lover Dapper Dan Williams and beat the rap. Dora's girls walked the streets at night; they got men out of cars. They lay naked in the window or stood on the sidewalk out front wearing only kimonos, flashing them open for passing men, even grabbing their privates and "plucking them in," as Norma called it, with the same vehemence, sometimes violence, as the women of Smoky Row. They were so prosperous that Dora opened another house at 304 Burgundy, which put Norma right between her two thriving bordellos.

In spite of the competition Norma continued to do well above Pete's Ringside Bar and Lounge, as did many others in the Tango Belt. Black women, who outnumbered white women better than two to one, did especially well. Camilla Turner and Juliet Washington worked only white girls out of the windows of their houses; Melba Moore drove girls around in a Cadillac to pick up men. Business was so good that both Camilla and Juliet bought property; Melba bought a second Cadillac.

There was enough business to keep everybody friendly and even take one night a week off. And there was enough liquor to keep everybody drunk during Prohibition. "Sunday night was our night for balling," Norma said, using her shorthand for "having a ball."

"We'd close up the house, and all the girls and their men would go to Pete's, La Vida, or the Little Club. We'd drink champagne and dance all night. The hustlers would get drunk enough to start breaking up the place. But the next day it was forgotten and everyone was friends again."

One Sunday night a fight broke out between a tough blonde who'd been around with prizefighters and a brunette who wasn't shy. They had enough liquor in them to decide that they didn't like each other much. Everyone in the bar talked them into going out to City Park at daybreak to duel it out.

"We all jumped into cars, just as full of rum as you can imagine. These two girls were into the show. They pulled hair and tore each other's clothes off with all the characters egging them on. After a while the police came, but instead of putting everyone in jail, they just told us to get on back where we belonged, which is what we all did. We went to bed and forgot about it, and the next day was another day."

Captain Theodore Ray continued to crack down on the prostitutes, but the Tango Belt was as rowdy as ever. To keep the peace, the chief of police put a beat cop in every block where girls hustled behind window blinds.

"The policeman would have had to be deaf, blind, and dumb not to know we were landladies and what was going on," Norma said. "He was good protection. One night a colored man took out his tool and shook it at one of the girls. The policeman ended that. He kept the drunks from pestering us. It was nice to know he was on the block."

Blue was a pretty redhead from Knoxville. She didn't have a pimp, as many of the girls did; she had a boyfriend, a nice Italian fellow who actually had a legitimate job. She paid her room and board at Norma's, twenty-five dollars a week, but also had a room around the corner on Dauphine Street. Norma assumed that Blue kept the other place so she and her boyfriend could have some privacy. She liked Blue and trusted her, sometimes leaving her in charge of the house.

Every night around midnight Blue asked Norma's permission to go out for a while. She returned in about half an hour, and she always came back happy. Norma assumed she went to see her boyfriend on Dauphine Street.

Blue never wanted a buyout—an all-night date with a man from out of town who wanted to take a girl out to the clubs. The other girls fought over buyouts, but not Blue. Again, Norma assumed that Blue would rather spend the night with the Italian fellow.

Then Blue fell in love with the policeman on the beat; he fell for her too. Blue was happier than she'd ever been and looked even younger than her twenty-four years. But without notice she gave up her room on Dauphine Street and stayed at Norma's house. She seemed sick. Within a week she was dead. She'd taken two mercury tablets—enough to poison her.

Later the cop told Norma that Blue had been on heroin, and he'd gotten her to take the cure. But she couldn't stay off junk, and her policeman quit her.

Norma would not knowingly let girls on drugs work for her. "Blue was the only girl I ever worked who was on heroin, and she gave me less trouble than all those young kids I had on Conti Street years later who took pills. I had no problems at all with Blue. Of course, I don't know what she would have done if she hadn't had her junk. She handled it so well I never had any reason to even suspect it." Norma paused, then said, "I should have."

Two things Norma had absolutely no use for were drugs and pimps, which often entered her house together. Most of the girls lived at Norma's house, many with their pimps. The pimps liked to get their women hooked on drugs so they had more control over them. During Prohibition marijuana—sometimes called muggles—was legal and smoked openly on the street. Heroin, morphine, and hop (opium) were used more covertly, as was cocaine, which went by the street name inchy, presumably because it was laid out in lines and snorted by the inch. Norma tried to keep the well-supplied pimps out of her house.

The house life of a pimp demanded that he get up, get dressed, and wait outside, whatever the hour, whenever a date (the polite term for a trick) came. Sometimes the pimps stood on Pete's corner, if Pete was still open, and smoked a little muggles. If it was cold they'd go over to the Chinaman's and drink coffee until the all-clear signal came. If a man came in and bought drinks, the wait could be several hours. A pimp might just get back in bed when someone else would arrive.

"They say a pimp's life is a tough life," Norma said sarcastically. "They really earn their money, don't they?"

Undaunted by the prostitutes' being released almost as soon as he picked them up, Captain Ray intensified his crusade to clean up the Tango Belt. Norma was arrested five times in three months. At the height of the antivice campaign, one of Norma's friends thought it would be amusing to present her with a police dog. She named the animal Vidalia.

Upriver from New Orleans, across the Mississippi from Natchez, was the town of Vidalia, Louisiana, but Norma didn't name the dog after the town. She just liked the ring of the word. She talked to the dog as if he were human, throwing the name Vidalia into nearly every sentence. One of the cabdrivers heard her talking to the dog, saying, "Vidalia this" and "Vidalia that," and he began calling his customers vidalias.

"How's the vidalia coming, Norma?" he would ask. "When will the vidalia be ready?"

Then the girls picked it up and started a language in code. If a country-looking man came in, someone the girls could tell had never been in a whorehouse, one might say to another, "Here's a vidalia on a holiday," which meant he only wanted to spend ten dollars. A "double Friday" meant twenty dollars.

Norma began using such codes in her book instead of putting down amounts of money, as well as entering the vidalias' and the girls' nicknames in case the book ever fell into the wrong hands.

Meanwhile, the word *vidalia* was catching on around New Orleans as part of the street slang. First the cabdrivers used it to identify a male passenger in search of a prostitute. But its use spread, and it became a tag for a sucker from out of town.

At three o'clock one Monday morning, a cabdriver named Rocco called Norma. "I got a vidalia from New York for you," he said. "He saw you over at La Vida the other night with Pete and wants to meet you."

Two well-dressed gentlemen arrived, the man from New York and a man he introduced as his secretary. They didn't want just two girls; they had Norma call every girl in the house to the bar. Bootlegged liquor began to flow. This went on all the next day and into the following night.

The vidalia finally picked a girl, but he didn't care about going upstairs. He just wanted to drink. His secretary remained sober, went off with a girl now and again, and returned to their hotel during the day, but only to check for messages. Norma sent out for steaks and fed them.

The man from New York continued to drink. He finally took off his clothes—but only to take a bath! He brought his drink and his girl with him to the tub. When he wanted to go to sleep, he asked his girl to come to the room with him, but all he wanted her to do was go to sleep too.

"He never did screw," Norma said.

She ran a tab for him. If a girl crossed in front of him, he would call out to Norma, "Put her down for twenty." With some regularity he would yell, "Put them *all* down for twenty!" This went on for three days.

"Believe me," Norma said, "my blood pressure was soaring, because a whore wants her money first, and when you have to wait for it, you're in a bad condition."

On the afternoon of the third day, the vidalia told Norma that he and his secretary would have to be heading back to New York.

"How much do I owe?" he asked. His bill was $4,500, the equivalent of nearly $75,000 today. "Write her a check," he told his secretary.

A check! This was a landlady's worst nightmare. A taxi driver's too. Poor Rocco had stayed at the house with his vidalia for three whole days, even eating and taking his showers there so he'd be around when it came time for the payoff, a commission of twelve hundred dollars. His face was long and sad when he saw his man write out what they all were thinking was a piece of rubber.

Norma tried to get the man to send his secretary to the hotel to cash the check. "Wouldn't that be better than having it go through with my name on it?" she asked.

"Oh, that's not necessary. You just put it in the bank. It's as good as gold," he told her.

Norma knew it would take four or five days for his check to clear; by that time she'd be out of her mind. But she also knew better than to push. Her instincts told her he was legit, a fine gentleman, very high class. Norma took the check, warmly thanking both men, telling them she hoped they'd be back.

It was too late in the day to do anything about it. She sweated it out that night, and the first thing the next morning she called a friend at a local bank. He told her he'd call New York to see if the check was good.

While she waited she instructed the girls to do useful things like scrub the sidewalk with a pink voodoo concoction that was supposed to draw clients. When her friend called, he said, "Very prominent family. His bank said his check is good for any amount."

That was no vidalia on a holiday. "*That*," said Norma, "is what you call a *good* vidalia!"

During the 1920s Norma was arrested thirteen times, not a bad record considering that many women were arrested over a hundred times. Her charges ran from "soliciting for prostitution" to "relative to accosting from doorway" and "relative to operating an immoral house," to which was added once "and also with insult and abuse." Captain Ray himself was the arresting officer on more than one occasion. Never, though, did Norma spend so much as a night in jail. "Happy" Russo, Dora's husband, was a friend of the night recorder, who let all the prostitutes walk.

If Captain Ray was frustrated by the apparent upper hand of the demimonde in the Tango Belt, he was soon to be vindicated. Federal agents had been conducting raids in New Orleans since the beginning of Prohibition; not even the Boston Club was immune—agents confiscated one hundred bottles of liquor there in 1924. The members were outraged! They should have felt lucky—no arrests were made. After a series of raids in 1925, agents dubbed New Orleans "the liquor capital of the world," for they netted more liquor than some claimed to have seen *before* Prohibition. Over the next two years they padlocked New Orleans speakeasies, more than in any other city in the nation, eighty-six the first year alone—including Bourbon Street's famous Old Absinthe House, on its hundredth anniversary. Many of these places were in the Tango Belt—cabarets, cafés, and establishments like the Little Club, a favorite haunt of the demimonde crowd and other underworld characters. The Little Club later reopened in the Central Business District, but most places in the Tango Belt never opened again. Pete Herman's club was one of the few that survived and stayed in the area.

Other places that didn't close permanently moved over to Bourbon Street, which in the late twenties began to change from a residential to a more commercial street. There were plenty of French Quarter dwellers to support it too, an all-time high of 20,000 by 1930. (The population of the Quarter today fluctuates between a shockingly low 3,500 and 5,000; tourists outnumber residents.) The irrepressible Count Arnaud, owner of Arnaud's restaurant, saw the opportunities on Bourbon Street and in 1925—raids be damned— opened the first nightclub as we know them today, with both a supper club and a floor show, at the corner of Bourbon and Bienville.

Changes had already been taking place on Canal Street as well. Businessmen didn't want the city's premier shopping district to resemble a European throwback. They wanted Fifth Avenue! They began removing the fabulous Victorian ironwork balconies and galleries from the façades of the buildings. Two of the biggest department stores, D. H. Holmes and Maison Blanche, needed warehouse space. They looked no farther than directly behind them—in the Tango Belt. The area began to resemble a freight entrance instead of the high-spirited, twenty-four-hour entertainment district it had been only a couple of years earlier.

Entertainment in the late twenties changed too. The Orpheum, right off Canal, which had opened as a vaudeville house and billed some of the most enduring performers of our time—Houdini, George Burns, and Gracie Allen among them—was converted into a movie house. Movies proved such a powerful draw that two more great movie palaces, the Loew's State and the Saenger, with its nighttime Florentine garden setting under a star-studded azure sky, were built on Canal Street.

There were theaters in the Tango Belt too: the two-thousand-seat Lyric on Iberville and Burgundy, with its cupola rising above the marquee, and the Greenwald, a burlesque theater which became the Palace, on Dauphine and Iberville. Most of the people who lived along Dauphine and Burgundy were black, and these theaters eventually catered only to black patrons as segregation took over the Tango Belt. (The Lyric, boasting such acts as Josephine Baker and Mamie Smith, is now a parking lot; the Palace operated as a movie house until it was torn down to build a parking garage.)

Prohibition left its mark on the Tango Belt and made it nearly unrecognizable; once risqué and exciting, now it was merely run-down. Its cabarets gave way to laundries and plumbing suppliers, trades that contributed to the warehouse look of the once rough-and-tumble, lively, exotic streets, a look that persists to this day.

The Tango Belt lost its name along with its identity as jazz and dancing infiltrated other parts of the French Quarter. One kind of entertainment, though, sub rosa and illegal, persisted.

In the momentum of the cleanup by the feds, Captain Ray saw his chance to further cripple the Tango Belt. In 1928 he asked the acting mayor, T. Semmes Walmsley, to issue vacate notices, evicting landladies and their tenants from known houses of prostitution. On August 8, 1928, the *New Orleans States* reported what was called "the most telling blow yet struck against vice in the section below Canal Street formerly known as the Tango Belt": Captain Ray's closing of six houses of prostitution and the elimination of several soft-drink establishments.

Dora Russo and Camilla Turner were specifically named in the article. Dora's house at 335 Burgundy and Camilla's on St. Louis Street were padlocked, which meant they could not be occupied for a year. Ray also brought charges against the night recorder, "Happy" Russo's friend. Ray's battle with the demimonde in the Tango Belt had become a war.

"My precinct is almost free of vice," he told the *States* reporter. "Almost all the women have moved out of the precinct and many have left the city. Those who have remained will find their places padlocked if there is a chance for it."

"Captain Ray was hell," Norma said. "The last thing I needed was to have my house padlocked for a year." The bar had been a good front, and Norma had made good money serving near beer (2.75 percent alcohol) and bootlegged liquor. Again, though, she needed to find another way.

The name Glen Evans was never mentioned in any police roundup. For nearly thirty-five years Glen had operated a classy and very discreet parlor house next door to Arnaud's restaurant on Bienville Street. Her girls never worked doorways. Business came from the taxi drivers and the restaurants. "She ran a very smooth operation, no publicity, but she was getting up in age," Norma said.

By 1928 Pete and Norma were having trouble. "We were making up and breaking up so much I decided I wanted to leave." She and Pete continued doing business, though, with Norma sending girls to his lounge and taking a share of the proceeds.

But when Norma leased a house at 410 Dauphine Street, it was clearly old Glen Evans's operation that held the greatest appeal for her. Norma renovated the Creole-style house, which was long and narrow, with a double parlor up front, the kitchen in back, a warren of bedrooms on the second floor, and a private room on the third. Then she filled it with antiques and claimed it was the nicest place in the French Quarter. She hired only the best-looking girls and dressed them in formals. She gave up doorways and worked her girls under a new set of rules.

First and foremost, if a girl had a pimp, he wasn't allowed within half a block of the premises. Anytime a girl appeared in public, she must be dressed as a lady—no suggestive clothing—with hat and gloves, purse and shoes to match, and no open-toe shoes. Bra and panties also had to match. She must be impeccably groomed, her hair professionally coiffed, and her lips and nails painted, but in chic, sophisticated shades, nothing garish. More than once Norma was heard to inquire as a girl entered the parlor, "Where do you think you're going, to a Mexican fiesta?" Then the girl was sent back upstairs to remove the offending color.

Girls were never to kiss the dates; if a girl came downstairs with her lipstick off or awry, she was fired—they were selling sex, not emotion. Norma's girls were expected to be unswervingly loyal to her and totally discreet, never divulging anything regarding the operation. They were not to take drugs, they were to be examined by the house doctor twice a week, and they were not supposed to work during their periods, although girls were known to use sponges, which sometimes had to be removed by the doctor. Finally, they must never, never roll a customer (steal his money) or shake him down (extort money). Any violation of the rules was grounds for dismissal. Utterly serious, Norma said, "My girls had to be of the highest moral caliber."

Norma's immaculate girls, her strict rules, and her new house resulted in a better class of client. "I began to get the best business. My clients were local men from the exclusive clubs across Canal Street—the Boston Club, the Pickwick, the Louisiana Club. They were from Uptown. They frequented the New Orleans Athletic Club on Rampart Street. These were not the vidalias," Norma said. "I called these men the Good Men."

These were the men who had the real power in New Orleans. They controlled the money. They met in the boardrooms at their banks or the cardrooms at their clubs, where they made the decisions that most affected the city, often without a single elected official present. They belonged to the old-line, secret carnival organizations— Comus, Momus, Proteus, and Rex, King of Carnival—that were all but impossible to get into without a birthright. As they ruled society in New Orleans, so they ruled politics and politicians. Their word was the last word; their power was absolute.

Norma claimed that, at her house, Good Men were not hard to find.

The Good Men weren't always on their best behavior, however.

The week before Mardi Gras, late at night, one of the Good Men arrived at 410 Dauphine Street. He was in high spirits, having just won $2,500 at a gambling house. He was also drunk, as though in training for the Mardi Gras bacchanalia. This year he was king of one of the big four carnival krewes, an honor in New Orleans akin to a royal knighting, reserved for those who have achieved prominence in business and society.

He pretended to wave his scepter over the girls, anointing them as he called for more drinks, spending his money freely. Norma tried to get him to take a couple of girls upstairs—it would take two to handle him—but the man wasn't interested in the beautiful girls in their ball gowns; he wanted the madam of the house. He held out a wad of money that looked like a head of lettuce in his hand. She recalled: "He started sticking money down my brassiere. He said it was mine, and, believe me, it was tempting, but I wouldn't do it. No one respects a madam who lets men maul her or a madam who turns tricks."

Norma resisted him, as nicely as she could, but his expansive, generous humor began to turn sour. He asked her to dance, but he pushed her around on the slick hardwood floor of the living room. He scuffled with her, playfully at first, but got more aggressive every time she said no. Finally, during one of his scuffles, he slipped on the floor and fell, hitting his head on the small wrought-iron coin receiver to play the music box.

Norma knew he was badly hurt, but now he was resisting her offers to take him to a doctor or hospital. In desperation she suggested a hotel, but he refused to go. So Norma called Gaspar Gulotta, Pete Herman's brother, who owned a nightclub on Bourbon Street.

Gaspar knew the man. He hurried over to Dauphine Street and tried to reason with him, but the man was still having none of it. Gaspar decided that the best thing to do was call the police—not an easy decision for either him or Norma to make, but Captain Ray had been promoted out of the precinct, and the French Quarter had begun to revert to its usual easygoing attitude. Gaspar didn't think there would be a problem.

Money was everywhere—on the floor, in the sofa, in Norma's bra. She picked up all the bills and wadded them into a ball just the way the man had come in with it, the entire twenty-five hundred. When the police arrived, they wanted to take the man to jail.

Norma said to the lieutenant, "Don't take him to jail. Here, take this." She put the wad in his coat pocket.

They took him to a hotel. A few hours later, after the man had sobered up some and collected himself, he called the district police station. He claimed Norma had rolled him and demanded her arrest. Police from a different shift arrived to search the house and question Norma. "I couldn't tell them the real story about where the money went; once a bribe is taken, mum's the word. I was just going to have to take it on the chin, but when the old boy found out he had a fractured skull, he came to his senses and decided he didn't want the publicity he was going to get if he got *me* put away."

The would-be king missed Mardi Gras altogether that year. Norma said dryly, "I guess you could say we crowned him."

CHAPTER FOUR

Such a Wicked City

 Two cabdrivers, brothers from Alabama, were known as Itchem and Scratchem because they looked and drawled so much alike. One night in the early thirties, before the Great Depression hit New Orleans, one of the brothers picked up a fare at Southern Railway on Canal Street. She was a woman of about forty who had with her a much younger woman, a sort of child-woman, very thin and petite with a high-pitched voice. The child-woman wasn't the older woman's maid, but she clearly wasn't in the same class.

Itchem didn't know who the woman was, but he knew that she was someone of importance. He could tell by the way she carried herself—her husky shoulders thrown back, her chin tipped upward ever so slightly; by the glamorous hairdo set in shiny, seductive waves; and by her cashmere coat, which grazed the back of his hand as he took her vanity case from her to put it in the trunk of the taxi. Her rings flashed in the soft interior light of the cab. He closed the door after she and her companion were settled. She told him what she wanted, and Itchem drove through the dark, run-down streets of the Tango Belt to Norma's beautiful parlor house at 410 Dauphine.

Norma recognized her the moment she walked through the front door. She was an actress. Norma, a great moviegoer—she often, in a rush, threw her fur coat on with nothing underneath to catch the last feature at the Saenger Theatre on Canal Street—had seen this actress in several movies and especially liked her when she costarred with Wallace Beery, one of Norma's favorites. Her name was Marjorie Rambeau.

"I can only stay for a couple of hours," Rambeau told Norma. "We're catching the last Sunset Limited back to Los Angeles." She was on her way from Florida, where she'd been vacationing with her husband. As she handed her coat to the maid, she gave Norma a coy but knowing look. "My husband told me not to get off the train in New Orleans because it's such a wicked city."

People carried cash in those days, and Norma had seen lots of men with big rolls, but never a woman with the kind of roll Rambeau had in her pocketbook. She peeled off a hundred-dollar bill and asked for a bottle of champagne. The maid went for the champagne, Norma put on some music, and Rambeau and the straggler, as Norma immediately thought of the younger woman, settled themselves in the back parlor. Norma had no doubt that Rambeau had picked up the straggler on the train.

Men weren't the only ones fascinated by the madam of the house. There were ten or fifteen girls in residence that night, but Rambeau took a shine to Norma. An hour passed, then two. Rambeau missed the Sunset Limited. She gave Itchem a couple of C-notes and told him to leave. The champagne flowed faster and faster (Norma poured hers into a plant behind the sofa). Rambeau began to paw Norma; she wanted Norma to dance with her. Ever since the carnival king fell and cracked his head, Norma and the girls had not danced with the customers, but they had danced for them. Several girls danced naked for Rambeau and the straggler, who started to carry on and giggle, her voice rising higher and higher the more she drank. When Rambeau wasn't petting on Norma, she and the straggler petted each other. Norma kept her eye on Rambeau's purse—she felt protective of the movie star, because she, too, was prone to throwing her money around when she had had too much to drink.

The night wore on, with Rambeau cracking those hundred-dollar bills for drinks and tips. She became spectacularly drunk. She wanted to go upstairs and get out of her clothes. She was at the stage of drunkenness where this was not something she could do by herself—she wanted Norma to help her.

Daybreak was not far off, and Norma didn't want Rambeau to fall asleep at the house and wake up feeling humiliated, so she called an entertainer at a French Quarter nightclub, the boyfriend of one of the girls, and asked him to drive Rambeau and her friend to the Roosevelt Hotel. She made sure Rambeau had all of her fabulous jewelry on, most notably the ring that Rambeau had claimed was worth twenty thousand dollars, and she made sure the boy knew that she knew exactly what jewelry Rambeau was wearing. He told Norma that he gave the two women over to the doorman at the Roosevelt, and that they'd had a hard time making it up the steps to the hotel.

Norma knew that Rambeau had spent a considerable sum that night, but she was shocked when she tallied it—thirty thousand dollars! It had happened too many times before—a beef the next day over a large amount of money. Norma decided soon after sunrise that she'd return half of it if Rambeau showed up at the house before getting on the train. By nightfall she assumed that the actress was on her way back to Hollywood. Norma's purse bulged with the money; it would be safely in the bank the next morning.

But at the Roosevelt Hotel, Rambeau and her young friend were barely able to get out of bed for dinner. Earlier in the afternoon, from her prone position, she'd called the cab company, looking for the driver who had taken her to Norma's house. Hungover, she realized she had no idea where she'd been. She became adamant with the dispatcher; she claimed there'd been a robbery, and the cab company would have hell to pay if they didn't help her find the culprits. Late in the afternoon the dispatcher located the address on Itchem's trip sheet. Rambeau ordered some beef broth and Coca-Cola from room service and went back to sleep.

The next morning Norma was getting ready to go to her bank in the Central Business District when she heard the front door open, followed by the maid saying, "Ma'am, please, you can't go in there. I'll call Miss Norma."

High heels struck the floorboards as a woman hurried toward the back parlor, her voice raised in anger. "I want my money!"

Norma hid her purse and met Rambeau at the door to the parlor. The poor little straggler was still with her, looking licked. "What money?" Norma asked.

Rambeau got right in Norma's face, hostile. "Look, I want some of the money I spent the other night. That's too much to drop in one place." Before Norma could reply, she said, "You rolled me." Norma recognized Rambeau's woman-on-the-tough role from her movies. "And if you don't give it to me . . ." Instead of finishing her threat, she stalked out to a pay phone in the hallway. Near the front door, Itchem nervously fingered the brim of his porkpie hat. Rambeau got out a nickel and lifted the receiver.

"Oh, do you want to use the phone?" Norma inquired. "Who are you going to call?" Even though she was shorter than Rambeau, she stared Miss High-and-Mighty down.

"I'm calling the police."

"Okay, honey," Norma said, "you're throwing your weight around pretty good here. You know, if you hadn't tried to muscle me I might have considered what you had to say. Instead, I think I'll do a little nickel dropping myself. You call the police, and I'll call *The Times-Picayune*. Now won't they have a juicy little story." Rambeau blanched. "I have nothing to lose," said Norma. "What about yourself?" She took the phone from Rambeau's rather limp hand, took her nickel as well, and started to drop it.

Rambeau put her hand over Norma's. "Let's not be hasty, Norma. What do you say we have a talk?"

"Fine with me." Norma hung up the phone.

The two women went into the parlor. Itchem tried to eavesdrop from down the hall. Norma gave the cabbie an arched eyebrow and banged the door.

By the time Rambeau sank into the sofa cushions, she had recovered her good humor. "How about some champagne," she asked, "for old times' sake?" Norma nodded to the maid.

Norma had been bluffed since she was nine years old, and she could smell a con coming. Rambeau kissed her, said she'd had a beautiful time, but, after all, that *was* a lot of money, could they talk about it? "You can't use it anyway, because it's all marked. My husband, when I left Florida, gave me that money, but he didn't approve of me carrying so much, so he said he had the serial numbers recorded on all of it."

Norma said nicely, "If I can't cash those hundred-dollar bills, shame on you, because you'll be reading about it." She let Rambeau take that in, then went on. "Look, if you had come in here right, instead of barging in and being hostile, I might have given you some of your money back. But I've decided there's nothing you're going to do about it."

Rambeau thought about it and recognized that Norma had the bigger muscle. "Okay, let's just forget this. I'll charge it off to experience, and if you ever come to Los Angeles, look me up and I'll show you one gorgeous time."

She gave Norma her card, and when the champagne was poured she made a toast to the hair of the dog that bit her, but she didn't take even a sip. Norma took a long draft as she thought, Yeah sure, old girl, I bet you'd show me a hell of a time on your stomping ground. Ain't no way I'm leaving mine—this town suits me real great.

The two women kissed goodbye, and Rambeau and the straggler were off to catch the eleven o'clock train.

Itchem, who'd nearly been fired because of the stink Rambeau made, came back to 410 Dauphine to wheedle more money out of Norma. She gave him a cut, but not the 40 percent he normally made. And Norma gave the girls who'd danced naked a cut of the money too, but not their full cut (40 percent of a cab fare, 60 percent otherwise). They'd knocked themselves out in the entertainment department, but, after all, they hadn't had to go to bed with Rambeau.

Norma kept $24,000 for herself and bought an annuity with it— for her retirement. Before it matured, Carrie Badon Schubert, Norma's aunt, and her husband, Billy Schubert, signed a notarized affidavit swearing that, in their presence, John Gauley Badon had given his daughter, Norma Badon, a gift of $24,000 in cash.

Back in Hollywood, Rambeau went on to have a long and lucrative career as a character actress. She specialized in aging harlots and fallen women and appeared in movie classics such as *Tobacco Road, The*

View from Pompey's Head, and *Man of a Thousand Faces.* She was twice nominated for an Academy Award for best supporting actress, for *Primrose Path* and *Torch Song.* Norma saw every movie Marjorie Rambeau ever made.

When Marjorie Rambeau's husband (probably her third, Francis Gudger) told her not to get off the train in New Orleans because it was "such a wicked city," he no doubt had in mind exactly the seamy scene that epitomized the Tango Belt in the twenties—naked girls lying in the windows of brothels, gambling behind every door, and incidents of people being mugged and robbed on the streets while that hot jazz played all night long.

But the city was wicked right down to the political infrastructure. When the local writer Jack Stewart was researching the music scene in the Tango Belt, he discovered that "a politically complicated game went on to keep things going as they were.

"After a public outcry to clean things up," Stewart explained, "some blue blood would be appointed commissioner of public safety, or whatever title, and he'd take off like a rocket—he was going to get the job done. Then he'd realize the mess he was mired in and that he was nothing but a figurehead, a pawn in the whole deal, a scapegoat. Ultimately, he would quit." And the status quo was maintained.

In the late 1920s, when Captain Ray was helping to change the Tango Belt irrevocably, T. Semmes Walmsley was the commissioner of finance. Walmsley was part of the Uptown social elite, a member of the Boston Club; his father had been Rex, King of Carnival, in 1890. When Mayor Arthur O'Keefe became ill and was forced to leave office in 1928, Walmsley became acting mayor. He had been Ray's biggest supporter in the cleanup of the Tango Belt. Now he appointed Ray to head the police department.

But he promoted Theodore Ray right out of the precinct where he'd been so effective. Ray held his new post for less than a year before he resigned from the police force. No reason was given.

At the time Norma had two good policemen on the beat patrolling Dauphine Street. She left the gate to her alley at the side of the house unlocked. Whenever the cops got tired, they'd come in through the alley, go upstairs, take one of the rooms, and go to sleep, leaving Norma's phone number with the precinct in case a crime was committed.

In 1928 Huey Long was elected governor of Louisiana. Known as the People's Governor, Long had a solid base everywhere in the state except New Orleans. He planned to rectify this problem by getting control of the Old Regulars, a New Orleans political machine with powerful leverage in the state legislature.

Then, in 1929, while the country sang along with popular songs like "I'm Sitting on Top of the World" and "Happy Days Are Here Again," the stock market crashed. Walmsley found himself mayor of a city with a crumbling infrastructure, where teachers, police, and firemen were poorly paid and poorly equipped, and there was no money in sight.

Officially elected mayor in 1930, Walmsley became the head of the Old Regulars, which put him in direct opposition to Long. In declaring war on New Orleans, Huey Long hung a demoralizing moniker on the tall, bony-faced Walmsley. He referred to him relentlessly as Turkey Head while he starved the city into submission by preventing banks from lending it any money and, later, burying it in trash by not releasing money to pay the garbage collectors and forcing a strike during a record-breaking heat wave.

At one point Long threatened to put New Orleans under military rule. He specifically ordered the militiamen he'd dispatched to search out prostitution in the "cesspool of iniquity" he claimed the city had become under old Turkey Head. Norma's police friends told her to close her house for a while. "Here I had this beautiful house, and suddenly we needed a new place to hustle," she said.

Jackie, her housekeeper who answered the phones and made appointments, knew of an apartment on Chartres Street. The place was gloomy and overdone, with drapes made of a heavy damask and matching couches and bed canopy. But it had a phone.

Norma stationed three or four girls in the apartment. That same evening she brought a few dates over in her car. "These were Good

Men," she said, "a few Good Men worth the risk." Since the crash Norma wasn't getting so many Good Men.

As soon as the men left, one of the girls called her. "I don't feel right in this place, Norma," she said. "There's something spooky here. It's just not normal. Maybe you'd better come over."

When Norma got there another girl said she had something to show her. "We didn't have enough bedrooms with three men here," she said. She opened the closet and pointed. "So, look, I turned a trick on the ironing board."

"That's no ironing board," Norma told her, "that's one of those boards they lay you out on when you're dead."

The apartment, it turned out, belonged to an undertaker. "You should have seen those whores running out of that building, down to Chartres Street," Norma said. "They never got over it. Every time I wanted to put them in another apartment, they had to investigate first."

By 1932 Long and Turkey Head had called a truce, and Norma was fully operational at 410 Dauphine again. "The police still had raids occasionally, but they were token raids. Next door to me was a colored lady, Mary. Over my alley was a balcony that looked right into her bedrooms. Whenever I had these token raids, we'd put planks from my balcony to her windows. The girls would walk the planks to Mary's and pull the boards in behind them. Then I would open the door and let the police go through the house."

The war between the two politicians was ended only when Long was assassinated in 1935, after which his successor made a deal with Walmsley, who agreed to resign two years before the end of his mayoral term in return for restoration of financial self-control to the city. But the city's political and financial travails didn't seem to hamper Norma's operation after 1932. One reason for this was that George Reyer became chief of police (subsequently called Police Superintendent) in 1931. As Norma told Howard Jacobs (for his *Times-Picayune* profile), "Reyer had a peculiar notion that real crime consisted of strong-arm plug-uglies preying on the public. He didn't have much time for the minor vices that menaced nobody."

Another factor was that New Orleans was feeling the full force of the Great Depression. The French Quarter especially had deteriorated to the point that people called it a slum, and there were murmurs of a plan to tear the old buildings down on a number of square blocks and erect a vast housing project in their place. But, savvy businessperson that she was, Norma found opportunity in the very worst of times. In fact, she made her first fortune.

Not only movie stars found their way to 410 Dauphine; so did bootleggers who carried cigar boxes full of gold coins. Norma bought more furniture for the house—antique tester beds, cheval mirrors, and upholstered Victorian boudoir chairs, along with the new furniture she purchased at Maestri's store on Rampart Street. What a relief it must have been to enter Norma's well-appointed, comfortable house after a night out on the town in the risqué but decaying French Quarter.

As she continued to refine her parlor house, Norma, in her early thirties now, also found her personal style. She began buying expensive tailored suits, the kind she wore for the rest of her life—when she wasn't wearing a smashing skintight cocktail or evening dress. Soon she would own luxury cars, usually Cadillacs, along with the odd Jaguar or Corvette. As fast as she could spend money, Norma made more. For while the Good Men were feeling the Depression, Norma had found another clientele: patrons of the seemingly endless stream of conventions that came to New Orleans even during the Depression.

The undertakers came to town. One came to the house, and the girl he went with claimed it was the easiest money she'd ever made. All she had to do was lie there—like she was dead. Norma and the other girls made sure they knew where he was from—they didn't want to get screwed *after* death!

When a convention of Baptists was in town, a nice-looking man came to the house. He went upstairs but was back down almost immediately, spluttering and enraged. Norma asked him what was wrong.

"Your girl won't take me," he told her, "says I have a dose."

"Well, if my girl says you have a dose, then you have a dose."

"I'm a preacher," he said, nearly shaking with outrage. "I've never been in a house before."

"Okay," Norma said, "I'll have my housekeeper take a look. She's a real expert in these matters."

Jackie took him to the next room. In less than two minutes, she was back. "Norma, that man's got the biggest dose I've ever seen!"

Norma said. "Sorry, no action," and the man raged around, insisting, "But I've never been with a hooker before!"

"Then, Reverend," Norma said, "you better go home and have a good talk with your wife. You sure as hell didn't get that on a toilet seat."

He left, fuming. But he wasn't gone long. About twenty minutes later he was back, meek and mild. He asked Norma what he should do about his problem. She sent him to the same doctor who checked her girls.

Unlike the Reverend, a lot of conventioneers had women with them and wanted to bring them to the house. Jackie had been trained as a classical ballet dancer, and she had a beautiful body. She and Norma came up with a way to promote her natural talent and make a lot of money.

Jackie put on a gorgeous negligee and did what she called interpretive dance. At a strategic moment her negligee would fall from her shoulders and float to the floor. "We had the first strip shows right there at 410 Dauphine," Norma said. "Jackie didn't shake it up because she didn't need to. She could have put any of those Bourbon Street strippers that came after her to shame."

The shows were such a success that the women got bolder. They came up with the "fake shows." In these Jackie and some of the other girls would act with men as if they were having sex in front of the audience. The men, though, were gay. "The only way this boy could get a hard-on was with a device known as the wimpus. It was a glass tube with a little pump. He'd go out in the hall before the show and pump that thing until his prick got hard—and he had a big one. Then he'd go in and mount the girls like a big deal was going on, but he never had an orgasm. I saw him put on numerous shows in one night when a big convention was in town, yet he'd never have an orgasm with a girl. It was all fake."

The fake shows were quite popular with the conventioneers' ladies. "We'd be booked all night, and it got to be that there were more couples coming to the shows than single men."

Norma talked to many men who told her that when it came time to vote on where they wanted to have their conventions, they would pick New Orleans because it was a wide open city. "That's what made New Orleans famous," Norma said.

Mardi Gras was big in 1933. The banks in the city were still operating; everything seemed fine. "In New Orleans," Norma said sardonically, "I think they waited until every last cent had been put in the banks, *then* they folded."

One day Norma was walking along Carondelet Street in the Central Business District, on the other side of Canal Street from the French Quarter, and a clock in the window of a bank caught her eye. It was the type of clock that would look great sitting on a mantel, Roman numerals on a round face embedded in antique wood. The clock was a premium for opening an account. "I always was sort of freaky for clocks," Norma admitted. "I went in and looked at it, and I thought, What the hell?"

To open an account, the bank charged a dollar. Norma estimated the cost of the clock to be about fifty cents. "But, oh, what a price I paid for that clock. I put all my money in, the bank went down, and I lost almost everything"—close to $90,000.

Still, Norma counted herself lucky. Many of her friends were not faring nearly as well. Some of the cabdrivers, especially the ones with families, had it rough. She brought syrup from Shady Pond, her Pearl River farm, and gave it to the drivers, along with butter that they could trade for oleo. She freely gave out groceries and clothes, and bought one chauffeur's children bicycles for Christmas. That cabbie appreciated what she had done for his family so much that when he got on his feet again he presented her with a new Frigidaire for the house.

All through Prohibition Norma had continued cheating with near beer and whiskey at 410 Dauphine. At a dollar a setup each for the men and girls, it had been too good a deal not to take the chance. Then in 1933 the Volstead Act was repealed, ending Prohibition and enabling Norma to open a bar again.

Norma had hoped to buy herself a house as well. She didn't like the street entrance on Dauphine, the box steps coming right down to the sidewalk, visible to anyone watching, as was the gate to the alley, the only other way to enter the property. She kept her lease at 410 Dauphine, but without the perfect location Norma wasn't certain that she wanted to stay in the business. She decided to take what money she had left and go to New York.

She arrived by train. At Grand Central Station, she told a cab-driver to take her to the Hotel Monticello on Sixty-fourth Street. He gave her a funny look. "Have you ever been in New York before? Do you know that hotel?"

"Is there any reason I shouldn't go there?" she countered, assuming that there must be hustling girls at the hotel. In her suit, hat, gloves, matching shoes and purse, she was sure *she* didn't look like *that* kind of girl.

Sure enough, characters—underworld characters—sat all around the lobby. From them she found out why the driver had grinned and squirmed: the gangster Legs Diamond had been shot down in the Monticello by an old friend he'd double-crossed.

One of the characters befriended Norma. He took her to an opium den in Chinatown where moving contraband for the so-called mayor of Chinatown gained him entrance.

They climbed many steps. Chinese children played on the landings. When they got to the third floor, to Norma's surprise a big blonde answered the door. Her name was Dolly, and she was distraught. That very day her Chinese boyfriend had been sent up for the tong wars; his sentence was fifteen years.

She welcomed Norma and her friend into a living room. Norma's eyes could hardly take it in—all around were poodles. Not live dogs. They had died and Dolly had had them stuffed. They were sitting, standing, lying all around the opium den. Norma had never been in such a place. She had never smoked hop—she didn't even smoke cigarettes.

They were taken into a room with bunks. Her friend bunked with one Chinaman; another took Norma off to another bunk. He rolled the ball, heated it, and let it burn. Then he loaded a pipe and gave her a big draw. The Chinaman took his draw and sat back with a seventh-heaven smile on his face.

Afterwards Norma's friend took her to a Chinese restaurant where they were the only Caucasians. The food was incredible; Norma was starving.

She asked her friend, "Did you get sick when you smoked?" He said he hadn't. "I didn't either," she said.

"You're supposed to get sick the first time you smoke," he informed her. "It upsets your stomach."

Norma had seen him lay down a hundred-dollar bill, and she hadn't seen him get any change. "Well," she said sympathetically, "you sure wasted a lot of money on me, because I don't know how to inhale!"

But what an experience she'd had. "I don't know why I was so amazed, because I knew girls in New Orleans smoking hop over on Tulane Avenue, where Chinatown used to be. But I felt wicked. I thought, Here I am smoking hop in New York City with a bunch of goddamned stuffed poodles!"

Norma returned from New York short on money but with a long lease left on her beautiful house at 410 Dauphine Street. Within a couple of years her business became more solidly established than it had been before the 1933 bank failure. But even better times were ahead.

In 1936 Robert Maestri, who owned Maestri's furniture store on Rampart Street, as well as a lot of the property that had once been the site of Storyville, became mayor. In a lucrative deal he sold this property to the city, which erected several acres of two-story, red-brick, four-family dwellings, the same kind of housing project the city was considering for the land the French Quarter occupied.

Maestri continued to corrupt the city's political infrastructure during his tenure as mayor. He was party to the graft and scandal that had often infiltrated city politics, and under him the spoils system flourished. He had legitimate civic achievements as well, such as decreasing the city's debt significantly, and under his leadership New Orleans supported cultural organizations like the ballet and the symphony, restored historically important buildings, and improved garbage collection. But the inbred practice of graft continued. The price tags at the Maestri furniture store, where all the madams bought their furniture, still included a markup, as they had through the twenties, sometimes more than a hundred percent, that went directly to police protection. With Bob Maestri mayor and George Reyer chief of police, the town was as wide open as at any time in its history.

In the wake of Huey Long's rule in New Orleans, Maestri didn't hear much hue and cry from concerned citizens about vice and corruption. Perhaps they were relieved to have money moving again and banks and business functioning normally. To keep up appearances Maestri appointed a respected doctor as commissioner of public safety. But Frank Gomila was not interested in reform. To ensure public safety, he included in his duties a twice-weekly inspection of the girls at Norma Wallace's house.

Norma bought influence when she bought furniture at Maestri's store, but as Clint Bolton said in his *New Orleans* magazine article, "Influence is not always a matter of dollars and cents."

At the top of the FBI's Ten Most Wanted list in 1936 was a hoodlum named Alvin Karpis, who was sought for bank and train robbery, kidnapping, and murder. Karpis fancied the girls at cathouses, and during the spring of that year all the hookers and madams in town seemed to know that a man who fit the FBI's description of Karpis was on the prowl in the New Orleans area. Circulating with his description was the detail that he sported a huge diamond ring.

J. Edgar Hoover, the director of the FBI, particularly wanted Karpis and had put out the word to every police chief in the country. George Reyer was the one who delivered. Bureau agents arrested Karpis at the corner of Canal and Jefferson Davis Parkway without a shot being fired. Hoover was whisked to New Orleans for a photo opportunity that made it look as if he'd been in on the capture.

Bolton said to Norma, "Reyer alerted the FBI. Who alerted Reyer?"

Norma answered, "Karpis was in my place a night or two before the FBI picked him up. When I saw the pictures in the paper after the arrest, I knew for a fact that it was Karpis. Especially when they mentioned his big diamond ring. Honey, that was a headlight! I figured him for something big-time, a gambler, crook, something. But he behaved well, was generous with the girls, and we always had a lot of high rollers comin' in, so I didn't think too much about it. Except that was a real beauty of a ring."

In the underworld no one admitted anything unless he absolutely had to, but with the capture of Alvin Karpis, the flamboyant Reyer made a name as chief of police, and Norma became a woman with influence. Reyer dropped in at her Dauphine Street house regularly, along with his equally colorful chief of detectives, John Grosch, who cut quite a figure in a white linen suit with a fresh rose in the lapel. The local FBI agents spent time in Norma's parlor too. She doled out the information, they doled out the protection. It was a fine line to walk—to keep her influence without getting a reputation as a stoolie. She walked it with perfect balance. With friends in high places and her wealth, Norma Wallace at thirty-five years old became one of the most powerful women in the New Orleans underworld.

CHAPTER FIVE

My Two
Most Exciting Lovers

"My husbands were all better than I was," Norma confided to her tape recorder. To Howard Jacobs she said wistfully, "All my marriages were beautiful. I'm the bossy, domineering type, and I'll take full responsibility for breaking 'em up. The trouble was, my husbands all considered themselves married, but I didn't."

Soon after Norma left her location above Pete Herman's club in 1928, she married for the first time. On any legal paperwork filed over the years, however, she always named Pete as her first husband. Her closest friends didn't know any different. It's no wonder: "My first marriage was to Alex Zolman, a racetrack figure, although we'll dismiss him because he didn't play as long or important a part in my life as did the other four." And she never said another word about him.

Before the other four, though, it seemed as if the men she loved the most she didn't marry. There were three of them, Andy Wallace first. The next two were her lovers during the ten years that Norma called the most glamorous period of her life.

Near ten o'clock on a Sunday night, Norma and a coterie of her girls emerged from the shadowy streets of the French Quarter onto Canal

Street, which New Orleans businessmen had turned into the brightest, widest main street in the country in their effort to create a first-class, modern shopping district.

To Norma's right was the palatial Saenger Theatre; to her left was McCrory's, the five-and-dime store with an Art Deco diner. Norma sometimes ate lunch in one of its booths lined with blue mirrors before a long afternoon of shopping. The stores where she was well known for large cash expenditures lined Canal Street almost to the Custom House near the Mississippi River. There were department stores, shoe stores, liquor stores, drugstores, and the furrier where she'd bought the mink she wore over her low-cut red dancing dress on this cold January night.

Norma and the girls crossed the Canal Street neutral ground, their high heels skittering over its polished red-and-white terrazzo squares as they hurried to beat the streetcar rumbling down its tracks to the river. Burgundy Street, where they crossed, became University Place on the other side. The Meal-a-Minit's sign, with its thousands of watts from incandescent bulbs, lit the corner in a blaze like high-noon sunlight. Half a block down a Phil Harris movie, *Double or Nothing,* played at the Orpheum. Across the street was the Roosevelt Hotel (now the Fairmont), where only a couple of years ago Huey Long had held court from a tenth-floor suite, and where the local politicos regularly convened. They sometimes called Norma to send girls, or drunkenly found their way to her house after one of their confabs.

The lobby of the Roosevelt stretched a city block between University Place and Baronne Street. Its walls were mirrored and marbled, and gilded columns ran its length. Stylish women, wearing long dresses, hats with peacock feathers, and exotic furs (Norma spotted ocelot, fox, and mink) strolled arm in arm with men in tuxedos and sharp double-breasted suits. Others lounged on the velvet-upholstered sofas and chairs, smoking and chatting while they waited for the show at the Blue Room to begin.

The Blue Room was the hottest nightclub in the city, and also one of the oldest in the country. It was a spacious room with a large dance floor under a midnight blue, star-studded sky, a padded circular bar, and candlelit tables both ringside and on terraces so the Blue Room Orchestra floor show was visible to all. Romantic, swank, and classy, it served the famous Ramos gin fizz and headlined such sizzling acts as the tango duo Enrica and Novello.

But the headliner that January broke all attendance records. In 1936 Phil Harris was one of the most popular entertainers in the country. He had starred as himself in a 1933 film called *So This Is Harris* and won an Oscar for best comedy short subject. He was such a star that he played himself in two subsequent films.

Norma, with her girls, was on her way to see him. At the stroke of ten she breezed through the big double doors to the nightclub, barely stopping to shrug out of her mink, which fell into the hands of the waiter following her. Heads turned as she floated to her usual front-row table, compliments of the star. When Charley Bagby, the piano player, saw her, he broke into "Be Still My Heart."

The first act was a ventriloquist, Edgar Bergen with his smart-aleck dummy Charlie McCarthy. Charlie sat on Edgar's knee, having a little trouble keeping his head upright. Edgar asked him why he was so groggy.

"Well, Charley and I," he said lifting his chin toward the piano player, "had a pretty rough night last night."

"What did you do?" Edgar asked.

"We went down to Dauphine Street to visit the Queen."

The crowd laughed, because by that time everybody knew who the Queen of Dauphine was. A reporter for the *Item* had picked up the reference earlier in the week and started using it in his column, "The Spotlight." Also, the show was broadcast over the radio, and Harris regularly preceded his songs, such as "That's What I Like About the South" and "Doo Wha Ditty, Oh So Small and Oh So Pretty," with "This one's dedicated to the Queen." During the broadcast he'd let his friends know where to meet him after the show too— over at the Queen's on Dauphine.

Norma had met Phil during the first week of his engagement at the Blue Room. His show was from ten to two nightly, and after hours he and his band had decamped to a bar on University Place. The bar was owned by one of Norma's friends, Louie—not her ex-boyfriend. One night when the band members were particularly wound up and didn't want to quit, Louie closed down his bar and took them all over to 410 Dauphine. Norma had taken one look at

Phil's large-featured, roughly handsome face, which was rarely without a smile, and fallen in love.

Every night after the show Phil and his band would head to Norma's, where they'd fix big pitchers of absinthe (a drink made from wormwood, a psychoactive substance that was banned in 1912), tell jokes, and play music. Phil wrote a song for Norma called "Queens Drink Absinthe in New Orleans." Norma loved all the attention he gave her, and she had never laughed so much in her life. "I discovered that when you're in love, everything is laughs."

So many people were clamoring for tickets to the Phil Harris show that the band's engagement was extended through February. Whenever they could Phil and Norma would go to her farm in Pearl River. Sometimes Jackie and a couple of the girls came along with a few guys in the band. One night Phil got a little loose and tried to bring one of the cows into the living room. They all laughed until Norma wasn't sure they would recover.

Norma had horses at the farm; she'd bought them after a tuberculosis scare that turned out to be a case of too much nightlife. She exercised and got as much fresh air as she could now. Phil had never ridden horses until he met Norma. He loved riding with her.

All too soon Phil had to leave New Orleans, though he returned for two more Blue Room engagements. In between, Norma visited him in Cincinnati, Dallas, and Los Angeles, where he played the big, fabulous nightspots. They'd spend a few nights together, until Norma needed to get back to her business. "Or I'd send out a distress signal," she said, "and he'd beeline for New Orleans."

Phil's fame and popularity continued to grow, and he joined the Jack Benny radio show. After that, on one of Norma's trips to California, he showed her the property he'd bought, formerly the actor Adolphe Menjou's, right in the heart of Los Angeles. But when Norma saw it, before Phil built his house, it was thick with orange trees and deer were jumping over the fence.

When Norma met Phil, he was unhappily married to a woman named Mascot, a former Miss Australia. Even though they divorced, Norma never allowed herself to think she had a future with this man who made her laugh as no one else did, one of the great loves of her life. She knew that his life would always be centered in Los Angeles and New York. "And I had a good business, enjoying it all so that I could never have given it up for love or money," she insisted. "I liked what I was doing too much; I liked the excitement of it all. So we enjoyed each other better knowing that it wasn't forever."

Phil eventually married the singer and actress Alice Faye. But he and Norma kept in touch, writing, sending telegrams, and hearing about each other through friends. Phil's engagements at the Blue Room had begun for him a lifelong love affair with New Orleans. He returned to the city often, to play his music, to reign at Mardi Gras as King of Bacchus in 1972, and to visit one of his and Alice Faye's daughters, who became a permanent resident of the city. He also visited Norma. "Over the years our love affair deepened into friendship," Norma said. Whenever he was in town, they got together for dinner or a few drinks. And always for a few laughs.

One night Louie called from his bar on University Place. "Norma, send over one of your best ladies," he said. "I got a good customer in here needs a smart cookie with athletic capabilities."

This vidalia sounded like he could be trouble, so Norma sent Eileen, a dazzling brunette who was as smart as she was beautiful. Eileen left Dauphine Street around midnight and didn't return until late the following morning.

"I never want to go out with that man again," she told Norma. "I couldn't stand him. He's mean and he's brazen. The word is he's from Chicago and connected to Capone."

That same night he called for Eileen. She handed Norma the phone. "It's the vidalia with the machine gun," she said, "you know, the one from last night."

In a voice icy with authority, Norma told the man she wasn't interested in his business. Right away he got smart with her. "Why, you little bitch," he said. "Nobody talks to Sam Hunt like that and gets away with it."

"Well, I just did, Sam Hunt, and I'm getting away with it. You can just go to hell."

"We'll see about that," he snarled. "I'm coming over there, and I'm going to beat your teeth in."

"You just better try that," Norma said and hung up.

She got her .410 shotgun from the hall closet. She didn't really expect him, but she was ready to scare the hell out of him if he showed.

A few hours later, just when she'd stopped carrying the gun from room to room with her, two men walked into the front parlor. She knew immediately which one was Sam Hunt. His frosty blue eyes had the cruelest, coldest expression she'd ever seen. She tried to remember where she'd last put the shotgun.

Standing an arm's length away, Norma faced him. He made a surprising move—he took off his hat.

"That was you on the phone?"

"It was," Norma said inching her shoulders back ever so slightly.

"Mind if I sit?"

She nodded. He never took his eyes off her. Before long Norma forgot she was angry with the man.

His drink was B & B. They talked into the night, and the spark they'd struck began to glow a little hotter.

Sam stayed with Norma for a week. They went out to dinner every night, they went dancing, and they slept together. Except Sam never made love to her. He'd hold her and pet her, but that was as far as he'd go. She began to wonder if he was normal.

A couple of nights later, as he held her in the crook of his arm, she decided to find out. "Sam? Are you awake?" He said he was. "Sam, there's almost nothing I like more than being held and petted. Almost nothing." She stopped, not sure how to go on.

Sam lifted himself on his elbow so he could look at her. The streetlight coming in through the shutters was just enough that they could make out each other's faces.

"Norma," he said, "I'll never lay you until I know that you really care for me, that you're not just turning a trick with me. I care too much." The gangster, it seemed, was a romantic.

After a week he invited Norma to the races in San Antonio. He told her to meet him at the Southern Railway station that night. She arrived in plenty of time to settle into a compartment. She stared out the window but saw no sign of Sam. Fifteen anxious minutes went by; the whistle blew; the train was ready to pull out—still Sam wasn't there. Norma wondered if she should get off the train. It was beginning to move when she saw him running toward the tracks from the terminal. When he found her in the compartment, he held her and kissed her with a passion she'd never encountered before in a man. She swooned with desire. Before the train was out of the New Orleans city limits, Sam drew the window shade and pulled her into the lower berth. This time he went all the way. He made love to her off and on for the next twelve hours, until they needed to eat and drink and pull themselves together so they could get off the train. By the time they reached San Antonio, Norma was crazy for Sam Hunt.

He told her he was married, one of those spur-of-the-moment deals, and he didn't love his wife any longer, but he had a baby daughter he loved very much. That was all right; Norma didn't want to break up his marriage. But Louie had told her some stories of his meanness—they were hard for her to believe. And there were rumors that he'd been in on the St. Valentine's Day Massacre. Louie told her they called him Golfbag Sam because he carried his machine gun in his golf bag, and that he'd served time in the Cook County jail.

"I won't ever tell you my business," Sam told Norma, "and don't you ever ask. I don't want you to know anything. I don't ever want to put you in that spot. Because I love you."

What he did didn't matter; it couldn't. Norma was already in too deep.

Louie had verified that Sam was affiliated with Al Capone's outfit. Capone was in Alcatraz, but when Sam took her to Chicago, he introduced her to Capone's brother, who ran a whorehouse with many women in it. They all wore shorts and bras, and they turned tricks like they were on an assembly line. A girl who worked there told Norma that after six months in the place she had to have a hysterectomy because she was so beat up.

When Sam and Norma were in Chicago, they never went out alone. Another man was always with them, she had no idea why. But they vacationed on their own, in Hot Springs, Arkansas, a big gambling town, and all the characters there knew Sam. Norma enjoyed every minute of it.

Norma and Sam were so much in love that every time they had to part they fought. Then they'd meet again and make up. This went on for some time, until they finally became jealous and distrustful of each other.

One Sunday afternoon Norma put Sam on a plane for Chicago. As she was leaving the airport, she stopped to talk to a pilot she knew, someone she'd had a brief affair with who was now a friend. Norma never fell out with lovers, even the ones she married. She always kept them as friends. Sam didn't understand friendships like that—with other men.

Norma drove to Pearl River to spend the night, to get a little peace and quiet and solitude before beginning another week. She was in bed when she heard a car roll up to the house. The engine was cut and the headlights were off. She got her robe and crept into the living room.

Before she could get a fix on what was happening, someone had a shoulder to the door, ready to break it down. Norma edged over to a window and looked out. Standing next to the car was Philip, who regularly chauffeured Sam when he was in town.

"Sam Hunt," she yelled, "is that you?" She sprang the door open so that he nearly fell into the living room. "What the hell are you doing?" she demanded.

"I want to know if anyone is here with you," he said, as cold and mean as she'd ever seen him.

He'd seen her talking to the pilot at the airport. It had been too late to get off the plane, so he'd gone on to Memphis, disembarked, then taken the first flight back to New Orleans. She tried to explain that the pilot was an old friend and going off with him was the last thing on her mind; she told Sam she knew he wasn't a man to play those kinds of games with, but he was primed for a fight and turned a deaf ear. Before it got too ugly, he left, and Philip drove him back to the airport.

Four days passed, and neither of them called, the worst lovers' quarrel they'd had. Norma was in love with a lunatic gangster. She needed someone to talk to. She went around the corner to see her closest, most trusted friend and business partner, Pete Herman.

They went to Pete's apartment over the nightclub. He had living quarters on the Conti Street side, with the adjacent building on

Burgundy walled off for business as it had been when Norma opened her operation there. Since Norma had moved to 410 Dauphine, a block away, Pete had married, been widowed, and been left with two daughters. He listened to Norma's troubles with Sam Hunt, and at once he knew the solution.

Pete saw his opportunity; he proposed to Norma. He seemed to think Sam would leave her alone once they were married.

Norma looked at him. He was completely blind; she knew he could no longer see her. She recalled the night soon after she'd moved above his lounge that he'd taken her up to the roof over his club to teach her some self-defense moves. He still had a little sight then, but he hadn't seen her right hook coming, and she'd decked him. She smiled. She felt great affection for him. They had been lovers off and on for so many years, and now they were the best of friends. She loved Pete, no doubt about that.

But Norma was not "in love" with Pete. Jumping into marriage with him reflected her emotional upset over Sam Hunt, a man she was deeply in love with but could never marry, not only because of his marriage and devotion to his child or his mob affiliations and criminal acts but because he wanted more of her than she would ever be willing to give. He wanted Norma to be *his* woman, and Norma was nobody's woman but her own.

Because Sam Hunt was a hot-blooded lover and a cold-blooded killer, Norma's decision to marry Pete proved to be one of the most dangerous things she could have done. It almost cost them their lives.

Pete and Norma were married on July 28, 1936. That night they listened to news of the Duke of Windsor, who would abdicate the English throne in order to marry his American lover, Wallis Simpson. It all seemed so romantic. Phil Harris sent a telegram from Dallas: I HEARD I LOST OUT AGAIN.

Pete's apartment was already beautiful, and now it was filled with all the wedding presents people had given them. Norma made just a few changes when she moved in, bringing only her clothes and personal possessions. She was happy; she thought she and Pete could make a go of it. It made her sad, though, to see Pete, a devout Catholic, leave for church every Tuesday to make a novena because he was having trouble facing his blindness. But Pete's failed eyesight didn't prevent his riding with Norma in Pearl River. They went nearly every Sunday after they'd closed their respective places and returned at noon on Monday. He rode Mike, the old mule, which he felt safe on, and he and Norma seemed not to have a care in the world.

But news of their marriage found its way to Chicago. Sam was furious. He knew Pete; he'd spent quite a lot of time and money in his nightclub, both with Norma and on his own. He felt betrayed. He called Norma and in his fury threatened her, and Norma understood that he was unleashing his anger and frustration. She assumed he would forget about it. She was upset and hurt—she didn't want to lose Sam, but he was married and now she was too. And she promised herself she would do her best to stay married.

On a beautiful Sunday in the fall, Pete and Norma went riding in Pearl River, enjoying the weather and the farmhouse, which Norma had been improving steadily since her father had died. It was a beautiful place, far off the highway. She'd had a good road built to it along with other improvements. But with all the expense Norma had never bothered to have a telephone installed.

That afternoon, as she and Pete relaxed after their ride, an urgent intuition seized Norma. She needed to call her house. She and Pete left immediately, driving ten miles to the town of Slidell, where Norma could find a pay phone. She called Jackie.

"Sam Hunt is here," Jackie told her, keeping her voice low. "He's been drinking B & B all day. He's so furious he's gone crazy, Norma. He built a fire under the couch in the living room. When I put it out, he built another one. He's being quiet right now, but I don't dare take my eyes off him. I've had no rest at all, trying to keep him from burning us up. Every time I try to talk to him, he tells me to mind my own business. He says he's going to wreck the house, and he's got a gun on him, Norma. He is really performing."

This wasn't the first time Norma was grateful for Jackie's cool head. Unsure what to do, she finally decided to let Jackie handle it, and she and Pete went on with their plan to spend Sunday night in the country.

It seemed she'd made the right decision. Sam left during the night, and Norma figured that once he sobered up he wouldn't cause any more trouble. He had good friends in town who would make him see the futility of all his commotion.

Monday went by, and Norma heard nothing. About one in the morning she left 410 Dauphine. She went down the concrete box steps, and as soon as she hit the sidewalk, a car engine roared and headlights blinded her. She leapt back on the steps as the car jumped the curb. Had she not moved so quickly, she would have been crushed against the front wall of the house. The concrete steps saved her. Through the windshield she saw Sam's cold and determined expression, and she managed to unlock the door and get inside before he could back off and come at her again.

She called Pete at the club. "We're in for trouble," she told him. "Sam's on the warpath." Pete said he would call Richie, a friend who could nail a half-dollar from a hundred yards. Meantime, Norma called Philip, who told her he was on his way to meet Sam at Pete's place.

Before Philip could get there, though, Sam arrived. He got out of the car with his gun and fired directly into the club, missing Pete by inches. Richie entered the club through an alley door on Conti Street. When Sam saw him with his gun drawn, he crossed Burgundy, and the two had a shoot-out. Philip heard all the gunfire, drove down Burgundy to Conti, and persuaded Sam to get in his car before anyone was killed.

Philip got Sam on a plane to Chicago. Norma thought it was over forever, she'd never see Sam again. But she'd have her memories of their torrid nights together, and she'd never take off the diamond ring he'd given her, a five-and-a-half-carat rock to help balance the memory of Andy Wallace on her other hand. The bullets in the green door on Burgundy Street would remind her of him for years. He was out of her life, and just as well. He was too volatile, too possessive, too dangerous. She accepted that he was gone forever; nevertheless, it hurt her to think so.

Once again, she was almost dead wrong.

·   ·   ·

Norma's marriage to Pete lasted less than a year. She explained the breakup this way: "We had reached the point where we didn't have fun anymore. Instead, we mostly tried to buck each other—we were antagonistic toward each other. The problem was jealousy. When I got a phone call, he would put his ear to the phone.

"Italians can really be something. They want a wife that's a madam and a nun and all of the saints combined, and I don't think I was capable of it."

She admitted that she was jealous of Pete too. "Because I'm self-ish," she said. "When I love, I want to be all of it." What it came down to was this: "I can dish it out but I can't take it."

Though Norma gave no details about the breakup of the marriage, she was honest about her feelings upon entering it. "I guess Pete was married and I wasn't because my heart wasn't in the marriage. I think," she added, "I'm the sort of person who never should have married in the first place. I'm a lot like a man; I like freedom. I liked the freedom of love affairs."

But Norma still cared a great deal about Pete, and she had sympathy for his handicap. "When a person is handicapped like he is," she said, "there's more sympathy in your love. I would do more for him than anybody else because of that and because he is a fine little man, no doubt about it. I would do anything for him except stay married."

So she moved back to 410 Dauphine, leaving all the wedding presents and things she'd bought for the apartment. "I knew it would hurt him if I took anything. All I took was my dough, my clothes, and an Oriental rug that was very precious to me because it had been a gift from Sam, and back to my whorehouse I went."

Norma did not tell Pete she was leaving, which shocked and undoubtedly hurt him, yet he remained her friend until he died.

Before long, sometime in 1937, Norma began going with a seaman named Bill Carver. Pete named Bill as corespondent in the divorce, and Norma eventually married him. She summed up her third marriage in a few words: "It was a nice enough marriage, and we had a nice life together for a while." They were married for six years, during which Norma bought a house at 512 Governor Nicholls Street in the Quarter, and Bill spent a lot of time at sea. Bill Carver was more than an "episode," as she'd called her marriage to Alex Zolman, but not much more. Talking to Clint Bolton, she couldn't remember his name. "Carver, Caron, something like that." His name appears both ways on legal documents.

"Isn't it terrible?" she asked Bolton. "I can't remember my husband's name."

Helen Moran remembered Bill Carver's name and the man. "I liked him," she said with feeling. "Norma married him about the same time John [J. G. Badon, Norma's half brother] and I married [1939]. She invited us to dinner to announce it.

"He was a sailor, and he was a handsome brute too." Helen broke into a lilting laugh. "Oh, yes, and he was younger than Norma. Except for Pete Herman, all her husbands were."

Norma said, "Whores make good wives, but madams don't. When you're making money in a whorehouse, that makes you independent and hard to get along with as a wife in the first place."

She talked about the girls she knew who'd married cabdrivers, policemen, and club owners, men who fell in love with them. Afterwards, these girls were never interested in hustling again. "But madams," she said, "don't make good wives because their way of life just doesn't fit into the domestic scene." She tested the veracity of this statement during her fourth marriage, to Charles McCoy.

Meanwhile, though, Sam Hunt may have heard about Pete and Norma's divorce, which was finalized near Christmas. He sent Norma a present, a diamond watch on a gold chain; she rushed out and reciprocated with a gold money clip engraved with his initials. She claimed some reticence, even though her act did not reflect it. "I didn't want to make up with this man because I knew I wasn't ready for that kind of settling down to anybody. I wanted to have this freedom I had left Pete for."

But Sam accepted the present and arrived at the house in short order. The love affair picked up again as if he had never tried to run Norma over in front of 410 Dauphine, as if the shoot-out on Burgundy Street had never happened.

. . .

In the late 1930s the French Quarter underwent another change, a result of the threat to demolish the historic buildings and replace them with a low-rent housing development. To prevent such destruction, the Vieux Carré Commission was established in 1937. But even earlier in the decade people interested in historic preservation had begun to restore and renovate the old dwellings. This renovation forced many of the poorer residents to move out of the Quarter. They left and the tourists arrived, courted by the restaurants, hotels, and nightclubs that had been springing up all over the area. Within the shrinking population of residents, a fear rose, as it had in the twenties, that the Quarter was losing its picturesque quality, this time to tourists and developers. Tennessee Williams, who arrived in New Orleans in 1938, was quoted some years later as saying that the French Quarter was in danger of turning into Kansas City. This change in the Quarter, though, marked the beginning of tourism as the number one growth industry in the city, with more job impact than either the port or the oil and gas industry by the end of the century. As merchants, hoteliers, and others catered heavily to tourism, the picturesqueness of the Vieux Carré was often so pronounced as to seem artificial, and rumors floated that Disney wanted to buy it and turn it into another theme park.

Norma in 1938 became part of the push to refurbish the Quarter in her quest for the ideal situation for her parlor house. She said that before she married Pete she had found the perfect location for her establishment at 1026 Conti Street. The Greyhound bus station was across the street, at the corner of Conti and North Rampart, providing plenty of customers, as it had for Juliet Washington, whose house at 1020 Conti flourished. Next door to the bus station, at 1019 Conti, was the New Orleans Transfer Company. At 1006 music and good spirits poured from the convivial Regal Beer Parlor, an outlet for the Regal Brewing Company over on Bourbon Street. A tailor was conveniently located at 935 Conti, and across from him Pete's nightclub still drew a full house several nights a week.

The house Norma found at 1026 Conti shared a parking lot with the next-door neighbor, the Holzer Sheet Metal Company. Cars could drive up the driveway to the lot, or they could enter from Rampart Street. At the time Norma said that from the Rampart side the back of the house was not visible, which meant that she could do what she couldn't at 410 Dauphine—keep the heat away from the front. The visibility factor changed through the years, until she finally erected a twelve-foot concrete wall.

The interior of the sixteen-room, green-stucco, 1830s classical-style town house offered great possibilities. One entered a long foyer, more like a vestibule, with a stairway to the second floor. Near the front door was a shuttered window where Norma and her girls could keep an eye on the customers coming up the driveway as well as on the constabulary. To the left of the hall were three rooms that Norma could turn into her private apartment, a luxury she didn't have on Dauphine Street. Past those rooms the hall went out to a courtyard on the side of the building, a long rectangle covered with blue Mexican tile. On one end was a sunroom, connected to Norma's apartment. On the opposite side was a door to the room Norma would use as her main parlor. It had an entrance from the back yard. Across the courtyard on the right was another large room, a second parlor or a show room. Next to it was the back stairway, which led to a balcony overlooking the courtyard. The balcony fronted numerous bedrooms, then led to a hall where the front stairway continued to the third floor, which consisted of a few large, airy rooms with casement windows and creamy white-marble fireplaces. An ideal house with an appropriate history: It had once belonged to Ernest Bellocq, the famed photographer of the Storyville prostitutes. The very best feature of it, though, was a secret space behind the main parlor—the perfect hideout!

It could be very nice, except, "The condition of this house—Oh Lord!" Norma said. "Colored people were living in it, and it took trucks and trucks from the city to move the stuff out of the community parking lot, where they had been dumping for years. They had painted over the beautiful black-marble mantels with green paint. And the place had to be fumigated. But I got it cheap, forty-five hundred dollars."

Some of Norma's friends say that Sam Hunt paid for the house. Norma didn't divulge that information, though it's likely that he did, since she bought her mother a house at 3830 Piedmont Drive in

Gentilly, a suburb with California-style bungalows set on grassy terraces, along with the lot next door, which she had fenced for her mother's three dogs. In her memoirs she said she had only enough money for those lots, yet the transactions for Conti Street and her mother's property took place together. She did mention, however, that Sam gave her a lot of jewelry, furs, and clothes, and he helped her decorate and furnish Conti Street. "As always," Norma said, "Sam was generous." By the new year she was in the house.

Sam wanted Norma to go out with him on New Year's Eve, a big night in New Orleans, the night before the Sugar Bowl and another excuse to line Bourbon Street with wall-to-wall party animals. Cabdrivers were picking up men and women all over the Quarter and taking them to the shows at 1026 Conti. Norma had a full house. She couldn't afford to leave at a time like that. "I was there to keep down any kind of beef; even with my love life and other problems, I never neglected my business. That's one reason I lasted as long as I did."

She told Sam she couldn't go out. He took her car and went to Louie's bar on University Place, where he drank B & B's until two in the morning. Loaded and belligerent, he let himself into the back parlor.

The first thing he saw was Norma sitting in a man's lap. Someone she'd passed had pulled her down, and she'd stayed to talk for a minute. Sam strode straight up and cursed her out.

Norma didn't scare easily. "I would cry at a bird's death and faint at the sight of blood, but when it came to things like this, I was made out of iron."

She defied him—stood up and stared him down. He threw the key to her house at her and left. But he didn't go far, only back to Louie's.

With a few more B & B's in him, Sam decided to wreck the house. When he returned the first thing he did was beat up Slim Williams and Johnny Packer, two cabdrivers who were waiting for their vidalias. He ran them both into the alley, then into the street. Norma said, "He had a bad habit of kicking people, which I detest."

The girls, frightened, began to leave, one telling a cabdriver, "Just go anywhere. He's crazy, *crazy!*"

Sam wanted to whip everybody. A couple lounged in the front parlor, drinking champagne after Jackie had danced for them. Sam barged in, threatening, "If you know what's good for you, you'll get out of here right now." People in the rooms upstairs had no clothes on; he ran up to the balcony shouting that they'd better get dressed and get out—and fast.

Norma knew then that she couldn't go on with Sam. Her one absolute: Don't fool with my business. She could take anything but that.

Sam headed back to Louie's and put down more B & B's. When he left he told Louie, "I'm going back to finish her off." Alarmed, Louie called Norma and suggested she call the law. But Norma knew better than to call the law on someone like Sam Hunt.

She opened the door; his hand shot out, hitting her in the face. "I know it's hard to believe, given everything else he did that night," Norma said, without a thought to what he'd done *before* that night, "but he wasn't the kind of man to hit a woman. He was mortally wounded by his own act. We went into the parlor. He was a hurt man, and I felt sorry and cried."

About that time the doorbell rang. It was the police. Somebody, either one of the cabdrivers or Louie, had called them. They asked Norma if there was any trouble. She told them no.

She went back to the parlor. Sam, ever the romantic, said, "Darling, you didn't have me arrested. Why?"

He spent the night with her, and they talked most of the next day. They decided that they weren't meant for each other, that if they tried to go on, something serious would happen.

"It must have been hard for him to look around ten twenty-six and see all the beautiful things he had given me, how much he'd helped me fix up the building. Also, it's a big thing to have the madam of the house. If I had been willing just to be his woman, we could have had a good life together. In a way, I'd shown him up quite a bit, and amongst his kind of people, a woman never does that to a man without getting her neck broke. I suppose I was just lucky. Sam and I never saw each other again. But it was a good love affair for me, never a dull moment—exciting, that's the word."

Sam Hunt died some years later in a shoot-out in Chicago.

CHAPTER SIX

Squaring Up

The war years came, and for Norma the money kept rolling in, largely because of the influx of servicemen on leave and the convenient proximity of her house to the bus station where they arrived. Sometimes the line of soldiers waiting for their turn with a girl stretched around the block. Norma had as many as thirty girls working for her then, and each would turn five or six tricks a day. And she had her regular customers too. Her gross of the proceeds was at least a hundred thousand dollars a year, but Norma had given up on banks after losing her money during the Depression. She stashed her savings behind a loose brick somewhere on Conti Street, either in the fireplace in her apartment or within the deep recess of the hideout—she never divulged the location. Before she tried to "square up" in 1946 and live the straight life with her fourth husband, Charles McCoy, she had accumulated over eighty thousand dollars, almost as much as she'd lost in 1933.

During the first half of the 1940s, most of Norma's money went into her property. She put full bathrooms in each of the rooms, and in her private bath she added a bidet of black marble, which she chose because it most closely matched the Italian marble of the fireplaces. After a lot of labor and money, the green paint had been stripped from them; now Norma had their ornate carvings edged with gold leaf. The back parlor, where the dates entered, was a low-ceilinged room, an addition to the early-nineteenth-century house. She made it cozy, with pecky cypress paneling on the walls, deep red Oriental carpets over the hardwood floor, a small crystal chandelier, easy chairs, a comfortable sofa, and an adjoining bar. The courtyard became a tropical paradise, with large trees and flowering plants, a glass-topped table with chairs, and eventually a toucan and a couple of parrots with foul mouths. She turned the sunroom into her office. To shelter the balcony and courtyard, she installed a translucent green corrugated cover that bathed the area in light like an aquarium. Then she commissioned a romantic mural of azaleas blooming in Mobile, Alabama, on the wall upstairs from which the balcony hung.

Norma also commissioned some nude paintings, one of Jackie dancing and others of a few of her most beautiful girls, and she bought some nudes by the Hungarian painter Pâl Fried. These she hung throughout her bordello, which she furnished with antiques, adding a few stunning pieces of Chinese ebony furniture as accents. She acquired one exceptional conversation piece—a bed that was supposed to have been in the Storyville madam Josie Arlington's house. At least that's what Bertha Anderson, once Josie's protégée, had told her when she sold Norma the bed.

Made of brass and exquisitely draped in red silk, the bed had a mirror in its canopy. Norma put it in her bedroom, but its first night there was also its last. "I looked up into it," Norma said, "and thought, Oh Christ, this is thirty years too late." So she put electric lights in it and moved the bed to her show room upstairs, and put it on a revolving dais. It proved to be a terrific gimmick. Some people came to the shows to see the bed, or so they said.

For the first time since the twenties, Norma was arrested in 1944, but not for prostitution. She was picked up for being drunk and disorderly, and for fighting and disturbing the peace on St. Louis Street between Chartres and Royal. For the record, she gave Pete Herman's address at 328 Burgundy, where she'd operated her first bordello and where Pete continued a prostitution operation, with Norma supplying some of the girls. Even after their divorce Pete and Norma remained business partners, and every night they cut the proceeds, Norma or Jackie bringing bank bags to Pete's to collect the night's take.

Under Robert Maestri's regime, gambling thrived along with prostitution throughout the war years, but Police Superintendent Reyer seemed reluctant to answer specific requests to clamp down on clear violators of the law, and his men were lax in their duties to crack down on slot machines and handbook (bookmaking) operations as well as prostitution. The mayor, after an easy victory in the 1942 election, seemed to lose touch with the public; city services deteriorated while he paid more attention to the management of the Old Regular coalition and responded only to friends. Favoritism flourished; vice and corruption were on public display as never before.

By 1945, when it was time to campaign again, Maestri and the Old Regulars were overconfident. Even a rift between Maestri and a city assessor, which resulted in two slates of Old Regular candidates, seemed not to worry him. He made fewer public appearances. He was ill at ease around other candidates. One of those candidates was deLesseps "Chep" Morrison.

Morrison was a handsome man of thirty-three, in superb physical condition, quite attractive in his military uniform. A lawyer from Uptown New Orleans, he became a state legislator at twenty-eight. Nearly his opposite, Maestri was swarthy, middle-aged, and out of shape; his formal education had stopped at the third grade. For him public speaking was difficult; even one-on-one his speech could be shockingly uncouth. One story recounts President Franklin Roosevelt's visit to the city. Dining at Antoine's, the President and his son Elliott had begun eating the restaurant's famed oysters Rockefeller when Maestri, at a loss for words, suddenly blurted across an otherwise silent table, "How ya like dem ersters?"

Aside from such obvious differences between Morrison and Maestri, the dynamic younger man was being groomed as the candidate of reform. Some of his strongest support came from the wealthy and social Uptown women, the "silk stockings," who considered Morrison one of their own, a "debutante's delight." They organized a citywide grassroots effort to promote him. Not only did they go door to door, hold rallies and receptions, and work the phones, but they underscored their candidate's promise for sweeping reforms with dramatic visuals. "A Clean Sweep for Morrison" was their theme. On the freezing Saturday night before the election, hundreds of Women for Morrison from across the city lined up in rank and file on Canal Street, shouldering their household brooms. Down Canal to St. Charles Avenue at Lee Circle, the March of Brooms swept the city clean of corruption as they swept their candidate to victory. The efforts of the women's "Broom Brigade," along with the veterans who nightly placed Elect Morrison signs all over town, made the difference: Morrison defeated Maestri and the Old Regulars' machine by four thousand votes.

Morrison's election in 1946 was a major event in the lives of the French Quarter landladies. "Everybody was scared to death that Morrison was going to eat them alive," Norma said. "His own lawyer, Henry somebody or another [she probably meant Henry Muller, who was not Morrison's lawyer but the owner of a restaurant supply company as well as proprietor of several houses], had a house, and he'd gotten all his girls out to vote, really plugged for Morrison. But when Morrison got in, Henry had to close the doors down. Morrison was going to reform the city, clean it all up. Big deal."

Henry Muller was one of Morrison's biggest campaign contributors, forty thousand dollars in 1946. According to Morrison's chauffeur, the money ensured that Muller could operate freely; he may have ceased operations for a short while as part of the show.

And to scare the other madams. But he was not the source of Norma's concern. "A man named Cody Morris was running a house [809 Baronne Street, in the Central Business District], and that was supposed to be okay with Morrison. Morris said as soon as Chep took office he was going to run all the other operators out of business, particularly me. Morris and I were bucking each other for quite a while there. I knew the town was about to go down, and I believed what he was telling me. I could have stayed and cheated, because I had a few spots and a couple of my girls had very nice apartments, but when this message came back to me, I said, To hell with it."

The other reason she said "to hell with it" was Charles McCoy.

McCoy was a Washington, D.C., policeman on shore patrol in New Orleans when he found his way to 1026 Conti Street. He was young, ten years younger than Norma (who was now forty-five), and heart-stoppingly handsome. He had a family and a job waiting back in Washington, but he was willing to leave all that behind. Norma was still married to Bill Carver, but she put her lawyer to work, and he somehow finagled McCoy out of the service while arranging Norma's divorce. She got the house on Governor Nicholls Street in the settlement and put it up for sale. With close to a hundred thousand dollars in cash and Morrison promising the crackdown Reyer and Maestri wouldn't deliver, Norma said, "I had been looking for an excuse to go live on my farm, so I shut down the shop and moved to Pearl River." The house there was beautiful, overlooking the water, with a guesthouse and a mile of woods behind it.

But Norma had put too much of her time and money into 1026 Conti Street—and too much of herself—to give it up. She listed it under the name Norma Lindsley; then her mother moved in and supposedly ran it as a rooming house while Norma and McCoy "went domestic," as she liked to say, at Shady Pond.

Norma had said she was quitting the business for McCoy's sake. He believed her, and she believed it herself, for a while. McCoy wanted to run a dairy farm, so Norma took her cash and bought five hundred cows. While he was being Farmer McCoy, Mrs. McCoy was into canning—orange preserves, blackberry jam, corn confit, tomato chutney, pickled green beans and okra. She also became a sharp-shooter and killed a wild boar in the woods one day.

But she kept in touch with her friends in the French Quarter too, talking regularly with Pete and his brother, Gaspar Gulotta, who had the inside track with the politicos and the police. Was she waiting for the all-clear sign from Gaspar? If so, she didn't get it; meanwhile, the years were passing and canning was beginning to get old.

Back in the city, Amanda may have been playing it straight and operating a rooming house, but during that time Elmo got married to a shy, sweet, and very young woman named Sarah Gentilly. Norma had met Sarah the Christmas before she left Conti Street, when Elmo dropped by to give his sister a present. He left Sarah in the car, but Norma insisted that he invite her in. Sarah was too naïve to understand the action at 1026 Conti Street; she thought Elmo's sister had a lot of pretty friends.

After she and Elmo married they moved into the house with Amanda. Sarah, a half century later, curled her lip and wrinkled her nose at the mention of Conti Street or, for that matter, anything having to do with the French Quarter. "I hated it," she said, "everything about it." But she didn't know if Amanda may have been playing madam in Norma's absence. She said that families lived in the house, yet she also said she never saw them.

She and Elmo weren't there long, though. Sarah told her new husband that if he didn't move her out, she was going home to her mother. Elmo bought her a house in Lakeview, a family-oriented section of town and a far cry from the Quarter in the late forties. But as long as Sarah was married to Elmo, which she was until he died in 1968, she couldn't get away from the part of the city she found so distasteful, because she kept the books for Elmo's various nightclubs in the French Quarter and across Canal in the Central Business District.

While Norma was in Pearl River, she developed a small cyst on one of her eyes. Her sister-in-law Helen took her into the city one day to have it removed. Norma talked more that day to Helen than she had to anyone since the move to the farm. Things were not good at Shady Pond. Everything was going wrong: The livestock was dwindling as cows seemed to be dropping dead overnight; some beautiful young heifers were under a tree during a thunderstorm when lightning struck and killed them all—"There went the future of our dairy!" Norma told Helen.

Also, McCoy's management was poor. "What does Mac know about running a dairy?" Norma said. "He's an ex-policeman. But you can't tell any city person there's no money to be made in the country. They don't believe it."

As they drove to New Orleans, Norma told Helen, "Your life is so different from mine. I'd trade shoes with you any day."

But at that time Norma's life was not very different from Helen's. Helen knew what she meant, though—that their backgrounds were different. "For Norma," Helen said in retrospect, "it was already too late."

Nearly five years after Norma and McCoy moved to Pearl River, Norma decided she'd had it with being domestic. In the kitchen were shelves and shelves of canned fruit and vegetables. She couldn't stand the sight. She went to her next-door neighbor's house, a mile away, and said, "Bring up your wagon," and she unloaded every last jar of corn and beans and preserves. Then she told McCoy she was selling the farm.

He was shocked. "Living with you is like sitting on a keg of dynamite!" he told Norma.

Norma didn't care. She wanted to get back to her old life, the one she'd grown accustomed to and understood, the life of danger, excitement, and action. She had begun to think she could actually die of boredom in the country. She called another dairy farmer she knew, Louie Ballaminte, who happened to be Carlos Marcello's brother-in-law. Marcello was reputedly the mob kingpin in New Orleans, though he had a number of vegetable trucks all over town and claimed to be nothing other than a lowly tomato salesman. Norma didn't know Marcello at the time; she didn't care who Louie Ballaminte's brother-in-law was anyway. She just wanted him to buy the farm. ("He stole it from me," she said after she let it go for a lot less than she thought it was worth in her hurry to leave Pearl River.)

McCoy went along with Norma's decision; he didn't have much of a choice since the farm belonged to her. But it was in his nature to be acquiescent; not only that, he loved Norma more than he loved any cows or land or dairy business. He loved her so much that he made a dire threat before they left Pearl River for good. "If you ever get in trouble," he told her, "if you ever go to jail, I'll leave you." Poor Mac. Money wasn't important to him. He didn't mind working; he always said he could make enough for them to live on.

Norma brushed off his threat. "I guess he figured this old girl was squared up and we were gonna get into canned goods," she said. "But all I could think about was what I was missing."

McCoy packed his belongings and followed Norma back to New Orleans, where he and Carlos Marcello became regular golf partners. He hoped he'd never have to follow through on his threat. At that time, he wasn't even sure he could.

CHAPTER SEVEN

Big Mayor, Little Mayor

"Without a doubt," Norma said of this time, "I picked the single worst moment to return to New Orleans."

When Gaspar finally gave her the all-clear signal to come home, it was late fall of 1949 and Chep Morrison had been mayor for nearly four years. He was riding a wave of popularity and had been written up in *Time* magazine as the "symbol of the bright new day which had come to the city of charming ruins." He was a busy man: changing the face of New Orleans with building projects like a new union station to replace the Southern Railway and Greyhound terminals; forging international trade programs that would turn New Orleans into the nation's second-largest trading port; and initiating civic improvements like garbage trucks to replace mule-drawn wagons. He was also conducting other affairs—his marriage to the socially prominent Corinne Waterman was faltering, but divorce was not a consideration since he had hope and promise to move on to national politics. As one of his former aides put it, "He went for hamburger when he had filet mignon at home." With all this on his plate, the sweeping cleanup of French Quarter vice and corruption that Morrison had promised dropped in priority. Not only that, he had his friend Gaspar Gulotta keeping an eye on things.

Howard Jacobs began his profile of Norma for *The Times-Picayune* with the following anecdote:

There was a mayor's convention in town, and the more adventurous of the visiting burgomasters found themselves at Norma Wallace's house of assignation in the French Quarter.

The delegation was about to depart after an evening of fun and frolic when the flamboyant Norma, peering out of the peephole at the front window, was horrified to espy a policeman lolling on the sidewalk. Quickly she telephoned her brother-in-law, Bourbon Street "Mayor" Gaspar Gulotta.

After informing him of her predicament and urging him to use his influence with the bona fide mayor to call off the law, she commented: "Do you realize if these men are busted the wheels of progress will grind to a halt in a dozen cities and an international incident might prevail?"

Replied Gulotta: "You mean a national incident?"

"An international incident," repeated Norma dryly. "One of 'em is the mayor of Barcelona."

Providentially, the poliziotto vanished in a few minutes. Norma gave the signal the coast was clear, and the city fathers eased furtively into the street and dispersed.

With the mayor tightly within Gaspar's sphere of influence, Gaspar gave Norma the signal, and Norma and Mac spent Christmas on Conti Street.

But the status quo was sharply interrupted by an incident on New Year's Eve 1949. A wealthy Nashville contractor who was in New Orleans for the Sugar Bowl was celebrating the new year in a French Quarter bar when he was slipped a Mickey Finn—a drink laced with chloral hydrate drops, which killed him. The mayor, under pressure from organizations such as the Chamber of Commerce, the Young Men's Business Club, the Kiwanis Club, Lions Club, and Optimist Club, and facing protests from the press about the vice-ridden state of the Vieux Carré, formed a citizens' committee to investigate crime in the Quarter. This committee included such stalwart citizens as Owen

Brennan, owner of Brennan's restaurant; Richard Foster, chairman of the police advisory board; Edgar Stern, who founded New Orleans's first television station (his estate, Longue Vue Gardens, is now owned by the city); and Gaspar Gulotta, the Little Mayor of Bourbon Street, so called because of his political influence.

No one on the committee had the personality and array of friends in both high and low places that Gaspar had. The pudgy Little Mayor greeted all the patrons of his Bourbon Street club equally, his cigar always stuck in the corner of his mouth, and when he wasn't tending to his own club he was off in a more splendid one, like New York's Copacabana, with pals like the stand-up comic Joe E. Lewis, who was played by Frank Sinatra in the 1957 movie *The Joker Is Wild*.

A newspaper reporter supposedly asked Gaspar how he came to be the Little Mayor. Gaspar grinned and talked around his fat cigar. "You know any udda guy in the street's gonna challenge?"

On April 4, 1950, a front-page article in the *States* implicated Gaspar in the Nashville contractor's death. The prime suspects, two women, had been in his nightclub five days before and attempted to steal fifty dollars from a sailor. Worse, a *States* reporter had been approached by a B-girl at Gaspar's. (B-drinking establishments hired girls to sell drinks to male patrons at extravagantly inflated prices in return for the pleasure of their company.) And she invited him to come back later for a sexual assignation.

Foster, chairman of the crime committee, demanded Gaspar's resignation. But the Little Mayor refused to resign, and Morrison, who was known to frequent Gaspar's, refused to dismiss him. Gaspar denied that any of the women worked for him, and he was given a vote of confidence by the rest of the committee.

After taking office Chep Morrison liked to remind the voters of the corruption and vice that had run rampant during the Maestri regime, keeping his image of reform before the public as much as possible, posturing as a knight in shining armor whose crusade was to save the city from its archaic afflictions. He replaced the lax police superintendent George Reyer with Adair Watters, a former marine colonel. A military man stiffened the reform image; no more weak spine on the side of law and order. But when Watters made too many public statements about municipal officers' corruption and acted to halt police graft, Morrison overruled the chief, and Watters resigned. He was replaced by Joseph Scheuring, the former chief of detectives. But Morrison's carefully polished reform image took on its first coat of tarnish after charges that more than 650 gambling establishments still operated in the city and that Scheuring was regularly taking advice from Maestri's partner in vice, Reyer.

Nevertheless, the committee continued its work, recommending the prohibition of taxis on Bourbon Street and convincing the City Council to strengthen municipal laws against prostitution. A new ordinance required mandatory jail sentences for prostitutes and their patrons. The promised cleanup seemed to be a thorough and organized effort, with pressure coming to bear particularly on the bordellos.

Norma saw the panic of all the landladies—Dora Russo, Juliet Washington, Gertie Yost, Bertha Anderson—everybody going Uptown. "So I went with the gang; I panicked and bought a house on Girod and Saratoga, a house near where the Italians killed Police Chief Hennessey before the turn of the century [another major New Orleans police scandal]." The house no longer exists; where it stood is now a parking lot, and its location is no longer considered Uptown but is on the periphery of the downtown business district, close to the Superdome.

Things eased off, but Norma continued to conduct business Uptown while she began new improvements to her property at 1026 Conti, with an eye to making money off it in another way. She put in kitchens and air-conditioning, turning the place into an apartment house, but she was apprehensive that no one would rent from her. "People knew who Norma Wallace was, and I sure didn't think they'd want to live in my house. At that time you were blackballed if you had a house; today it would be good for business."

A friend suggested she rent to Blue Room musicians. The word spread from outgoing to incoming bands, and Norma had no trouble keeping the place full at top dollar.

Meanwhile, from Chief Hennessey's old neighborhood, she established a friendship with Superintendent Scheuring. "He said I had a nice place and he would go along with it as long as he could."

Many believed that Chep Morrison wanted reform but that greed, corruption, and commercialized vice had become too ingrained over the city's two-hundred-year history. Then, on November 15, 1950, the *Item* reporter Tom Sancton interviewed Criminal Sheriff John Grosch, once George Reyer's chief of detectives. Sancton wrote that Grosch gave a "horse laugh" to the belief that Morrison was running a "reform administration." He went on to claim that seventeen houses of prostitution were being run with police protection, as well as over a hundred handbook operations. He charged that innumerable police officers were still taking graft.

Seven months later the investigating committee's head, Richard Foster, pointed out to the mayor that still the police had taken no action to reduce crime in the Quarter. At the mayor's request he wrote Scheuring, naming establishments and violations of the law. Scheuring did nothing. One month later Morrison asked Foster for his resignation from the police advisory board and appointed him chairman of the Bienville Monument Commission, a post even lower than commissioner of public safety!

By then Senator Estes Kefauver had arrived in New Orleans. His focus was organized crime in Louisiana. Under intense questioning John Grosch, wearing the only uniform he ever wore—his white linen suit and rose boutonniere—admitted that he had allowed gambling while he was chief of detectives, but he skirted other issues. His estranged wife, however, was happy to fill in for Kefauver: She testified that Grosch had received money and gifts from gamblers and proprietors of houses of prostitution, namely Henry Muller, and $150,000 in graft while he was a patrolman. As the damaging testimony grew, Reyer admitted to owning part interest in several gambling casinos. Then Morrison conceded that he'd taken campaign contributions from pinball operators, although he denied that he'd promised any favors.

Revelations continued until a newly called Orleans Parish grand jury demanded a private probe of police ties to vice. Many people were questioned by the Orleans grand jury, but few gave answers. One police captain refused to explain how he could afford a summer home, other real estate, and a yacht, and how he maintained various bank accounts on his salary. He was suspended. Then Cody Morris, Norma's adversary and the chief reason for her exile to Pearl River, took a jail sentence rather than answer such questions as did he have paid protection to run his bawdy houses and did he supply girls for policemen. News leaked out that several witnesses for the grand jury had asked for protection after receiving threats, and that thirty-eight high-ranking police officers had refused to answer questions.

Even though each grand jury served only a six-month term, the foreman was satisfied at the end of his term that if the police wanted to do something about stopping vice, they could. Provosty Dayries, the last police superintendent under Morrison, later proved this to be an accurate assessment, but to his own detriment.

A federal grand jury was formed to continue the probe. Norma was called before that jury on April 17, 1952, along with other Quarter madams, Dora Russo, Gertie Yost, and Marie Bernard. Cody Morris was called with another male operator, BeBe Anselmo, and a gambler and close friend of Gaspar, John Saia.

Norma's thirteen arrests for prostitution in the 1920s were cited in the newspaper account of the federal grand jury probe, along with the other witnesses' records, many dating back to the twenties. The more information that surfaced, the clearer it became that from the 1920s to the 1950s, little had changed.

The 1950s police scandals gave rise to one of the smartest, crassest, and most shameless scoundrels in the history of New Orleans. For most of three decades the mere mention of the name Pershing Gervais had New Orleanians sitting up and sniffing the air for scandal, and the antics of the volatile Gervais made *The Times-Picayune* read like a tabloid.

The son of deaf-mutes, Gervais had a trace of a speech impediment, the slightest pause before he began to talk, as if he had to untie his tongue first. His political life—and his life in the underworld—had started when he was a boy, brazen enough to hire out to the highest bidder (though his allegiance was usually to the Old Regulars) to stuff the ballot box or, if he didn't have time to stuff it, to pour ink into it. He grew up to become a police officer, but he was always on the lookout for money. In old New Orleans, heavy with corruption and graft, Gervais was quick to see moneymaking opportunities and take advantage of them. According to a story he told the reporter Rosemary James (*New Orleans* magazine, July 1970), one of those opportunities started the 1950s police scandals. Such a claim was only more of Gervais's theatrics: The police scandals were well under way, but his story was, at the very least, ingenious.

Fearless and completely amoral, as a police detective Gervais openly associated with known underworld characters. But when he began flaunting some very expensive jewelry, then went on "business" to New York City, Superintendent Scheuring, who was out of favor with Morrison and looking to ingratiate himself, decided to investigate Gervais.

Gervais told James that one morning he arrived at police headquarters late; roll call had already begun. Thinking the precinct captain might still be in his office, Gervais opened the captain's door and saw money spread all over the top of his desk. He scooped it up.

He told James, "I took a trip to New York. I rented not one, but two fancy suites in a fancy hotel. I rented fifty-dollar-a-day limousines with chauffeurs, too. In those days, La Vie en Rose was a big nightspot. Jersey Joe Walcott hung out there, and Pearl Bailey was the headliner. The minute I would walk in I would get a fine table, because if anybody smiled at me I handed him a hundred-dollar tip. I know exactly how it feels to be a millionaire, because . . . for weeks . . . I lived like one . . . on police graft."

But the story a colleague told differed significantly from Gervais's. Two supposedly well-known criminals had just been released from jail. They broke into the lakefront home of a Bourbon Street club owner who ran a B-drinking establishment and was also a bookmaker. He kept a large amount of cash in the safe of his house to hide it from the Internal Revenue Service. The ex-cons demanded that the club owner open the safe. The man refused, so the ex-cons began to bind his mother's and wife's wrists and ankles with copper wire, coming frighteningly close to cutting them off. The man opened the safe. The criminals got away with $150,000.

Since he had not claimed the money as taxable, the club owner told the police he'd lost five thousand dollars. Gervais and his partner

Sal Marchese caught the criminals and took the money, saying they'd recovered none of it. And off to New York went Gervais.

Meanwhile, back in New Orleans, Mayor Morrison was busy defending the police in spite of the blatant revelations of graft and greed. He claimed that police were underpaid and that most officers were honest, that only rumors were at the root of the police scandals. But it was a line some people weren't buying.

Perhaps Chep Morrison shouldn't have been so hasty to remove Richard Foster from the police advisory board. In 1952 Foster organized and became president of the Metropolitan Crime Commission of New Orleans, Inc., which still operates. The commission helped form the Special Citizens Investigating Committee (SCIC) (similar to but superseding the original crime committee), which in turn was responsible for hiring Aaron M. Kohn, a lawyer and former FBI agent hot from a ten-month study of corruption in the Chicago police department. Kohn was to conduct a similar investigation in New Orleans. With his arrival in New Orleans in June 1953, Morrison found a thorn in his side that resisted removal for most of the decade.

Pershing Gervais finally ran out of money in New York, and when he returned Scheuring fired him. But Gervais wasn't worried: He soon found a new job as an undercover agent—for Aaron Kohn.

In a letter to Clint Bolton, Norma wrote:

> I think Aaron Kohn is all wrong about organized crime. In my line I had the nicest place in town, so why didn't they come to me? I asked everyone I know if they were ever propositioned or had ever been shook down. They all assured me no. I had a music box, but I chose the man to put it in and he was not a character. As for dope, where I had very little contact with dope, I heard things. But I never heard some people's names Kohn talks about, and for two years I went to the Town and Country every Sunday nite. [Carlos Marcello owned the Town and Country.] That was my nite out of the whorehouse. I knew the Vice Squad was off on Sundays since they worked

late on Sat. nite trying to set some girl up either in a hotel or as a B-drinker. I knew almost everything I should not know. I tried to keep from hearing dangerous things because I had a successful whorehouse and characters are quick to put the finger on you for a stoolie. But I would hear who was on stuff and who was peddling. Kohn, I honestly believe, was wrong.

When Kohn hit town he convinced the department store heads that New Orleans would be a more prosperous city without gambling. I was a good customer in all the best stores, and as time went on I had all the sales people tell me he hurt business. Still, they give money to the Metropolitan Crime Commission so they can get rid of the gamblers and whorehouses and wind up with more serious crime than some whore selling her ass or some man betting on a horse. That's Kohn's idea about cleaning up crime today. This paid reformer is out of date, so he picks on Carlos. It amazes me how intelligent men keep letting him con them. I know he had coffee with that bucket head Supt. Joseph Giarrusso [Giarrusso became superintendent of police in 1960] often. Kohn should not have needled him so much about me. I could have been his whipping boy for a long time.

Because Norma used the Town and Country Motel when her house on Conti Street was hot, it's an easy assumption that she was tied to Marcello, that she was part of his network of cronies or paid him in order to operate undisturbed in the French Quarter. No doubt she paid for the use of the rooms at Marcello's motel, but there is no other evidence that Norma had business ties to the New Orleans "mafia," nor is there any evidence that Marcello had much interest in prostitution. Rosemary James, after years of investigative reporting, believed that Marcello wasn't interested in controlling prostitution. She said, "New Orleans was called the Wall Street of the Mafia because it had always been a money-laundering place."

Kohn, however, continued to investigate vice in New Orleans and its link to organized crime. Gervais told James, "In the old days, you couldn't open a whorehouse, you couldn't open a lottery shop, you couldn't even beg on Canal Street . . . unless the police said okay. That was crime that was organized."

Kohn stuck to his investigation, in spite of threatening letters calling him a "Jew bastard" and all imaginable forms of obstruction and interference, including having money planted on his person at one point and being refused access to public records by police officials. He hired undercover agents from other cities as well as local informers like Gervais.

Kohn found that gambling, graft, and prostitution saturated the city as thoroughly as the spring rains, not least among the police. He conducted public hearings against the mayor's wishes, but Morrison knew it would be political suicide to refuse. Cooperating witnesses included Doris Gellman, a prostitute who had worked in several houses, including Norma's, and Pershing Gervais and Salvatore Marchese, both of whom had been dismissed from the police department because of "unbecoming conduct."

Gervais went undercover for Kohn and testified about police corruption, then ran around town boasting that he was on both Aaron Kohn's and Norma Wallace's payrolls. Gellman testified that the madams called the money they paid the police for protection "towel money." According to Gellman, after two narcotics squad officers arrested two of Norma's prostitutes at Pete Herman's place, the charges were dropped and the officers were transferred to a different assignment. In another case she cited a lone policeman who attempted to raid Norma's house one night and was assigned to a patrol wagon as punishment.

At one point while Gellman was on the witness stand, she looked around the room and told Kohn that nine out of ten men present at the hearing were customers at Norma Wallace's house.

Morrison interrupted the proceedings. "Just a minute, Miss Gellman," he said. "I happen to be presiding at this meeting, and I am admonishing you not to make any statements that nine out of ten people sitting in the Commission Council Chambers have frequented houses of prostitution. I think that is a very false statement. I know it doesn't apply to a great number of people here who I happen to know personally, and I think it's a conclusion that isn't called for in this Council Chamber at all. We are here to investigate the police department and not to criticize or cast aspersions upon the public. Just stick to the facts. Stick to the things you know. If you know any person present who did that—but that is another question."

Morrison struck out at Kohn through such witnesses. He questioned their moral caliber, and he received editorial backing from the *States* and *The Times-Picayune*. He was a master at double-talk. When Kohn called the mayor to the witness stand, Morrison told Kohn that he had heard of allegations of police graft, but he said, "No one who ever does the wrongdoing had any authority or was permitted in any way to commit the wrongdoing" (SCIC report, December 23, 1953). He accused "evil influences" in the city of attempting to defeat his good administration and return to the days when the city was wide open, "a gambler's paradise."

Norma's brother, Elmo, appeared at Kohn's hearings, but only to testify that he rented his property at 231 Bourbon Street, the Moulin Rouge, an alleged B-drinking establishment, to someone who had apparently used it for prostitution. "But I don't know," Elmo said. "I wasn't there." Kohn asked him if he knew Superintendent Scheuring. Elmo said he did, that he played cards with the superintendent at his home on a regular basis.

Elmo hadn't wanted to testify at the hearings and was ill at ease, but when Gaspar Gulotta got up on the witness stand he appeared to be having the time of his life. On January 6, 1954, *The Times-Picayune* reported part of his cross-examination by Kohn. When asked if he knew a certain police officer, Gaspar replied, "There are a thousand policemen and I know nine hundred and fifty of them. The other fifty know me." When asked if he knew Louie the Pimp, Gaspar said, "I don't know anyone by that name, and if I did I would not call him that." He admitted knowing Dora Russo, even carrying on business with her: "A few years ago she asked me to get her some airplane tickets, and I almost got into a lot of trouble. I nearly was charged with causing transportation into another state." Then Kohn asked if Gaspar ever got an envelope from Dora Russo. "Sure," Gaspar said. "I borrow money from her. No longer ago than last week she sent me four hundred dollars in one of those brown envelopes."

Gaspar allegedly had taken Robert Maestri's place as collector and distributor of police payoffs from madams and landlords. But at Kohn's public hearings he had (according to J. A. Walker in *New Orleans* magazine, May 1971) a "nimble tongue and mental agility [that] rivaled his brother's deftness in the ring."

When Gaspar died only a few years later, his pallbearers included former Police Superintendent George Reyer and Mayor Chep Morrison.

CHAPTER EIGHT

Big Mo

Norma walked up the marble steps to 1026 Conti Street. The afternoon sun washed the façade of the three-story town house to a light moss green. Pots of brilliant red geraniums lined the second- and third-floor galleries behind the filigreed ironwork adorned with fleurs-de-lis.

Norma was wearing an expensively tailored cocoa-colored wool suit, matching high-heeled pumps, and a small-brimmed hat, a feminine version of a fedora. She wore it jauntily askew, the brim slanting across her right eyebrow. She carried her brown handbag and a folded newspaper tucked under her arm. Thrown casually over one shoulder was a fur stole, which she'd needed earlier to ward off the December chill. The temperature, though, was climbing, and Norma felt uncomfortably warm.

She unlocked the ornate iron gate between the gleaming white, fluted columns flanking the recessed front door, stepped into the foyer, and entered her apartment through the French doors. Inside it was cool and dark. She kicked off her shoes and stripped down to a cream-colored silk slip. Barefoot, she crossed the red Oriental rug in her bedroom, picked up the newspaper she'd tossed on the bed, and went out into the sunroom off the courtyard, her office. She sat at the desk and opened the newspaper to the section devoted to city news. On the top page were two rows of photographs, the fall graduating class of the police academy. From the desk drawer Norma took a pair of scissors and cut out the photos, trimming closely around each face. She lay the head shots, widely spaced, on pieces of blank white paper. Carefully, she studied each one. Then, with a pencil, she began to draw hats on the paper over their heads, mustaches on some of the faces. She tried a full beard on one, a goatee on another. She switched the faces to different hats and facial hair. After a while she sat back, satisfied.

She checked the diamond watch hanging around her neck on its long gold chain. Nearly coffee-break time. She went back to her bedroom and sat at her dressing table. Artfully, she applied a coat of pale pink lipstick, coloring outside the natural lip line to make her lips look fuller. She rubbed two small spots of rouge on each cheekbone the way old ladies do, as if they can't see well enough to blend the color properly. Next she put on a cheap pastel blue suit with a boxy jacket that made her large breasts look matronly, and a frumpy skirt, a little too long to be fashionable, that covered most of her shapely legs. She completed the outfit with white net gloves, a pair of low-heeled, black, sensible shoes, and a brimless blue hat, a few shades darker than the suit, which she perched squarely on top of her head, bringing its little blue veil down over her brows. She let her shoulders slump. The image in the mirror was of a woman twenty years older, undistinguished and, she hoped, unrecognizable.

Norma walked through the Quarter to Canal Street. She headed for the corner of University Place, to the Meal-a-Minit. She went in— taking mincing, old-lady steps—and sat at a table in the back where she could see the door and most of the restaurant. Opening the newspaper to the society section, she perused the pages for Dorothy Dix's advice column and pretended to read while she watched the door.

They started swaggering in, the men in blue, shiny silver badges, black-strapped nightsticks. They sat at the tables, talking, smoking, slurping coffee, giving the waitresses the eye. Some of them, even the young ones, Norma knew because they'd visited the house; she scrunched lower in her seat, her head bent over the paper. A few new ones came in, and from under her veil she memorized their faces. Half an hour later they drifted out, no bills to pay, just tips for the waitresses.

Norma waited until they were back on the street, paid for her coffee, and walked with her little, halting steps across Canal Street. As soon as she was in the Quarter, she threw her shoulders back and lengthened her stride. She'd done a good day's work. Now she was ready for whatever the night would bring.

Captain Joseph Guillot was the reason Norma began memorizing the faces of policemen. Big Mo, as he was called because his voice boomed as loud as the guns on the battleship *Missouri,* had been dispatched to the French Quarter by Superintendent Joe Scheuring soon after the Nashville contractor died to "break the Quarter loose," Norma said.

At one point during Aaron Kohn's hearings early in 1953, Norma had realized that she was the only madam operating. Everyone else had shut down, frightened by the depth of the SCIC probe. So she sold the house on Girod and Saratoga and bought one at 520 Governor Nicholls Street, one house up from where she had lived with Bill Carver. She and Mac moved in and began renovations while Norma continued to rent the apartments at 1026 Conti to Blue Room musicians. Mac was happy with this arrangement. Then one day Norma ran into one of the Good Men on Canal Street. He said, "Why don't you call me a girl?"

She couldn't stand it: She just had to "cheat" a little, her term for arranging tricks during times of intense police activity. She cheated whenever Mac played golf. He didn't know a thing about it until she kicked all the musicians out of 1026 and went back to work. "It was just too slow," Norma said. "I had to have action."

Then Big Mo Guillot did all the landladies a big favor: "He ran all the pimps out of the French Quarter so fast it wasn't funny," Norma said. "They were all scared to death."

The word went around that Captain Guillot was a "good" policeman. For the landladies that meant business as usual. The following

Christmas many of them decided to show their appreciation by sending the captain a gift. Norma did not join in. She told Jackie, "Those idiots didn't keep the sense they were born with." Norma knew that if you called your man wrong, you went to jail, and she didn't know Guillot well enough yet.

Big Mo was not amused. He packed all the gifts in a police wagon and hauled them back to the houses. It was more than a warning: He began "the inspections," as Norma termed them—entering the houses, peering into every nook, checking under every rug. He came to Norma's at all hours of the night, arriving with a policeman so small that Norma wondered how he'd ever gotten into the police academy. They'd ring the side doorbell, and when Norma opened the door, Big Mo would lift the tiny policeman in and they'd go through the house. They tapped on the pecky cypress walls of the parlor, checked each room, and searched the depths of every armoire. Sometimes this could take hours. Not only that, but the inspections occurred routinely, often more than once a week. Big Mo suspected that Norma had a hideout, and she was afraid he would find it; she decided it was time for elaborate security measures.

The hideout was behind the parlor, the entrance to it in the courtyard, to the side of the stairway. At one time there had been a dungeon with a wall where slaves were shackled, and the hideout had been a runway to the dungeon. It needed a new, undetectable door. The inside wall of the courtyard was tongue in groove; her carpenter made the door fit so flush that it was difficult to see any lines where it met the wall. Once the iron bar inside was slid into place, it was nearly impossible to find a crack. For extra camouflage, Norma put tall tropical trees—palms, ficus, hibiscus, and banana—in rolling boxes. When the door to the hideout was bolted, she rolled the trees in front of the entrance.

She also had a buzzer system installed. A girl was stationed at the window in the entrance hall during operating hours. If she spotted a police lookout or a suspicious looking car drove into the alley, she threw the buzzer, which meant, Get to the hideout as quickly as possible!

Norma developed a system of spies. Her spies kept Big Mo's house under surveillance until his car was in the driveway and all lights were out, then called Norma to tell her that the captain was away for the night.

As another precaution, she rented a condemned building around the corner on North Rampart Street. When Big Mo and the little policeman arrived, the girls could escape through the gate at the end of the Conti Street driveway and into the boarded-up building until the inspection was over.

One night a police lookout was across from the house when a regular customer, weaving a little with all the drinks he'd had over on Bourbon Street, came up the driveway and rang the back doorbell. Norma slid open the little barred window she'd installed in the door.

"You idiot," she said, "don't you see that policeman across the street?"

"But, Norma," the date slurred, "I wanna come in!"

Norma nearly took his nose off when she slammed the little window in his face. She turned to Jackie. "Tricks don't have a lick of brains!" Jackie nodded.

Another night the girl at the front window threw the buzzer—Big Mo was driving up the alley. Norma led two other girls and their dates through the gate to Rampart Street. The dates took off; she and the girls entered the condemned building through a specially rigged piece of plywood. But this time Big Mo got Norma. Norma was arrested three times in 1953, twice by Big Mo. He personally took her to be photographed and fingerprinted.

The young sergeant behind the desk asked Norma her age. As usual, she lied. "Thirty-eight," she replied.

Big Mo laughed. "Oh, come on, you old bitch," he taunted, "you're as old as I am. Don't tell that boy that!"

"Okay, forty-seven," Norma said, and Big Mo laughed some more.

Norma made a hundred-dollar bail and left while the night was still young. The story was on the front page of *The Times-Picayune* the next day, October 13, 1953. The second time Big Mo got her was four days later, in a surprise ambush at 1026 Conti—he had the door down before anyone could respond to the buzzer and get to the hideout. As always, though, Norma didn't spend so much as a night behind bars.

One night shortly afterward, Elmo called Norma from the Moulin Rouge, as he often did, wanting to know if he could send a customer over. Norma decided she'd better send a girl to the Roosevelt to meet him. She chose a new girl, unknown in town. The girl dressed up in her hat and gloves and carried her overnight case up the steps to the hotel. Big Mo happened to be driving by and called out to her from his police car before she could get through the door. Norma said to Jackie after she paid the girl's fine, "That man can *smell* a whore!"

Big Mo sabotaged Norma's spies. One evening Norma got a call that he was down for the night, and no sooner did that spy hang up than another called saying he was on the way. She went to the foyer window just in time to see him wheeling into the driveway. She threw the buzzer; he jumped out and rang the side bell.

Norma had trained her girls to act fast. It took only a couple of minutes for them to get into the hideout. She opened the door and said pleasantly, "You're always coming here when I'm changing clothes, Captain." Big Mo laughed.

He lifted his tiny partner inside. Jackie was sitting in the courtyard, her long, stockinged legs crossed at the knees, wearing a low-cut black sheath with a wide, leopard-print belt. Big Mo asked her what she was doing there.

"I live here, Captain," Jackie answered.

"Then where're your flimsies?" He meant her clothes.

Jackie explained that she occupied a room upstairs. A girl named Mary actually lived in the room; Jackie was living with a doctor by that time. Guillot went upstairs and came down with two tiny dresses, a top, and a kimono that belonged to the petite Mary.

"Do these things fit you?" he asked Jackie. "Let's see you try them on."

Jackie waved her hand at the skimpy dresses Big Mo held. "Oh, Captain, I outgrew all those clothes."

Big Mo and the little policeman laughed; Norma and Jackie laughed. "You know," Big Mo said to Norma, "I'll never frame you, but if I get you fair and square, I'll get you good."

"Oh, I believe you, Captain," Norma said demurely. And in one way, she did. Big Mo was interested in her—she knew all the signs—but so far he'd made no moves.

The cat-and-mouse game continued. Norma sometimes wondered how she managed to survive it, but it was exciting—she couldn't deny that. Big Mo made it exciting. One night, though, he gave her nerves more of a workout than even he knew.

Norma had a regular Saturday night customer, a very good customer. He would take one girl right after another, five or six of them, buy drinks for everyone, and run up an exorbitant bill. But he was also a very unusual customer: He didn't want to take any of the girls to bed; instead, he wanted to dress up in their clothes—their bras, girdles, dresses, even their shoes. Every Saturday he ruined most of the clothes he wore, stretching them out so they were useless to the girls. After a few weeks Norma bought him his own wardrobe—a padded lace bra, a boned corset, high-heeled shoes, a black silk kimono, and, best of all, a wig of long curly black hair. He dressed up, the girls combed his hair, and he danced in front of the wall of mirrors in one of the upstairs bedrooms. Norma's girls clapped and whistled and told him he was beautiful. After the last dance he masturbated, paid, and went home.

This man amazed Norma. He was one of the Good Men, with a wife and family Uptown. She thought perhaps he was looking for a man, and this would have been no problem. Many people came to Norma's for something other than straight sex. Norma knew one man in particular she could have called for him, a cabdriver who liked to make a little money on the side. He was so well endowed that the girls called him Frankenstein. But when she suggested such a possibility, the man turned her down. All he wanted was to look in the mirror and see a girl.

One Saturday night while this man was upstairs, Big Mo, reportedly tucked away for the evening, drove into the alley. Norma threw the buzzer. The girl with the man from Uptown grabbed his hand and led him down the stairs. He was dressed in his underwear and flimsy silk kimono, his long, black hair flying as the girl hurried him into the hideout. Norma heard them when they reached the patio, her high heels and his high heels on the blue Mexican tiles—*clickety-clickety-click*. As she rolled the plant boxes in front of the door, the girl told her the trick's male clothes were still lying on the bed.

"Hurry, Jackie," Norma said, "go hide them. I don't have the nerve to tell Guillot you like to dress in men's clothes."

Norma was frightened as she let Big Mo in that night, but not of the friendly, flirtatious policeman with the booming voice. She was afraid her Good Man from Uptown, who'd been coming to the house for a little over a year, would never come back. She whispered to Jackie while Big Mo was tapping all the walls and checking each room in the house, "We've lost a customer, and what a customer! We'll never see him again, I just know it."

Big Mo was in a particularly expansive mood that night, and any other time Norma would have found herself enjoying the game. But that night all she could think about was her good customer imprisoned in the dark hideout, four feet wide and twenty feet long, its brick walls damp with condensation. She thought Big Mo would never leave; he even accepted a drink, something he rarely did, saying her house was his last stop that night, and sat in the courtyard—only a few feet from the entrance to the hideout!—to drink it.

When he finally left and Norma's girl opened the hideout, she expected the trick to go *clickety-click-click* off into the night. Instead he came out aflutter with happiness. "Oh," he breathed, "I've been in a raid! I'm Madeleine, a girl in a raid!" He went directly up the stairs and carried on with the night.

But Norma and Jackie held their breath during the following week. Norma said, "He'll think about it and we'll lose him, I bet you."

The next Saturday night, though, the doorbell rang, and there he was. On the off chance he'd come, Norma had bought him a new pair of red satin high heels, the biggest size she could find. When he saw those shoes, he went into ecstasy.

CHAPTER NINE

Birds on the Wire

Norma was fifty-three years old in 1954. It was a memorable year—the year she bought the property in Waggaman and the year she seduced Wayne Bernard, an act that would change her life. In the meantime she was caught up in politics, police probes, and federal grand juries.

After her first grand jury appearance in 1952, her photograph had made the front page of *The Times-Picayune*. She could have been a politician's wife in her modest below-the-knee shirtdress, pulling on her white gloves—except for the company she was in. Gertie Yost, a grandmotherly-looking woman wearing sensible shoes, and Dora Russo, who had pulled her coat up to hide her face, were walking out of the Fifth Circuit Courthouse with Norma. Both Gertie and Dora were notorious madams, but neither had Norma's glamour, or her dark glasses, which added a touch of intrigue.

The newspaper photographs of Norma through the years, especially in the fifties, are large and shot close up, suggesting that she was a media favorite. She is always dressed in tailored suits and dresses that were ladylike rather than madamlike. An earlier photo shows "Norma in her heyday," wearing another of those cockeyed hats she favored, her hair short and dark. She looks like one of the girls from the Lucky

Strike Hit Parade, big smile, head at a coy angle, an innocent come-hither look.

In 1954, called for the second time before the grand jury, she was once again front-page news, caught by the *States* photographer as she walked into the hearing. She is in a dark suit with a nipped-in waist and her dark glasses. She exudes the imperturbable aura of an underworld figure with the seductive allure of a 1950s movie queen. She is all mystery and sex, powerful as an absinthe aphrodisiac.

By 1954 Norma and McCoy's marriage, nearly ten years old, was in trouble. Mac, uncomfortable with his wife's making front-page news as a known proprietor of a house of prostitution, kept after Norma to give up the business. He sometimes chauffeured the girls to hotels or to Bourbon Street in his black Buick, but according to the SCIC report he'd also been arrested twice in connection with prostitution, though the records of these arrests had disappeared. He didn't like staying at the Conti Street apartment with her, and Norma often thought that their place on Governor Nicholls Street wasn't far enough away. She was straining at the bit of marriage again, torn between wanting her freedom and her love for her good and kind husband, who needed something to do besides play golf, drink, and keep an eye on her.

Norma found ten acres in Waggaman, only twenty minutes by car from downtown New Orleans. It had been the site of the old Cedar Grove Plantation and was located on River Road on the West Bank of the Mississippi, just upriver from Avondale Shipyards. Over the years the main house had been changed—taken off its tall piers when it was moved farther from the river. A smaller house, a barn, and stables were also on the land. Behind them ran railroad tracks, the property's only drawback. Otherwise it was beautiful, romantic because of the ancient live oaks dripping with moss that surrounded the house. Norma and Mac could have horses there, and Mac would have plenty to do to improve the property. And, business never far from her thoughts, Norma saw the place as a definite option should Conti Street get too hot.

Norma and Mac introduced themselves to their new neighbors as Mr. and Mrs. Patterson, owners of the Patterson Trucking Line. A family named Bernard lived next door with their sons and Snapbean, their tall, thin grandfather. Behind them lived Earl and Elise Rolling. Elise was Helen Bernard's sister. What Norma didn't know when she bought the place was that Earl Rolling worked for the Jefferson Parish Sheriff's Department.

"Oh, Lord," she moaned when she found out, "what have I done now? I've moved right next door to a policeman!"

But Elise and Bubba Rolling were sociable and liked to party, Norma's and Mac's kind of people. Before long the two couples were seeing each other regularly and forming a genuine, solid friendship. Norma and Elise cooked together, shopped together, and sometimes sat on the patio behind Norma's house to chat and have a few drinks. Norma hired Elise's nephew Wayne Bernard to do yard work and small repairs, and to help Mac fence the property. Wayne liked working for Mrs. Patterson. He'd work three or four hours and she'd pay him twenty dollars. He knew guys who worked a whole week at the shipyards for that.

One warm summer afternoon the two women made up a pitcher of martinis and brought it out to the table and chairs nestled into the L of the house. Wayne was working in the flower beds. He'd taken his shirt off, and his naturally bronzed skin had a burnished sheen in the sunlight. He was only fourteen years old, but he was tall and strong and had thick, wavy black hair.

He heard Mrs. Patterson and Nan Ease, as he called his aunt, laughing. They tried to muffle it at first, but then they started whispering and giggling unabashedly. They were watching two sparrows mating on an electric wire, feathers flying everywhere. But Wayne had no idea what was happening and, true to his nature, ignored the women and got on with his work in the beds.

After a while Nan Ease returned home. Norma called out to Wayne that there was something she wanted him to do in the house. "Yes, ma'am, Mrs. Patterson," he said and followed her inside, up the stairs, and into the bedroom as she explained the job to him.

In the summertime Mrs. Patterson liked to wear loose dresses with scooped tops. That afternoon her dress kept falling off one shoulder, exposing her ample cleavage. Wayne couldn't keep himself from staring. He was embarrassed and tried to look away, but he was also fascinated.

Suddenly Mrs. Patterson stopped talking. When Wayne noticed, he looked up at her. "Do you like what you see?" she inquired. Wayne was so frightened that he couldn't answer. "Come on over here," she said. Wayne moved a little closer. "Come on," she told him again. When he got close enough, she took his hand and put it on her breast. "Do you like that?"

Wayne's legs were shaking so hard that they might have gone out from under him, he wasn't sure; all he knew was that he ended up on the bed. Mrs. Patterson started touching him and caressing him, all the while talking softly, saying, "It's okay, you don't have to be afraid, I'm not going to hurt you."

Afterwards she asked, "Now, did that hurt?"

Wayne said, "God, no."

The next afternoon Mrs. Patterson asked Wayne if he'd like to go riding. He scrambled up from the flower bed he was tending, and Mrs. Patterson told him to go saddle the horses. They rode up a trail to the top of the levee, then ran the horses for a couple of miles. On the way back Mrs. Patterson was friendly, her usual self, but she never said a word about what had happened between them.

At the stables, as Wayne was hanging the saddles, Mrs. Patterson said, "Sometimes I walk in those woods at night." She pointed toward a small coppice growing up between two oaks, forming a natural fence between her and the Bernards' property. Wayne didn't know what to say, so he just nodded. "I know how to whistle," she continued, then added pointedly, "and sometimes I whistle in the woods." Again, Wayne nodded. "I *like* to whistle in the woods," she said. He still didn't get it. Mrs. Patterson looked him straight in the eye. "*You* might hear me whistling in the woods some night."

It took Wayne another minute; then he said, "Oh! Well, if I hear you whistling, I'll come out."

That night he began a routine of walking in the lane at the side of his parents' house. He strained to hear a whistle. For a few nights he heard nothing. Then, there it was! When he found Mrs. Patterson under one of the big oaks, they held each other and kissed, but she seemed in a hurry to get back to her house.

A few more nights passed, and Wayne frantically paced the edge of the woods. The night he finally heard her whistle again, Mrs.

Patterson didn't seem to be in such a hurry. They kissed, their hands were all over each other, and then they got down on the ground under the big oak. He had managed to deal with both his and her clothing and was finally in the act when they heard a peculiar shuffling, as if someone were kicking up gravel and dragging something through the leaves that covered the ground.

Both Wayne and Mrs. Patterson froze, breathing hard. Wayne knew that sound, but he was too scared to think. Then someone called out, "Anybody there?"

It was Snapbean, Wayne's grandfather! Since Snapbean's wife had died, he had taken to wandering at night, one foot dragging, kicking up gravel and leaves. And he'd heard them! Wayne's breathing became loud and ragged. Mrs. Patterson put her hand over his mouth. He could feel her heart revving in her chest.

There was more shuffling; if Snapbean got any closer he was going to step on them. "Anybody there?" Snapbean called again. An eternity passed in ten seconds before they heard that foot dragging and Snapbean easing back over to the lane.

Snapbean had scared the life right out of Wayne, so he and Mrs. Patterson didn't finish what they'd started. After that, whenever Wayne worked at Mrs. Patterson's house, Mr. Mac showed him what to do. They still went riding, but Mr. Mac was always with them. Wayne would sweat, wondering if Mrs. Patterson had ever told her husband, but then he'd think that he'd probably be dead already if she had. He continued to be paid very well.

The friendship between the Pattersons and the Rollings deepened. If Norma saw a dress she liked on Canal Street, she bought one like it, perhaps in a different color, for Elise. She gave Elise a pair of yellow high heels Elise wore until her arches fell a number of years later. Bubba invited Mac to go duck hunting and deer hunting, but Mac finally had to admit he'd rather be on the golf course. The two couples spent holidays together.

Bubba Rolling had raised fighting cocks since he was fifteen years old. Behind his house he kept them in individual pens, the floors covered with cornhusks and straw so they had to scratch for their food, which made their legs strong. He worked with his roosters every day until they were ready to fight with tiny boxing gloves on their spurs, then until their spurs were ready to be cut off so that small, knifelike razors could be tied to their legs. Bubba had done very well with his roosters, fighting them and selling them, supplementing his policeman's salary and occasionally traveling to Central America because his roosters had such a reputation.

He also kept a kennel full of hunting dogs. Both the dogs and the roosters helped him put food on the table, so he was very careful to feed the animals properly to keep them in strong working condition. But soon after Norma bought her property, he noticed that his dogs were putting on weight. He took a couple of his best roosters to a derby, but they weighed in at two pounds more than when he'd started training them. He was mystified. Then he caught Norma feeding the animals bread and milk, two loaves and a gallon a day!

"But, Bubba," Norma said, "they look hungry."

Bubba just adored Norma, even though she was a disaster with his animals. He learned not to talk to her about fighting the roosters— the chickaroos she called them—or she'd cry! And Norma learned that Bubba was the kind of policeman she understood and liked. He was fond of saying, "The only way you can do police work—you gotta swap a dozen eggs for a crate of chickens," which was his way of saying that good information was worth a blind eye. It wasn't long before the Rollings were the only people in Waggaman who knew the Pattersons' real names and the reason for their deception.

So when Wayne was fifteen or sixteen years old, his uncle Bubba phoned one day and said, "Come on, we gotta get dressed up, we're going downtown."

Wayne put on his Sunday suit, and he and Uncle Bubba drove to the French Quarter in Bubba's police car. They pulled up in front of a huge green house with galleries and a lot of fancy ironwork, and when they got out of the car Bubba said, "I'm taking you to a place where there're a lot of pretty girls." Bubba walked him up the alley to the back door.

Bubba was doing what all good tribal elders are supposed to do in New Orleans, seeing to it that the rite of passage to manhood was conducted properly. He had no idea that Wayne had been initiated already.

They walked into Norma's back parlor. Wayne stopped cold just inside the door—a dozen of the prettiest girls he'd ever seen were all looking at him. Bubba sat in a chair and watched Wayne perch on the edge of the sofa. The poor boy was so nervous that he couldn't stop his leg from jumping.

Bubba patted his own leg and said to one of the girls, "Come on over here." The girl sat on his lap. He said to Wayne, "Pick yourself one of these girls." He saw that Wayne kept eyeing a blonde, Ruthie. "How about Ruthie?" Ruthie sat next to Wayne. "When you want to go upstairs, boy, you just go. 'Cause I'm gonna take off with this one in a minute."

Wayne sat for a moment, then leaned toward his uncle. "You know what I'm thinkin, Bubba?" he whispered. "What if Nan Ease comes in here?"

Bubba yelled, "Whoa, man! If *that* happens, you just follow me, 'cause I'm gonna make a hole in that wall and run through it!"

After a while Wayne went upstairs with Ruthie. She sat on the bed, under a canopy, and lifted her short skirt to unsnap her stockings from her garter belt. Wayne had never seen a woman peel off her stockings before. He was so enthralled that he forgot all about undressing himself. Ruthie took off her dress and very carefully, very neatly hung it over a high-backed chair. Wayne was looking and trying not to look at the same time.

Standing before him stark naked, Ruthie said in a soft, gentle voice, "Aren't you going to take your little suit off?" Wayne snapped to attention. It didn't take him long. He threw everything over the back of another chair.

Downstairs, Norma came out of hiding to bring Bubba a Scotch and water in a tall highball glass. The girl who had been sitting on his lap was now hanging over the back of the chair, her arms around his neck. But Bubba declined to go upstairs, which turned out to be a prudent move that day. Because upstairs Wayne was already getting dressed, though he was fumbling with zippers and buttons and trying to get his tie prim and proper. Ruthie took over, dressing him so that he thought even *that* was something. He came down the stairs before Bubba was half finished with his Scotch.

Bubba was astonished. "Hey, man," he said, "didn't you like that girl?"

"Yeah."

"Well"—Bubba cleared his throat—"did you do anything?"

"Oh, yeah. Two times."

They left, and as they were walking down the driveway Wayne said, "*Cooo-eeee!* What *is* this place?"

On his own Wayne returned to the house on Conti Street two or three times, until Jackie wouldn't let him in. With his characteristic sangfroid, he shrugged it off and went about his business. Soon after he quit school and went to work at Avondale Shipyards. Over the next five years he saw Mrs. Patterson only rarely.

CHAPTER TEN

The Game

Big Mo Guillot and Norma continued to play cat-and-mouse through the midfifties. Norma always knew when Big Mo's men were following her—they tailed her so closely she could spot them with no trouble. She enjoyed giving them the slip and disappearing into St. Bernard or Jefferson Parish, on either side of Orleans Parish, where they had no authority. Big Mo stepped up his inspections; Norma darkened her house and operated elsewhere for a few nights, writing Big Mo anonymous letters to specify the elusive madam's whereabouts, which sent his men scurrying all over the city. One night Marie Bernard, a madam Norma liked, called Norma to say that a cop was watching her house (at 6975 Canal Boulevard) and preventing a trick from leaving. Norma drove by slowly in her Cadillac. The cop recognized her and left Marie's to tail her to the St. Bernard line. But Marie, unlike Norma, was not gifted in her line of work. "She had a lot of bad luck," Norma said, "and never did succeed in having a really fine house; she was battling it all the time." Marie certainly didn't know how to make friends with the federal agents; she was eventually sent to jail for tax evasion. The feds located the linen service Marie used, counted each towel as a trick, and sent her up.

Big Mo was promoted to colonel, and Presley Trosclair, nick-named Foots because he liked to kick people in the rear end—even his own men—became the new vice squad commander. He operated very differently from Big Mo. Whereas Guillot was straightforward in his approach, Foots liked the setup. When it came to catching the prostitutes, he sent in young, eager-beaver graduates fresh from the academy. Norma spent more time studying the graduates' pictures and drinking coffee at the Meal-a-Minit, disguised as an old lady.

One of these young cops managed to learn one of Norma's pass-words. He called the house and asked for a girl, but he wanted the girl to meet him somewhere other than 1026 Conti. At the time Norma was using a house near City Park, a couple of miles out Esplanade Avenue from the Quarter. She decided to send Terry, a petite girl of French extraction with skin like white porcelain against her deep black hair. Terry was beautiful, and she knew it. She fit Norma's defi-nition of a chippie, a girl who never went with any man for very long, but men loved Terry—she was known around town as Yum-Yum because of her specialty—and Norma trusted and liked Terry. She would leave the house with her, and Terry was one of the few girls Norma socialized with.

Terry met the young man at the City Park house and took him to a bedroom. He gave her money, she undressed, and he pulled his badge. Then Foots made his entrance. This would have been all there was to it, because Terry refused to talk, except that Terry liked the young cop. As Foots stormed around the house, Terry said to her handsome captor, "What a pity that you have to be a copper and pull a badge just when I thought I was going to enjoy myself."

Norma said, "Just like all men—they think they are God's gift to the human race—his ego swelled. I knew Terry loved me and would never betray me. She wanted to date the policeman, but she said that if he ever asked her any of my business, that would end the romance. But this Paul was a stud, bragging to other cops about his free piece of ass. I had connections; I knew what he was saying—'I'm gonna get Norma Wallace because I'm screwin one of her girls.'

"Every boy that graduated out of the police academy, I was his ambition. I don't know what it was with these guys. Seemed like they thought if they could bust Norma Wallace they would be made captain."

Norma said nothing to Terry, and Terry continued meeting Paul at her own apartment. But the next thing Norma heard from her contact within the police department was nothing short of a call to arms. "This boy," her informer said, "knows your girl has a kid. He says she's no good and he's gonna rack her up and take her kid away."

Norma had always told her girls to be on the lookout for unusual body marks on men. "Just in case a beef came up, I kept a record: What was the size of his tool? Was it especially big or little? Did it have any marks on it?"

When Terry heard what Paul had said about her child, she told Norma he had scars on one of his thighs. Norma called her connection in the department.

Paul was brought in and accused of consorting with a known prostitute. He was asked for his resignation, at which point he denied the allegation. His superior demanded that he drop his pants. Paul resigned from the department.

"Actually," Norma said cooly, "he owes me a lot. Today he has a very fine business, has made a great success of it. If it wasn't for me, he'd still be on his lousy little salary, might even have been killed by now. I think about him and hope he doesn't hate me. I don't hate him; I just wanted to show him that wasn't how you played the game."

On Sunday nights Norma and Terry liked to go to the Town and Country to dance and have some drinks. Norma especially liked the piano player there, Sam Adams, who was also a tenant on Governor Nicholls Street, and always stopped whatever he was playing to sing "Mona Lisa" as Norma came in, segueing into a spoof of "It's So Nice to Have a Man Around the House." For Terry, Sam would sing, "Don't sit under the Yum-Yum tree with anyone but Terr-eee!" Foots thought they were soliciting men at the Town and Country, but the motel was in Jefferson Parish, out of his jurisdiction. Then Norma discovered the Black Orchid on Foy Street in Gentilly, a place with great Italian food and an intimate lounge. She and Terry often invited some of the other girls and started the night there. So Foots sent in a good-looking young vice cop named Nick Macheca.

The first several times Macheca went to the Black Orchid, he brought a date with him and spent the city's money on dinner and drinks. He watched Norma; he watched the girls; he didn't see any of them working out of the lounge. But he knew they were slick, and, anyway, he liked the place—it was becoming a home away from home for him. He stopped bringing dates. He bought drinks for Norma's girls, he danced with them, he tried to get dates with them, he put the move on Yum-Yum—that was for himself, not his job—but not one of them tumbled.

Foots demanded action. Macheca and his partner, Norman Macaluso, found out that "Mr. Royal" was one of the passwords to get into the house. They phoned and said Mr. Royal told them to call when they got to town. Jackie asked several questions, but she didn't like the answers; they didn't get in.

So Macheca and Macaluso decided to stake out the place. They picked a cold, drizzly night and sat in a van, nothing but a shell of metal, and shivered as they watched for men going up the driveway at 1026 Conti. A couple of hours went by. No one went in, but someone was coming out.

Marie, the maid, came down the driveway in her starched white dress, holding a red umbrella over her head. Macheca and Macaluso watched her cross Conti Street and walk toward North Rampart. She disappeared around the corner. They sat back to wait some more, hugging themselves to keep warm and fogging the windows in the van with their breath.

A half hour later a sharp rapping on the side of the van startled them. "Who the hell knows we're here?" Macaluso whispered to Macheca. Macheca shrugged. He opened the van window.

Marie held out a silver tray. "Miss Norma says she knows it's cold out here, so she sent y'all some chicken sandwiches and hot coffee."

Setups and surveillance were not producing results for Foots. He seemed to be nothing more than a footnote in Norma's life. He needed to find another way.

Straight through the fifties the fake shows continued to be popular, especially with couples. On the way to the house the cabdrivers
liked to tell their fares about the dog and pony shows at Norma
Wallace's. Word got around about a show with a pony and a girl, but
that the girl would only do it if the audience was large enough. When
the couples got to the house, they'd ask Norma if the girl and pony
were going to perform that night. Norma would say, "Oh, the girl
was oversexed; she screwed the pony to death." Then they'd want to
know if the girl was there. "No," Norma would tell them, "she's dead
from screwin too."

Norma said, "What the hell. I was selling something. And the
people kept flocking in!"

Then there were tales about the greased-girl show, in which a guy
tried to catch an oil-coated girl in thirty seconds or less. Soon rumor
had it that on the third floor Norma had installed a two-way mirror
with four rows of bleacher-type seats behind it. Now the word was
that the guy chasing the girl was some poor sap who had no idea people were watching as he tried to catch the greased girl fast enough so
that he didn't have to pay for her. Simone was the girl who screwed
the pony (it's really a small donkey, those in the know said); she was
the greased girl too. She was known as Norma's all-around girl—
she'd do *anything* if the price was right. Norma did, in fact, have a girl
named Simone who was called the all-around girl. Fact and legend
meshed, and the legend of Norma Wallace's house grew.

And it made Foots Trosclair hot under the collar, especially after
he'd lost one of his most promising young vice cops because of
Norma. He became determined to close her house down on a crime-
against-nature charge. He thought of a different kind of setup; he'd
use a woman this time. He sent a woman traffic cop to the Davis
Beauty Salon, where Norma had been a client for nearly ten years and
had a standing appointment every other afternoon. The cop made an
appointment, and as she was having her hair dyed an ungodly shade of
red, she chatted away to Norma.

The next time Norma saw her, the cop left the busy downtown
intersection where she was directing traffic and talked to Norma
through her car window. "You know, Miss Norma," she said, "I'm
out here directing traffic in the hot summer and the cold winter. I'd

sure rather work for you." Through the grapevine Norma already knew the woman was thick with Foots.

She looked the cop up and down. She had feet like doorstops— must have worn at least a size ten shoe—and that hair! "Honey," Norma said, "you couldn't even be a maid in my house." She shook her head sadly. "You look like death took a holiday."

Norma had a good friend, Poppy, a very pretty young homosexual man who lived Uptown. One evening Poppy and his burly housemate threw a big party. Norma went with Darlene Ford, a hefty woman who owned a beauty parlor in the Quarter. Norma wore a satin moiré dress with a trumpet skirt that dragged the floor in the back and a fluffy boa so long that she had to wrap it around her neck twice so she wouldn't trip on it—all in her favorite color, a luscious crimson. Darlene swathed her ample girth in yards of luminous purple and gold silk. But they were only pinpoints of phosphorescence in a sea of color that sparkled and glittered and waved and flowed, fabulous dresses that were jeweled and sequined and beaded and bugled, with necklines that plunged in the front and stood up in the back to showcase mile-high hairdos, many of which Darlene had created.

What a spectacle! Men dressed in women's clothes and some of them so beautiful no one would have known they weren't women. Everyone was drinking champagne and eating the delicious food that Poppy had spent days cooking. They were having a wonderful time— until the next-door neighbor came out on his porch and yelled that he had called the police.

The crowd broke and began running down the long steps from Poppy's raised house, tripping on their skirts and twisting their ankles in their high heels so that it was a wonder they didn't kill themselves. Norma's long, gold Cadillac Coupe De Ville was parked right in front. "I jumped in my car, and you've never seen anything like it. Fairies with dresses on jumped in with me. Some were riding on the hood. Darlene, who weighed about two hundred and fifty pounds, couldn't get in the car because it was so loaded. So she jumped up on the running board, and I took off. The car was tilting; wigs, high heels, and purses were flying."

Norma drove a couple of blocks. Everyone looked back to see the cops pulling up in front of Poppy's house; they all screamed. Norma whisked them away.

"I always did say there were three sexes—the male, the female, and the otherwise. I can guarantee you we would have made front-page headlines on that one."

It seemed like everybody heard about it anyway. Norma's police buddies kidded her for days. But it got Foots thinking. He had arrested a young homosexual on a crime-against-nature charge. He figured the boy knew Norma, so he offered him a deal.

A few weeks later Norma's young friend called her: He had a couple from out of town who wanted to see a show, could he send them over? Norma turned him down flat. Jackie tried to talk her into it, but Norma refused. Later her friend leveled with her—the couple was a vice cop and a policewoman, and Foots had set it up.

"Gee, I must have been born with a veil," Norma said.

Headlines across the front pages of the city's newspapers charged Chep Morrison and Joe Scheuring with laxity and called for Scheuring's removal as police superintendent. Scheuring had been indicted by the Orleans Parish grand jury for malfeasance in office, but Judge Bernard Cocke dismissed the charge. One of the city councilmen, Fred Cassibry, decided to take on Scheuring's ouster as his personal cause. Morrison, more stubborn than ever in the face of this adversity, stood up for his appointee while Scheuring insisted that Aaron Kohn had gathered his information from "the scum of the underworld." But when the Special Citizens Investigating Committee delivered its final report in April 1954, the first of its thirty-nine recommendations was the dismissal of Scheuring. Morrison, for the public record, traced the committee's information on lotteries and prostitution to that gleaned during the early days of his administration, when Adair Watters was superintendent. He insisted that Scheuring had eradicated these problems. In November 1954 the Louisiana Supreme Court reversed Judge Cocke's decision to dismiss the malfeasance charge against Scheuring. Still, the mayor refused to fire Scheuring.

So Judge Cocke cleared Scheuring of the charge the following January, and Scheuring immediately filed a lawsuit against Councilman Cassibry for defamation of character, asking a hundred thousand dollars in damages. Morrison and Scheuring seemed invincible.

The tables turned when Kohn served a ten-day jail term for contempt rather than divulge his sources to the grand jury. After his release he came to be regarded as a martyr for the cause of law enforcement. Irate citizens saw him as a victim of political intimidation. They wrote letters and made phone calls. Finally, they marched on City Hall.

The demonstration got to Morrison. With more underhanded machinations he had one of his loyal administrators call for the removal of Scheuring. Morrison continued to defend his chief publicly; the chief continued to refuse to resign. Whatever took place behind closed doors will remain a secret, but less than a month later Scheuring retired with accolades for his accomplishments and sacrifice.

Morrison had escaped total disgrace, but Kohn, the SCIC, and his own stubbornness had damaged his reputation as a progressive administrator. The mayor, though, still had ambitious political aspirations. Second in command to Scheuring was a retired army officer and a churchgoing resident of silk-stocking Uptown. In a savvy political move that gave his administration a fresh image of credibility and respectability, Morrison named Provosty Dayries as his new police superintendent in 1955.

Dayries was known as a man of honesty, integrity, and, above all, fairness. He adhered to a strict moral code; he remained above the political fray. He liked to wear a uniform reminiscent of World War II—brown jodhpurs, khaki shirt, short brown jacket, and big black boots. He carried a riding crop, which he snapped smartly against his boot with good effect. Around City Hall, though, the outfit and the attitude got him called Mr. Military, the Iron Man, and Mr. Stoic.

Too fair-minded to consider a frame, Dayries continued inspections in the mode of Big Mo Guillot. Norma, however, assessed him as a "goon," meaning not the gangster type but someone who is not street-smart.

Late one night she was looking out the front shuttered window toward the alley when a big Buick swooshed up fast to the door. Four men flew out of it, three uniforms and one in what appeared to be an English riding outfit—boots, whip, the whole nine yards. He strode directly to the window. Norma slammed it down. He called out, "I'm the superintendent of police."

Norma had never seen Dayries. Her response was to pull the shade and put out the hall light. The next thing she heard was "Break down the door."

Norma was home alone, and, as usual when she was in, the front door was unlocked. A few minutes later, though, down came the unlocked door. She heard one of the uniformed cops coming around from the back say, "I could have told you the door was unlocked."

Dayries walked into the hall and found Norma standing with her arms folded. "Now you've done it!" she said.

Irate, Dayries countered, "You pulled that window down in front of my face!"

Norma knew two of the cops who had come in with him; they'd been trying to catch her for a long time. She called them by name. "They brought you here, and you're going to be terribly disappointed," she told Dayries. "But come along—I'll give you a tour of the house."

On every wall hung the nude paintings. Dayries looked at each one, making no comment. He stopped in front of a nude girl on a horse. Norma waited; still, he remained mum. "Superintendent," she said finally, "isn't that a beautiful girl?"

He took his time answering, then amazed her by saying, "I think the horse is pretty too."

"Yes," Norma agreed, "but nobody wants to screw a horse."

Dayries tapped his crop against his boot, then continued through the house. He knocked on walls and opened drawers and closets on the first and second floors. Norma led him up the stairs to the third floor. She knew what he was looking for; sure enough, he spied a cabinet and became fixated, but only for a moment. He moved on, bending to peep under a low bed.

"Superintendent, please," Norma said, "it's dusty under there. You don't want to crawl in all that dust, do you?"

He rose. "I've had a lot of complaints about this place," he told her. He looked out the window to the alley below. "Men come down that alley."

"Yes," Norma agreed, "every drunk ever passed puked in it. They named it Puke Alley, in fact. They urinate in it too. It's had a lot of play. One night a couple of girls had a knife fight down there. Some poor do-gooder came along and tried to put a stop to it. They cut all his clothes right off him, left him nothing but his tie."

Dayries made no comment but turned his attention to the cabinet. "What have you got in there?"

"Listen," Norma said, "I can't hide anybody in that cabinet. It's way too small, right?"

"Where's the key to it?" He rapped his crop against the door.

"I tell you what—why don't you bust it open and see what's in it?"

He looked at her. "I'll take your word for it."

Back downstairs he asked her for her maiden name. When she told him Badon, he wanted to know if she was kin to the Badon from Covington who had been in the army with him. She said that was her cousin, and Dayries began chatting about the army as he strolled to the back of the house. Norma's maid, Marie, sat in the kitchen.

"What's she doing here?" Dayries wanted to know.

"She's keeping me company, Superintendent. With your permission."

Once he had satisfied himself that he'd been through the house thoroughly and was preparing to leave, Norma said, "Who's going to fix my door?" Dayries didn't reply—more of his strong, silent routine. Norma pressed the issue. "Are you going to send over a carpenter?"

She decided she had stumped him. "Never mind," she said dismissively, "I'll fix the door. You can go."

When Morrison appointed Dayries, he asked his new superintendent how long it would take him to clean up the city. Dayries thought about it and said he could do it in two years. The mayor gave him the command to get started. But either Morrison didn't know his man or he underestimated him. Dayries approached his charge with alacrity, high standards, and a true determination to institute change, qualities that are not always appreciated in the Big Easy.

One evening one of the city's politicos was being fêted for his upcoming marriage. The party was taking place at Lenfant's, a restaurant on Canal Boulevard that had an enormous banquet room. The mayor, the district attorney, the councilmen and assessors, the sheriff, judges—everyone who was anyone in city politics was there. Even the legislators had come in from Baton Rouge. Everyone was drinking and eating the mounds of shrimp and crawfish heaped on the tables. The room was dark; they were watching a movie.

Whenever Severn Darden, the district attorney, raided a house of ill repute, he confiscated any pornographic films he found and stored them in the basement at City Hall (now Gallier Hall), where the mayor's office was. The films were shown any time there was a stag party.

One of the mayor's aides was running the projector. The only sounds he heard other than the movie were the sucking of crawfish heads, the slurping of drinks, and the guffaws and whistles of the men in the room, until there was a loud *bump-bump-bumping* at the door. He stopped chewing and turned the volume down. The door flew open, someone switched the lights on, and the superintendent of police bounded into the room. He wore his jodhpurs, boots, and a felt hat. In one hand was his whip, in the other his police whistle, which he began to blow with a piercing *breeh! breeh! breeh!* stopping only to bellow, "This place is raided!" as the room flooded with uniformed cops.

Judges, councilmen, assessors threw down their napkins, spit out their crawfish, and hauled ass to the opposite door of the room. Only two people didn't move, the mayor and the aide running the projector. The aide calmly popped a crawfish tail into his mouth; he wasn't about to get up for anybody. After all, he was eating his crawfish, and, anyway, he was with the mayor. What could possibly happen to them?

Morrison wiped his mouth and slowly rose from the table. Dayries stopped the whistle screaming; he stood at attention. Behind him were naked people, larger than life, as the movie continued to roll.

"What the fuck do you think you're doing?" the mayor said. Then he began to yell, his voice getting louder and louder. "You stupid son of a bitch, you Uptown asshole, what the *fuck* do you think you're doing?" He shook with rage. "If you and your men are not out of here in the next minute"—he raised a fist—"you and every goddamned cop in here is *fired!*"

From his chair the aide watched as the tide changed directions. Now policemen were hauling ass out the door and councilmen and assessors and judges were turning back toward the tables. Dayries was red in the face, but with great aplomb he cracked his whip, just a little off his mark—he aimed for his boot but caught himself on the thigh. To his credit, he didn't wince. Instead, he clicked his bootheels together and executed a perfect military turn.

The door slammed shut. The aide was the first to break the silence in the banquet room. "Oooooo, ooooo," he wailed, "hit me, beat me, make me write bad checks!"

The men at the stag party went wild.

Norma was miffed about the expense to replace her front door. When she heard about the Lenfant's fiasco from her myriad contacts and customers in city government, she went directly to her lawyer's office. "You tell him," she said to Arthur de la Houssaye, himself an Uptowner and member of the Boston Club, "I've been inspected for lunch, dinner, and supper. They ring the bell when I'm bathing, I let them in. I get out of a sound sleep for an inspection. I've had it!" The truth of it was that the stiff-spined, aristocratic superintendent just wasn't as much fun as Big Mo Guillot. He didn't know how to play the game.

De la Houssaye went to see Dayries. He reported to Norma that, without any hesitation at all, the superintendent had agreed there would be no more inspections without a search warrant.

Dayries never went to Norma's again, but Joseph Giarrusso, the head of narcotics and soon-to-be assistant superintendent of police, arrived with the first warrant. He'd acted on good information, but when he got to the house, Norma was home alone. Gracious as an Uptown socialite, she invited him in and offered the commander a glimpse of her collection of nudes. As they walked around the house, Giarrusso found himself wondering how old Norma was. He knew she was older than he was, but just how much older was hard to tell. She was attractive—shapely, not sloppy like some middle-aged women; she kept herself well.

Twice more Giarrusso got warrants. Each time he was well informed and each time the house was as quiet as a graveyard. He understood that Norma was as well informed as he was.

Years later Norma told Wayne Bernard that, after those three trips to the house, Joe Giarrusso extended an invitation of his own. "Giarrusso got Bubba to set him up with Norma," Wayne said. "He asked her to meet him on the levee behind Ochsner Hospital, out in Jefferson Parish. She met him, but nothing took place. She said, 'If he wants to meet me somewhere, let's go to the Royal Orleans, the Roosevelt, someplace nice like the Blue Room. Don't tell me to meet you on the Mississippi River levee, for God's sake!'"

That's when Norma gave Joe Giarrusso the nickname Old Bucket Head. He was to become the next superintendent of police, but even if Norma had known that she wouldn't have cared. In the late 1950s Norma was at the absolute top of her game. She was irreverent, she was cavalier, and, above all, *she* picked the men she wanted to go to bed with.

Norma spotted John Datri at the head of a Mardi Gras parade, carrying the flag. He was part of the mounted police unit. She liked his tall, lean good looks—he was dark haired and young, just her kind of man. Not only that, she liked how he looked on a horse.

"Who's that guy?" she asked the friend who was with her at the parade.

"Aw, you don't want to mess with him—he's trouble," her friend said.

But Norma was looking for trouble. In the couple of years since she'd bought the Waggaman property, her marriage to McCoy had not gotten any better; it was almost finished if their sex life was any indication. John Datri was young—younger than Mac—and virile.

On Decatur Street was a place where off-duty police met. Norma and Terry haunted the joint until they found Datri and a friend there one afternoon. Norma sent Datri a beer. He told the bartender to send it back.

"Do you know who that is?" the bartender asked.

"Yeah, I know. She's that old ex-whore, that madam—I don't want to mess with her. I get in enough trouble without looking for it."

Norma brought the beer back herself. "What's the matter?" she asked. "You won't drink my beer?"

"I don't want to get involved," Datri said.

"You won't get involved," Norma assured him. "No one's trying to set you up." So he drank a few beers with her.

She then proceeded to set Datri up. She got Terry (Yum-Yum) to arrange a double date with Datri's friend—Yum-Yum with Datri, Norma with the friend. They were to meet at the Black Orchid. Datri's friend had some trouble convincing him they should go, but in the end Datri couldn't resist Yum-Yum.

At the Black Orchid, as arranged, Yum-Yum asked Datri's friend to dance; Norma asked Datri. They danced and talked, then Norma said, "Do you see what's happening here?" Datri didn't. "We're going to swap dates."

"Whose idea is that?" Datri wanted to know. He'd been having a few ideas about Yum-Yum.

Norma told him it was her idea; she told him how she'd always liked a man on a horse. When she finished she asked him, "So, do you mind?" By that time Datri didn't mind at all.

Datri's friend called him off to the side. "I've got bad news for you," he said. "Yum-Yum wants me."

"Son of a bitch!" Datri snarled, trying to keep a straight face.

Norma called Datri the Wild One. "Date-tree," she told him, "you're crazy." Datri claimed he was crazy because he'd been on the USS *Enterprise* when the Japanese bombed it. He would take a dare on anything, like playing chicken at night on horseback on the narrow top of the Mississippi River levee, or getting in the middle of a bunch of bikers fighting with broken bottles and breaking it up. Or throwing an envelope with his cut of bribe money in it back at a fellow police officer, saying, "Stick it up your ass." Or cockily telling Big Mo Guillot that he knew Norma Wallace paid him off.

Norma Wallace, 1920s, with her beloved Vidalia, a police dog whose name became a local term for an out-of-towner seeking a prostitute.

Norma, standing behind Andy Wallace and his bootlegger cronies. She took his name and the seven-carat diamond ring she's wearing before he eventually shot and wounded her.

Norma, 1930s. "Whores make good wives, but madams don't. When you're making money in a whorehouse, that makes you independent and hard to get along with as a wife in the first place."

Norma with her second husband, Pete Herman, at Shady Pond, her farm in Pearl River, 1936.

Pete Herman was twice the world bantamweight boxing champion before becoming a French Quarter nightclub owner. Norma first operated above Pete's Ringside Bar and Lounge on the corner of Conti and Burgundy.

1026 Conti Street, late 1940s. Once owned by Ernest Bellocq, the famed photographer of the Storyville prostitutes, and located across the street from the Greyhound station, Norma's third business address was in many ways ideal.

Canal Street, early 1950s. At the Meal-a-Minit, Norma disguised herself as an old lady to spy on the cops who frequented it and to learn the new faces.

Norma first saw John Datri mounted, at the head of a Mardi Gras parade, carrying the police flag. Off duty, he would soon dress in cashmere and drive the gold Coupe DeVille that marked him as Norma's new companion.

Norma Wallace at her second grand jury appearance, 1954.

In 1962, every cadet out of the police academy wanted the instant prestige that would come with shutting down Norma Wallace's forty-two-year operation. Top left, Big Jim Garrison, the New Orleans DA, who sought to reform the French Quarter; top right, Officer Paul Nazar, whose upset stomach and Mediterranean eyes gained him entrance to 1026 Conti Street; left, Frederick Soulé (center, with bowtie), commander of the vice squad that finally busted Norma.

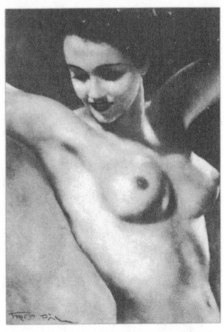

Below: Norma's house in Waggaman, later the Tchoupitoulas Plantation Restaurant, where men paid well to finally introduce Norma to their wives. The nudes that once hung at 1026 Conti (above) were transferred to the walls of the restaurant; there, however, the patrons were required to keep their clothes on.

Wayne Bernard, the boy next door who fell in love with "Mrs. Patterson," at their getaway in Poplarville, Mississippi, 1972.

"It's amazing what a little Bacardi and Coke will do": Norma in the living room of Tchoupitoulas, circa 1965, when her relationship with her youngest husband was at its stormiest and most romantic.

"If the truth will make you clean, I'll come clean . . . all the way." Norma's tell-all interview at age seventy-one won her an invitation to speak at the New Orleans Press Club, where she received a key to the city.

Or getting a vasectomy.

"What's that?" he asked Norma.

"They just go clip-clip." Norma scissored her fingers through the air.

"Wait a minute!" the Wild One yelled.

"Date-tree, you can't go on having children like this." His fourth had just been born. "You can't afford what you've got." Then she dared him to get a vasectomy. He went to Dr. Frank Gomila's office and had it done.

Datri liked going to bed with Norma. He liked her body, which was better than those of some twenty-five-year-olds he'd slept with— her large, perfect, creamy white breasts, her milk white pubic hair. He liked it when she told him, "Date-tree, you Italians are the best lovers in the world," and he'd say, "Aw, go ahead. You gotta tell that to all the dagos."

And he liked talking to Norma. He liked her stories about the house, because he never went to Conti Street. She told him that when a girl wanted to work for her, she made her strip down. If she passed the inspection, Norma hired her and got her a new wardrobe. Norma told him that she paid the IRS every year, like religion, in the neighborhood of five thousand dollars; that she'd had a fabulous love affair with Phil Harris; that of all the movie stars who'd ever come to her place, Don Ameche was the pussiest-eatin son of a bitch she'd ever seen—"He ate every girl in the house!" And Norma told Datri why she liked younger men: "When I feel like I want to get laid, I want somebody who can get a good hard-on, not some old boy who can't."

Datri also liked to go out with Norma. One night they arrived at the Black Orchid just as a fight broke out. Datri spun one of the guys around and decked him. "Good shot, Date-tree," Norma said, and they walked into the lounge as if nothing had happened.

Datri was getting his kicks. He tooled around in Norma's gold Coupe De Ville like he owned it. At first he didn't like the cashmere sports coat she wanted him to wear to the Town and Country— "Button the top button of your shirt," she said, "I like the hood look"—but he got used to it and started liking it enough that she bought him another one. He liked the leather jacket too and the cigarette case with the built-in lighter and the money she put in his pocket every night they spent together. He especially liked the outboard motor Norma gave him for Christmas. She'd sent George, her porter, to get it but told Datri, "He doesn't know an outboard from an outhouse," and gave him the money to get it himself.

Foots Trosclair heard about the outboard, and he wanted to nail Datri and take another shot at Norma too. One night he went to Datri's house and told him to take a ride. In the car he casually asked Datri what time it was. Datri looked at the heavy gold watch on his wrist and gave him the time.

"Where'd you get the watch?" Foots asked.

"You know where I got it," Datri growled. The watch had been a gift from Norma and was engraved with both their initials on the back.

"Give it to me," Foots demanded.

"Over my dead body! The only way you're gonna get this watch is to cut my arm off!"

Foots took Datri downtown. He wanted him to make a statement about his relationship with Norma. Datri started, "I, John Datri, am making this statement under duress and against my will."

"No, no, no!" Foots yelled. "That's not what I want!" He ripped the paper out of the typewriter. Datri continued to start each statement the same way; Foots ripped out each page and stomped it on the floor. They shouted, they threatened violence. They went on like that until one of the other officers made them both go home. Foots eventually got Datri by sheer luck—he walked into a barroom brawl and found Datri in the middle of it. Datri got fired.

But that was some time after he and Norma had drifted apart, no big scene, just a natural end to their yearlong affair. A few weeks later Datri ran into Yum-Yum at a country-western bar on Magazine Street.

"Ummmmmm," Yum-Yum said, "I've been waiting a long time." She drove him to the Town and Country Motel. Datri had half his clothes off when Yum-Yum took him in the chair.

Datri didn't think Yum-Yum was better in bed than Norma—well, except perhaps in one category. "That's why they called her Yum-Yum," he said.

.   .   .

Late one afternoon Norma drove over to the Davis Beauty Salon. It wasn't her regular appointment day, but sometimes she popped in for a quick fix if she had special plans. Davis didn't mind that Norma never bothered to phone ahead; she always tipped him well, often as much as fifty bucks.

The salon was being painted, and cans of terra-cotta paint had been stored under the carport behind the building when the painters left for the day. Norma nosed her spotless white Cadillac, only a few months old, between the carport posts and crashed into the paint cans.

Janice Roussel, one of the stylists, heard the clatter and yelled to Davis, "Franky, I told you to tell those painters to move the cans!" She was mortified when the back door opened and Norma walked in.

"Franky, baby," Norma said, "you won't believe what just happened." She leaned back in one of the shampoo chairs and closed her eyes, completely relaxed.

Davis chuckled and kept working on his customer. Janice grabbed a handful of towels, went out to the car, and tried to wipe off the paint. She came back in, crying with frustration.

"What the hell, Janice," Norma said. "I can buy another Cadillac."

Davis was so amused by the episode that he told two hairdresser friends about it. "You do Norma Wallace?" they shrieked. They insisted that he take them to one of the girlie shows.

Davis had never been to the house on Conti Street. Norma told him to drive to the back, where she'd be waiting at the door to the parlor. She gave the three men drinks, then took them to the second parlor off to the side of the courtyard, where a big blonde was playing the piano and several girls were dancing. They took their seats, Davis next to Norma. The piano player thumbed a run down the keyboard, gave a flourish, and a girl jumped up on the chair in front of one of Davis's friends, where she did a slow strip. Moving to the music, she writhed and rubbed her hands down her bare body, dancing closer and closer until she was right in the guy's face. Then she started on the next fellow.

Just when it was Davis's turn, there came a thumping on the outside wall. The piano player abruptly stopped, and she and the girls disappeared, swift and silent. Norma took an envelope from the drawer of a small mahogany table and stuck it through a slot in the wall Davis hadn't noticed. Then she called the girls back, but Davis was ready to call it a night.

"Don't worry, Franky," Norma said. "It's all part of the game." His two friends still wanted a free trip upstairs.

But Davis was thinking about his car parked out back and newspaper headlines and the business he might lose. He didn't care if he hadn't gotten his turn; he wanted to leave. "I guess I just don't have enough of the animal in me," he told Norma, his car keys jangling in his hand.

Norma picked up the phone. "Bubba, I got something for you, honey." A couple of her girls had been working at the Sugar Bowl Courts on Airline Highway when they spotted four high rollers driving around in a Cadillac. Four men were wanted in connection with a series of robberies in Jefferson Parish. The previous night they'd hit the Chesterfield Southport, tied up the night watchman with venetian blind cords, taped his mouth, knocked him out, and left him in the casino.

Bubba went out alone, riding reconnaissance as he did almost every night. Around midnight he spotted a car pulled up behind some hedges. Sure enough, it was a Cadillac, and four hoods were sitting in it. Without thinking Bubba pulled his big nickel-plated gun and approached the car. It was only after he'd announced himself and declared the men under arrest that he realized he had no idea how he was going to get four armed robbers out of the car by himself.

Coming down the sidewalk he heard *clip-clop, clip-clop,* a woman out walking alone. "Hey, lady," he called to her, "I'm from the sheriff's office. Will you call over there and tell them I need some help here?"

The woman looked at Bubba's big, shiny gat and took off at a dead run. That woman ain't gonna call nobody, Bubba thought. He held the gun steady, but he could feel himself breaking out in a cold sweat. Any minute these bozos were going to get smart enough to realize they had him.

The howl of sirens coming from all directions was a sweet sound indeed. The robbers were caught red-handed with the money from the casino, cordless venetian blinds, and a roll of tape. They'd also stolen a sack of brand-new chips, which they planned to take back to the Chesterfield and cash in.

Norma's brother, Elmo, got in on the game too. In the late fifties Elmo was running a couple of lounges, one of them the Gold Room on St. Charles Avenue. He heard on the radio that a girl had been brutally murdered and found in a canal down in Plaquemines Parish, below New Orleans. He had a feeling she was the girl who'd left his lounge about four that morning with a man Elmo knew by name. He called Norma; Norma relayed the information to Bubba; Bubba called a friend in the Plaquemines sheriff's office. About an hour later the officer called back and said, "Bubba, you hit it right on the head." They'd located the man's car and found strands of the girl's hair as well as a bloody hatchet in the trunk.

Another time Norma called Bubba to tell him that an escaped convict had been showing up at about four or five o'clock in the morning to see one of her girls. Bubba hid out in a truck belonging to the Holzer Sheet Metal Company, next door to 1026 Conti. He had a clear view of Norma's driveway and back entrance. In the very early morning he saw a lone man coming up the drive. Bubba scrunched farther down behind the wheel of the truck. Then he sat up a bit—the guy walked exactly like someone he knew.

The man got close enough for Bubba to see his face, and Bubba practically fell on the floor of the truck. This was a big-name judge. He walked right up to Norma's back door. When Norma slid open the little window, the judge said, "Is the coast clear, baby?"

"Yeah, honey," Norma said, opening the door, "come on in." Later she told Bubba, "He'd have soiled his pants if he'd seen you."

It took a few nights, but Bubba got his man, and the escapee was returned to prison. His colleagues were impressed. "What's the deal, Bubba, you got a crystal ball?" they asked.

"Yeah, I got me a crystal ball," Bubba told them. He just didn't say that it had gray hair.

Bubba Rolling became chief of detectives in Jefferson Parish, but Norma never paid him one dime for protection. With Bubba, information bought another kind of insurance.

Many big-time politicians patronized Norma's house regularly. Most of them, like the judge, had charge accounts. Occasionally, though, these big boys would get out of hand, which was a sticky situation for Norma. She couldn't call the New Orleans police; they would have loved to throw a few judges, or even the governor, in jail—Earl Long used to plan gubernatorial campaigns in Norma's kitchen, then his driver would take him over to pick up Earl's paramour, the Bourbon Street sensation Blaze Starr. So Norma would call Bubba, as she did the night the legislators came in from Baton Rouge and got drunk and rowdy, then belligerent, and started pushing her girls around. Bubba brought them back to Baton Rouge in his police car, even paid the girls for them. The next day the legislators were hungover, humble, and apologetic.

Norma kept information on everybody who was anybody in her big black book: their identification marks, their nicknames—like Uncle, Sunshine, Shoestring, Pin, Toothpick, Licorice Stick, Cowboy—how much they owed, how much they paid, when they were there, the girls they liked. She had them all, should it ever come to that. In the late fifties, at the height of her power and influence, someone asked Norma if there was anyone she *didn't* have in her pocket. It took her a moment, then she said, "The President."

CHAPTER ELEVEN

At the Mercy of the Trick

Norma never thought she'd survive in the business long enough to see a third generation of Good Men begin frequenting her house in the late fifties.

J. Cornelius Rathborne III (Cocie, pronounced "Cokie," to his friends) went to Norma's for the first time when he was fourteen years old. He was taken there not by one of his family elders but by a friend who was a year or so older than he was. Norma opened the little window in the back door and recognized the young man. In the parlor she asked the new fellow his name, and Cocie told her. "Oh, yes," she said, giving him the distinct impression that the name was familiar to her. She offered the boys a beer and chatted with them about school and where they'd been earlier in the evening. Then she asked how much money they had. The going rate was twenty dollars, but Cocie had only fifteen.

"Ten will do," Norma said. She always left the boys a little "mad" money in case they had some emergency or needed a taxi.

The girls came into the parlor, some dressed formally, others in sexy little dresses, all with beautiful long hair—Norma wore the only short do in the house. The boys made their choices, Cocie's girl brought him upstairs, and he found that he was a little nervous, somewhat embarrassed too. But not because this was his first time; his father had already seen to it that he'd been initiated properly—he'd left nothing to chance and had one of his mistresses take Cocie to bed, a half Cherokee woman who told Cocie, "Make a woman happy, you'll be happy."

Cocie was embarrassed this night because Norma's girl gave him quite a look-over. She began washing him carefully, explaining to him that he'd never have to worry about getting anything at Norma's house. Cocie saw the wisdom of this and felt better. He remembered what his father's Cherokee mistress had told him and had a damned good time that night.

Cocie went away to boarding school soon afterwards, but whenever he was home on break, he went down to the French Quarter. First he and his friends would go over to Bourbon Street, where they'd catch an act at one of the clubs, not dives with strippers but exotic dancers like Kalantan or Lilly Christine the Tiger Lady or Evangeline the Oyster Girl, who made her entrance out of a giant oyster shell and had green seaweed hair. Or they'd go to the Paddock Lounge to hear Fats Pichon, the Dukes of Dixieland, or Papa Celestin. Then they'd wind up the night at Norma's, where they'd run into their friends and have a few drinks before going upstairs. They knew better than to show up drunk; if they did she wouldn't let them in.

One night Norma turned them down, but not because they'd been drinking. She opened the little window, and when she saw them she said, "There are some people here I don't think you boys would want to be seen by." Cocie assumed somebody's father had gotten there first.

Cocie unabashedly admitted going to Norma's and said, "Hell, yes, use my name. I'm not embarrassed that I went there. Going to Norma's was part of growing up in New Orleans—those of us lucky enough to have some money."

But not all of the Good Men were willing to be so open. Another of Norma's third-generation clients preferred that his name not be used.

The first time he introduced himself to Norma, she said, "I know your daddy." She also knew his uncles, from a family of Jewish merchants. "Come on in, Sonny," Norma said.

Sonny and his friends had a few drinks, then Norma let them know it was time to drink up and leave or go with one of the girls. Sonny followed his girl out to the courtyard and up the stairs to the balcony. The steps were low. She said, "Watch your head!"

"Yeah, right," Sonny answered and walked right into a beam, which he did almost every time he went upstairs at Norma's because his attention was always focused elsewhere—say on the nice way the girl's dress stretched across her rear end.

Sonny and his friends liked to sit around the parlor and drink; it was a great late-night destination after they dropped off their dates. Sometimes their dates would sneak out after they got home, take the keys to their parents' cars, and drive to Conti Street to see if the boys' cars were parked at Norma's. The boys felt as if they were at their own private country club.

But Norma's was nothing so ordinary as a country club. For Sonny the biggest thrill came from knowing that what he was doing was against the law. He and his friends liked to talk about it afterwards; for Sonny the sex was anticlimactic.

Sonny didn't know that after he grew up and went into the family business he would suddenly yearn to be a police officer. Eventually he joined the police reserves and went out on night patrol; he had a beat on Mardi Gras; he chased armed robbers; he was even shot. But when he was at Norma's he got a taste of what it was like to be on the other side of the law.

A New Orleans lawyer whose family was from Colorado started going to Norma's while he was a student at Tulane University. He wasn't one of Norma's third-generation Good Men who never needed a password; the first time he went to the house he had a password, but he had to talk his way in anyway. Norma started calling him Waterproof when he arrived one evening during a rainstorm.

Waterproof liked the passwords and the nicknames; he liked that it was all so risqué and that the police station was only a block away. But Waterproof never felt that he was in any particular danger.

Most of the Good Men, including the college students, went to Norma's on a lark, with an innocent desire to live life in the fast lane for a night now and then. They were made to feel important there, and they could have sex with girls who had the reputation of being the best in the business. They might not have known that some of the Good Women were going to Norma's too—for sex with a man who broke the law of averages with his endowments: Pershing Gervais, who once charged a wealthy Uptown woman fifteen hundred dollars for his services, or Frankenstein the cabdriver.

But those were the people who were interested in straight sex. Some came for companionship—wealthy people who needed someone to talk to more than they needed sex. Others had indulged every hedonistic whim they could think of and went to Norma's when they had run out of thrills. A girl like Simone would bathe them in golden showers and serve up hot lunches, fare not out of the ordinary in a lot of brothels.

Beyond the kinky and degenerate, though, were the true deviates, those who came to Norma's with a desperate need they were unable to satisfy anywhere else.

One of these was a man from North Carolina. He wanted someone, anyone who would do it, to beat on his penis as hard as possible, even with a hammer. Most of the girls couldn't handle that. They tried putting bobby pins on the skin of his prick, but that didn't satisfy him.

He dealt mostly with Jackie, and it was several months before Norma met him. She was surprised by his looks. He was pale and terribly emaciated; she thought he looked as if he needed a transfusion. When she shook hands with him, his hand was like ice.

He continued to make trips to New Orleans every two to three months. One trip he got Terry, but he was not at all interested in Yum-Yum's specialty. He asked her to stick needles in his penis. Terry did. She also hammered it. She didn't mind the blood. The crueler she was, the more pleasurable it was to him, the more orgasms he had, and the sooner he had them.

After a while, though, needles and hammers weren't enough; he asked Terry to cut his testicles with a razor blade and sew them back up. Terry complied. He had multiple orgasms. But this was very messy. Terry went out and bought a cover for the bed.

When Norma saw the room after one of these episodes, she was appalled: "This room looks like you've been butchering hogs!" Terry told her about the razor. Norma never would have dreamed that Terry, a pretty, dainty girl she knew to be very fastidious, could do such things. Terry was unfazed. "He pays well for it," she said, "and he leaves happy."

Norma, though, couldn't get over thinking that Terry was callous. The razor blades were too much; she didn't want the man to come to her house any longer.

The story got around, first to the girls at the house and then to the nightspots where they went, and Terry got a new nickname. Yum-Yum became known as Terry the Cutter.

One way Norma hid income was to have Gaspar Gulotta cash checks people gave her and run them through his business. Once a man gave her traveler's checks for an evening of entertainment, and a week later Gaspar got a notice that the checks had bounced. According to a letter from American Express, they had been stolen.

Norma headed straight to the American Express office, where she described her customer as "outstanding because he was very short and inclined to be a humpback." The clerk practically went into shock as she continued. "He has a big prick, and on one side of his leg not far from his prick is a birthmark."

She informed the officer that she would contest it if the man continued to claim that his checks had been stolen. "I'm going to tell how he dropped his pants at Ten Twenty-six Conti Street for three or four hours and enjoyed it to the fullest." Norma got her money.

Norma understood that, because she ran an illegitimate business, people were always going to try to take advantage of her, whether they were soldiers who demanded their money back after their fun upstairs and called the shore patrol to muscle her or Good Men's progeny who liked the free drinks at the house. Even the Good Men themselves sometimes made unreasonable demands. Once one of them begged Norma to let a girl come to his house. He assured her that his wife was out of town. Against her better judgment, because the man was such a good customer, Norma relented on a rule she'd made based on experience. Only an hour after her girl arrived the wife barged in—she'd set her husband up with a phony vacation story. She took a swipe at the girl and threw her outside naked, refusing to give her her clothes. Norma said, "The poor kid was in a predicament, but, worse, she could have been killed. No matter what, you're always at the mercy of the trick."

On Conti Street, Norma always had a large, strong man on the premises during working hours. If the house got hot, though, and the girls were forced to conduct business in hotels and motels, they were completely vulnerable. In the late fifties, when Norma seemed as invincible as some of the politicians who had charge accounts at her house, one of the most gruesome acts of her career took place.

Norma had been warned by a police contact that a warrant to search 1026 Conti had been issued for the following Saturday night. As usual, that evening Jackie fielded the calls and dispatched girls to various hotels. One man was unknown to her, but he had impeccable credentials, a good reference, the right password, and all the right answers to her questions. She sent a girl to meet him at one of the Airline Highway motels.

When the girl got there, the man brutalized her over several hours. He bit off both her nipples and her clitoris. When he was finished he hung her from a coat hook on the back of the door. The hook pulled away from the door, and the girl survived. But the man seemed to have materialized from that dark place that was more frightening than any threat from the law or any act by a masochistic deviate, and he disappeared into the dark again, never to be found.

CHAPTER TWELVE

Tricks of the Trade

 The younger sister of one of the girls asked for a job at Norma's. She was a very pretty girl, younger looking than her seventeen years, small boned and delicate, her face a sweet and perfect oval.

On the girl's first night of work, just before four in the morning, a car slid up in front of 1026 Conti and parked. When the girl finished with her last trick shortly after four, she ran quickly to the car, got into the backseat, and the car drove off. The next evening the car arrived again, same time, parking so that part of Norma's driveway was blocked. Norma watched from the window as her new girl ran out and opened the rear passenger door. A man and a woman sat in front. It dawned on Norma that the girl's parents were picking her up after work every morning.

Norma figured that the parents didn't want their daughter running in the Quarter, getting mixed up with dope fiends, and she was sympathetic for a while. But after a few weeks she began to get irritated. "It looked like hell," she said. "My parents knew what business I was in, but even when I was hustling, they didn't come pick me up." She finally buttonholed the mother one night and asked her what the deal was.

"Well," the woman said apologetically, "our daughter has always lived a very sheltered life."

But that was one of the more unusual stories about how girls got into prostitution. More often they had been turned out by their parents or they were runaways who had fallen on hard times.

In 1957 a girl named Rose Mary, barely eighteen years of age, came to Norma's house. She was a tall, slim, striking brunette. Her mother, a devout Catholic, had not allowed her daughter to date, so Rose Mary had fallen for the first sweet-talking rogue to come on to her, though she refused to sleep with him unless they were married.

On her wedding night, still a virgin, Rose Mary called her mother to ask her what to do. Her mother replied, "You made your bed, lie in it." A month later Rose Mary's husband told her she could make a lot of money modeling. He sent her to Norma's house with another woman, because it was well known that the one thing Norma truly hated was a pimp. When Rose Mary found out what was really expected of her, she called her mother to ask if she could come home, but her mother refused to speak to her.

Shortly after that Norma heard from a character she knew, John Miorana, a good-looking man, wild, unpredictable, charismatic, and a natural-born criminal. He called Norma from jail after learning from his outside contacts that Rose Mary, his younger sister, was working at her house. He told Norma that Rose Mary had married a bad actor and a pimp, and he asked Norma to take care of her.

It wasn't easy to get to know Norma. She held herself back, as if she was wary of newcomers, which she was—she hadn't been in the business for almost forty years by being anything other than extremely cautious. Instead she drew Rose Mary out, getting her to talk about her parents and her home life, her marriage, her hopes and dreams. She found out that Rose Mary was a nurturer and had a strong maternal instinct. There would be time for all that, but first the young woman had to learn how to make a living. Norma began teaching her the tricks of the trade.

The first order of business was to inspect each date carefully, get him over to the sink and wash him with soap and water. And of course, while you were doing this, you were putting him at ease, especially if he was younger, letting the date know he wasn't going to end up with a syphilitic brain from frequenting Conti Street.

The second step required a little more finesse. Norma and Rose Mary were in the kitchen as Norma was explaining how to check for disease. One of the porters walked in.

"Come over here," Norma said. Quicker than he could protest, Norma unzipped his pants and pulled out his penis; grasping the head, she used a rapid, rather clinical movement to milk it. "One drop is all you need," she said and held up her index finger. She told the porter he could go. He scuttled out of the kitchen, zipping up as he went.

"Feel that," Norma said to Rose Mary. "Rub it between your fingers." Rose Mary, her nose wrinkled in distaste, complied. "How does it feel?" Norma asked. Rose Mary shrugged. "Is it smooth?" She said it was. "Then he's all right. If it's even a little gritty, like it has sand in it, something's wrong with him. If it's real gritty, drop him like a hot potato and get away from him as fast as you can."

Not long after that a date came to the house and picked Rose Mary from the girls in the parlor. Upstairs she took him to the bathroom sink and began the ritual washing, all charm and reassurance—as though it was his first time, not hers. The man told her he was a doctor. Rose Mary expressed the proper awe. She looked down. She thought she saw something jump into the sink. She looked more closely. Several things were jumping; not only that, they were crawling all over him; his pubic hair was infested.

"Norma!" Rose Mary called loudly. She smiled sweetly at the man. "I've never seen those before," she said.

"Neither have I before I came here," the doctor said hotly.

Rose Mary was about to go out to the balcony to call Norma again when the bedroom door opened. "What is it?" Norma said, irritated.

Rose Mary pointed. Norma peered at the doctor. "How dare you come in here like this," she snapped. To Rose Mary she said, "Get away from him."

"What do you mean?" the doctor said. "I didn't have those when I walked in here." He gestured toward Rose Mary.

"Like hell you didn't! And don't you dare say this girl gave you that. I know a case of crabs when I see one, and you've had that case for quite a while."

"He's a doctor, Norma," Rose Mary said.

"A doctor! You put your clothes on right now! You should be ashamed of yourself. You're a sorry son of a bitch for a doctor. Don't you ever come to this house in that condition. Go home and give it to your wife, anybody, but don't bring it here!" Norma continued her ranting until she drove the doctor straight out of the house. She rushed back, issuing orders like a drill sergeant: Remove those sheets, take a bath, wash your hair, wash your clothes, no more work until Dr. Gomila checks you. When Rose Mary asked her to slow down, Norma nearly bit her head off: "What's the matter—are you deaf?" Norma expected everyone's brain to work as fast as hers did. She continued her rapid fire as she sprayed the room down.

Next Norma told Rose Mary to get some pointers from Terry. Terry showed her some new tricks, giving her a few of the techniques responsible for her first nickname, Yum-Yum. She explained it in musical terms. "Imagine that you're playing a flute," Terry said. "You've got to close certain holes to get one sound and stretch your lips to get another." Rose Mary looked skeptical. Terry said, "They don't call it a blow job for nothin, honey. Look, just think to yourself, Ummmm, delicious, yum-yum."

"I don't know if I can do that," Rose Mary said.

"Sure you can. A lot of the girls prefer it. It's easy and it's not as messy. A lot quicker too."

The first time a customer asked Rose Mary for this, she tried to remember everything Terry had told her, from the deep sucking pull to the whirling dervish tongue, but in her enthusiasm she went too deep, gagged, and threw up on the man.

She told Norma she didn't think she ever wanted to do that again; Norma told her she'd get over it.

One evening Rose Mary went upstairs with a husky man who wore wire-rim glasses. When he disrobed she saw that he had the largest prick she'd ever seen. She called for Norma.

Norma opened the door to the room. "What is it now?" Rose Mary pointed to the man's penis. Norma called out over the balcony, "Jackie, who's the man in this room with the big dick?"

They dubbed him the Womb Scraper, and Norma told him that he could not enter any of the girls—that was the rule if he wanted to keep coming to the house.

One of Norma's strictest rules was the one insisting that there be no locked doors while a girl was in a room with a date. Rose Mary went upstairs with the Womb Scraper the second time he came to the house, and as she walked toward the bathroom, he tried to turn the lock, which was old and used so infrequently that it didn't yield immediately. When Rose Mary saw what he was doing, she rushed back toward the door, yelling, "Norma! Norma! He's trying to lock the door!"

Footsteps pounded on the stairs, then Norma rushed into the room. She lunged for the Womb Scraper like a she-lion, scratching his face and screaming at him. George the porter had to get her off him. This time Norma banned the man from the house for good. A few weeks later they heard that he'd been arrested on Canal Street for masturbating in front of some children.

Not only did Norma have rules but she had rituals. Every night just before seven o'clock, for example, when the house opened for the evening, she asked one of the girls to give her a pubic hair or two. She'd wet her finger and stretch the hair over the keyhole of the parlor door, where it would stick with the moisture. Then she'd put a lighted match to the hair. And the men would start arriving.

She'd been asking Rose Mary for pubic hair for a couple of weeks running. Once again she called Rose Mary over to the door and asked her for a couple of hairs. Rose Mary sighed and started to hitch up her dress, then changed her mind. "Get somebody else to donate them tonight," she said. "I'm going bald down there." She walked off, through the parlor, toward the courtyard.

Nothing happened for a moment. Then Norma rushed past Rose Mary, her heels striking the courtyard tiles hard enough to create sparks. At the top of her lungs she demanded, "Did you hear that? She's going bald! Jackie, get her pay!" She turned just enough to yell back at Rose Mary, "That's it—you're fired!" Jackie rolled her eyes and gave Rose Mary a hundred dollars.

Rose Mary went upstairs, changed clothes, and left the house. She called Norma the next evening. "I'll be there in an hour," she said.

"Oh?" Norma inquired archly. "Are you finished partying?"

Rose Mary hung up the phone. No pity; she'd never get any pity from Norma. But she was developing backbone.

Rose Mary started telling Norma what she was willing to do and what she wasn't, and she was fired regularly, nearly once a week. She always came back, but then the men started complaining. One said, "Your girl won't go down."

Rose Mary said to Norma, "I told you I wouldn't do that anymore." She got fired.

Or Rose Mary would come flying down the stairs, tying her kimono around her. "He wants me to get on my hands and knees— like a dog! He wants to come in the back door. I won't do it. Not now, not ever!" And Norma would fire her again.

One week Dr. Gomila came for the girls' regular checkup. "I need sedatives," Rose Mary told him. "She's impossible." Dr. Gomila agreed and gave her a prescription.

One night Rose Mary told Norma that she wouldn't go with a certain man anymore because he always wanted her to go to the bathroom with him. "I'm telling you, Norma," Rose Mary warned, "I'll throw up."

Norma was exasperated. "Rose Mary," she said, "I am at my wit's end with you. I spend half my time listening to what you won't do and the other half running up those stairs after your ass. You are the world's worst hooker!" She told Rose Mary to start answering the door and assisting Jackie, who had also stopped hooking early in her career.

Rose Mary cried with relief. Norma was the biggest bitch she'd ever known; she loved her dearly.

CHAPTER THIRTEEN

A Different Kind of Trick

 Through the fifties Norma's Conti Street neighborhood saw more change. The Greyhound bus station had been moved out of the French Quarter, and Mike Persia's car dealership opened next door to Norma's house.

Also, there were fewer landladies than ever in the Quarter. Dora Russo had left for a less visible location, 2130 Bayou Road, where she ran a comfortable but not first-rate house known for quick business and gin rummy games. Mayor Chep Morrison, who didn't want to run into his Uptown neighbors at Norma's, dropped in at Dora's now and again until he began his affair with Zsa Zsa Gabor in 1959. Shortly after that Gertie Yost's high-rent establishment at 935 Esplanade became a day nursery and kindergarten. Marie Bernard, jailed for tax evasion, left two addresses where she operated, 509 St. Louis and 505 Decatur Street. After many years Uptown at 1618 Melpomene Street, Bertha Anderson had returned to the Quarter, to 818 Royal Street, but she had died. Juliet Washington had given up her house two doors down from Norma's, and Melba Moore's Cadillacs brimming with prostitutes had long since disappeared from the streets of the Quarter. Camilla Turner killed herself by wrecking her car on the Chef Menteur Highway, returning from the Gulf Coast, where she'd found her lover with another woman.

But Pete Herman was still running his nightclub a block away and, with a few of his own girls and a few of Norma's, the brothel above it, which the locals referred to as Pete Herman's Chippie Inn.

Rose Mary laid out brown envelopes on the desk in the sunroom and stuffed them with payoffs. Some she left at the house, where the beat cops picked them up via the slot in the second parlor; others she brought to the precincts where Norma's contacts were assigned; still others went to the police department's Broad Street building. When Big Mo got his envelope, he usually responded by sending Norma violets. She liked the gesture but not the flowers—they reminded her of flowers old ladies would get. She gave them to her mother.

The money in Pete Herman's envelope wasn't a payoff but his cut of some business he and Norma had shared. Pete had some good regular customers, though, that he didn't like to share, just as Norma didn't share all of hers.

On one occasion Norma nabbed one of Pete's hundred-dollar men, took his money, then told him to go back to Pete's, where her girl would meet him and take him to a hotel. She told Rose Mary she didn't know the man well enough to have him at the house. The following evening she sent Rose Mary to the lounge with Pete's 30 percent cut. Sometimes Rose Mary would just give the envelope to Poke Chop or Coffee Pot (because of the big bump on his forehead) or Chilie Beans, Pete's emcees at the club, and that would be the end of it. More often, like this night, Pete answered the door himself.

Rose Mary handed him the envelope. "What's the matter with her?" he asked, and Rose Mary knew she'd be there at least an hour. He opened the envelope, fingered the money—he claimed he could tell the denomination by feeling it—and said, "She took my customer, she took my money, and I'm still talking to her? She wants to send me my own tricks and charge me?" Rose Mary let him blow off steam, knowing full well that Pete still loved Norma, that if anyone said a thing against her, there'd be hell to pay.

Mac still loved Norma too, though more and more she seemed to be pushing him away. The girls had heard her curse him out, then they had watched him leave, his golf bag slung over his shoulder, and they couldn't understand why she was so angry with him. He was so nice and he loved her so much—and he was *so* good looking. They all would have tumbled had he only asked, but Mac never hit on any of them. The girls knew that when Norma was angry with Mac, they'd better get out of her way.

Marcia, a raven-haired beauty who had a dramatic widow's peak, arrived at the house one evening just as Norma slammed the door behind Mac. She went upstairs to get dressed for work and came down the courtyard stairway. Norma saw her and went into a rage. "Don't you know how much I hate widow's peaks?" she yelled. "Go upstairs this instant and get rid of it!"

Marcia protested, "But, Norma, it's my *hair*!" Norma told her to shave it off or she'd be fired. Marcia cried and begged, but to no avail. Finally, she went upstairs and shaved off her widow's peak.

That Christmas Norma was so angry with everyone in the house that she held back the bonuses, and instead of the large bottles of Joy perfume that were always part of their Christmas presents, she gave them small bottles. Only the animals escaped Norma's fury, and they were like a bunch of spoiled brats. Norma doted on them, feeding them shrimp and choice liver, then getting Rose Mary to call the vet at two in the morning if a cat threw up or had the runs. The parrots were out of control. "Screw the bastard!" they shrieked as the girls led their dates up the stairs.

Poodles were all the rage in the late fifties, and Norma had several. She called one Carmen Miranda and dressed the white miniature in a skirt and Carmen Miranda–type bra, perching a fruit hat on its head. If a banana shook, Norma would accuse Rose Mary: "You fooled with her hat." Rose Mary wanted to strangle Carmen Miranda. Then there was the monkey, a little spider that liked to sit on a wide piece of molding above the back door. Rose Mary came in one evening and the monkey let loose on her head. "Norma!" she screamed. Norma laughed as she hadn't for weeks when she saw the mess. "Go ahead, laugh," Rose Mary said. "You're two of a kind—you're both crazy!" It got to where Rose Mary dreaded the appearance of a new pet.

Norma began sneaking around with men. One night after she and Mac had argued until Norma ordered him to leave, Rose Mary found her standing in front of the bathroom mirror, plucking hairs and getting ready for a night on the town.

"Oh, these little white hairs," she said, tweezing one from her chin. She turned around. "Make sure they're all gone, will you?" she asked, and as Rose Mary inspected her face, Norma added, "Even when I'm dead, or I'll come back to haunt you."

She got dressed in one of her hot little red numbers and put on her diamond earrings. Then she told Rose Mary to keep an eye on things in the parlor and made her escape through the front door, as if Rose Mary had no idea what was going on.

Mac had been spending most of his time in Waggaman, but, as he often did, that morning he came back sometime after four to try to make amends with Norma. The last trick had not been gone long when Rose Mary saw him park behind the house. As always he walked around to let himself in the front door. He wasn't halfway down the driveway when Norma burst through the back door.

"Rose Mary, Rose Mary," she yelled, "hurry up, hurry!" She tore off her red dress and threw it on the floor of the parlor. The diamond earrings landed behind the couch.

"You think I was born yesterday?" Rose Mary snapped. "Like I don't know what's going on? I know who you were out with." Her brother John was recently out of jail.

Norma paid her no attention. "Mess up the hair, Rose Mary," she said. "Hurry!"

If Norma was angry with Mac, she'd fire Rose Mary. Sometimes she'd fire her, then say, "Come on, let's go get a drink." They'd go over to Bourbon Street to Dan's International or Lafitte's Blacksmith Shop. When it came time to pay, Rose Mary would say, "I don't have a dime."

"You should have worked," Norma would answer, paying the bill.

"I got fired, remember?"

Sometimes when Rose Mary got fired, she'd take a hundred dollars from Norma's purse and go out alone. But the next day she always told Norma that she'd taken the money.

"Oh, so now you're a common thief," Norma would say, but she'd never take the money back.

During that time Norma's mother moved to one of the rooms on the third floor of the house. Rose Mary was getting fired so much that she decided to move into another room. That way when Norma fired her she'd just go upstairs and talk to Amanda for the rest of the night.

But Amanda was not well. Her alcoholism had reached a point that she was sick most of the time, and she had Parkinson's disease as well. Once, in the early morning hours, she started a fire. It was only luck that Mac had decided to hang around that night. He broke the door down and got to Amanda before she burned herself up. They didn't know if the fire was accidental or not; Amanda had tried to kill herself several times with pills. She had a rage to match Norma's, especially if she was drinking. She would throw bottles at Norma and scream at her. But Norma, so volatile herself, never raised her voice to her mother. She would try to soothe her and tell her everything would be all right.

But her mother, her marriage—everything seemed to be working on Norma. She would walk through the house, pulling at her hair until it was standing on end. Rose Mary would say, "Pleeeze, Norma, go brush that hair!" And if Norma thought about it, she'd tell Rose Mary she was fired.

By this time Rose Mary had been fired so much that she hardly even acknowledged it, unless she wanted to make a point. Norma had stopped going to Canal Street to shop. Instead, she had the stores send over racks of clothes that she tried on in the privacy of her apartment. One night after she'd just fired Rose Mary, she told her to pick a dress from the rack.

"I've just been fired," Rose Mary said. "I get fired so much that I don't have any money to buy clothes."

"Oh, go ahead," Norma told her, "pick out a dress. I'll pay for it." It was that night that Rose Mary found out Norma had been calling her mother, letting her know that Rose Mary was safe. She told Rose Mary to pick out a dress and go see her mother. The reconciliation made Rose Mary enormously happy, though she remained with Norma.

• • •

And so things continued as a new decade began. The year 1960 marked Norma's fortieth year in the business. Norma put her mother in a nursing home and took Big Mo's violets to the ladies there. She spent time in Waggaman, though she made no pretense that her marriage made her happy. She saw men, like John Miorana, but no one in particular after John Datri.

Norma was accustomed to having men offer a lot of money for the madam of the house, but she had never accepted those offers, no matter how tempting. Now, though, she came home more than once and held a sheaf of bills out in front of Rose Mary, on one occasion twenty hundred-dollar bills, which the man she'd been out with had offered her to spend the night with him. She took him to the Roosevelt Hotel, put the money in her purse, told him to go freshen up, and while he was in the bathroom, she left.

"What the hell, Rose Mary?" she said, handing her five hundred dollars. "He was stupid to give it to me, don't you think?"

Not one man ever came back to protest. It seemed that Norma had come full circle, duping men out of money just as she'd duped Dr. Silvester so many years ago.

Norma peered at the man standing on the other side of the parlor door. She had to put her face up close to the bars over the sliding window to see him because he was so tall. He introduced himself as Jim Garrison, a local attorney. His voice was a deep bass; his eyes were intense; he stood six foot seven. When Norma opened the door, he had to duck to get inside.

Norma gave Garrison a drink and sat with him in the parlor. It was just after six o'clock, and the house wasn't open for business yet; she told Garrison she'd see if any of her girls was available. But he didn't want to go upstairs; he wanted to give her his card. He told her that he had been an assistant district attorney and now he was in private practice. He gave her an engaging smile. "It's an advantage to know how to play both sides of the fence," he said, adding that he'd appreciate any business she could send his way.

Norma had left the door to the courtyard open. The phones began ringing. She got up and closed the door. Garrison clearly knew what business she was in, but Norma didn't want him to hear Jackie on the phone. Even though he was charming, quite personable, Norma thought that he seemed strange and she didn't trust him. He finished his drink and left, appearing to stalk rather than walk away. She put his card in her desk and, for the time being, didn't give him another thought.

There were too many other things to think about. The 1960 elections resulted in a complete change of guard. Chep Morrison ran for governor of Louisiana instead of mayor of New Orleans and lost. Vic Schiro was elected mayor, Provosty Dayries resigned as police chief, Schiro named Joseph Giarrusso (a friend of both Big Mo Guillot and Foots Trosclair) as his successor—and a decade of police scandal came to an end.

Giarrusso was the right man for the job; he was not only a capable administrator but good at public relations. He knew how to address his officers and win their loyalty; he knew how to speak to the people and reassure them.

Norma figured she'd better get on the good side of the new superintendent. Every evening around nine o'clock, Joe and his brother Clarence Giarrusso (who became head of narcotics) and a few of their cronies would stop in at Dan's International, a Chinese restaurant and lounge at the corner of Toulouse and Bourbon, for a cup of coffee. Dan's was one of Norma's favorite Quarter hangouts. She took to arriving in time to have a drink and chat with the Giarrusso brothers. When she felt the timing was right, she arranged a meeting with Joe.

Giarrusso agreed to meet Norma at City Park late one evening. He drove to their specified meeting place near the Dueling Oaks, parked his car, and got into her Cadillac. He had no idea what she wanted to talk to him about, and he was thinking perhaps he'd been naïve to agree to see her, but his curiosity had won over any caution. Not only that, it was possible she had some information for him. He gunned his throat, but nothing cleared his husky, watery voice. "So what's up, Norma?" he asked, cutting straight to the chase, his vowels gurgling.

Norma drove slowly through the empty, winding streets of the park, dark even with a harvest moon because of the dense canopy of oak trees. "What's your hurry?" she wanted to know. She was a naturally flirtatious woman, a quality Giarrusso appreciated, but he knew she was devious too. His instincts were going against any notion that she had asked for the meeting because she'd decided she wanted to have an affair with him.

"No particular hurry," he said. "I'm just curious."

He saw her glance down at the seat beside her, where a brown envelope lay. Her manicured hand came away from the steering wheel. She picked up the envelope and tossed it in Giarrusso's lap. "That's yours," she said.

Giarrusso tossed the envelope back into the space between them. "I'm not gonna take it," he told her.

Norma tried her sweet talk with him, the oh–come–on–we–all–know–how–to–play–this–game routine, but Giarrusso kept shaking his head. "Why won't you take it?" she asked.

Giarrusso thought about it a moment. "Because I don't trust that you won't spill your guts one day," he said.

"I'd *never* do that," Norma told him.

"I don't know," Giarrusso said. "If you thought it would cleanse your soul to tell the truth, you might."

"My soul is the soul of discretion," Norma said, "you know that." She cut her eyes toward the envelope again. "Go on, take it."

"I don't want to do that," Giarrusso said emphatically.

Norma drove him back to the Dueling Oaks. She'd lost this point, but now they were even, one strike each, and there would always be another match. After all, he hadn't arrested her for attempted bribery, and anyway, the new mayor was deep in her pocket. He was getting so bold about his visits to the house that he'd begun to drive the city car over and park out front. She'd heard that Schiro's backers had asked the mayor not to use the city car, but they certainly hadn't gone so far as to ask him to stop frequenting the house. How could they? Most of them put in their fair amount of time too.

Norma's house was a New Orleans institution. What the hell—it had been an *American* institution ever since John Wayne, the Duke himself, had visited when he was in town, even if he didn't go upstairs with the rest of the movie folk he was with. (He'd spent the evening talking to Rose Mary, mostly about Pilar, his wife, then he gave her five hundred dollars, "For takin up so much of your time t'night.")

After forty years, Norma wasn't worried; she'd always found a way to protect herself. She still had good contacts in the police department, and new ones arriving with each class from the academy. One of those recent graduates, a smart young copper who was called Donald Pryce, had fallen head over heels in love with Terry. He was going to college at night, for which Norma respected him. Recruited for the vice squad, Pryce had learned quickly that there were many ways to supplement a policeman's salary. He was already tipping off half the people Norma knew over on Bourbon Street, and he told Norma that he would check warrants for her as well. She added Pryce's name to her roster of envelope recipients.

Around that time Elmo, who was always on the lookout for a deal on liquor to supply his B-drinking business, was arrested for attempting to buy bootlegged liquor from a ship at the New Orleans port. He was sentenced to eighteen months in the federal penitentiary at Seagoville, Texas. While there he contracted tuberculosis, but the prison authorities did not consider it bad enough to hospitalize him. Sarah, Elmo's wife, dutifully ran Elmo's lounge, the Moulin Rouge on Bourbon Street (he'd sold the Gold Room in the business district), though she complained and said she hated the French Quarter; and Norma drove to the prison outside Dallas as often as she could, usually accompanied by Elmo's mistress. The last time she'd gone, she'd been shocked by her brother's appearance, but she was unable to get any satisfaction from the prison authorities.

Early one evening shortly after that Jim Garrison dropped by. Acting against her instincts, because she was sick with worry about Elmo, Norma asked him to help her brother. He agreed to take the case. One of Norma's girls, Faye, was in some trouble too. She'd been arrested for possessing marijuana, and her Cadillac had been seized. Garrison took Faye's case as well, and Norma paid him a stiff legal fee. Again, he wasn't interested in going upstairs, but he did ask Norma if he could open a charge account with her. She told him to consider it done, even while telling herself that there was something strange about him. After that he called for girls to meet him at a hotel. Never was he a trick at her house, and Norma sometimes wondered if it was because he didn't want to be where he could be nabbed for his bill, which he was always slow to pay. Whatever the reason, Garrison proved to be an entirely different kind of trick.

Suzanne Robbins was living out a young girl's fantasy.

When she was sixteen Suzanne left North Carolina after being run out of her house by her stepmother. For as long as she could remember she'd had dreams of a life of excitement and glamour, possibly wealth and fame, and New Orleans was the city of her dreams. She hitchhiked her way down, and when she saw Bourbon Street, which when Suzanne arrived in 1954 boasted good restaurants, Las Vegas–type entertainment, and classy nightclubs instead of the current corn-dog stands, strip joints, and T-shirt shops, she knew she'd found the place where at least some of her dreams could come true.

Suzanne, a beautiful young woman with long, curly hair and a lithe, shapely body, had a natural glamour about her. But she also had a practical side, and she took the first job she could find as a cocktail waitress at a Canal Street club. She found out soon enough that the club was a B-drinking establishment. After the men got drunk, the management either kicked them out or gave them rides a distance from the lounge, then dumped them. Suzanne didn't much like the job, but she needed money, and beyond flirtatious talk there were no requirements.

The Bourbon Street entertainers—vocalists, comedians, and dancers—were like a big, established family, not transients taking off their clothes for a buck and then leaving town. It wasn't long before Suzanne became part of the family. She had an openness about her, she was vivacious and had a quick wit, and she wasn't afraid of hard work. She became an exotic dancer, first as the redheaded Wild Cat Frenchie, the Sadie Thompson of New Orleans, then as blonde bombshell Jezebel, the girl with a thousand moves, at the Poodle's Patio. Suzanne was one of the most popular acts on the strip. People sought her autograph; she was being featured in national magazines and offered parts in movies. Much more than the glitter and glitz of her youthful fantasies had become reality.

Suzanne knew Jim Garrison from the club and from around the Quarter. After hours she and her friends liked to go to the piano bars, like the Old Absinthe House and Lafitte's Blacksmith Shop, where they saw him sometimes. One night she saw Garrison at a party, and when she was ready to leave he offered to walk her home. When they got to her apartment, Suzanne said good night, but as she turned to go inside, Garrison grabbed her. He wanted to go in with her. Suzanne tried to put him off nicely. He wasn't her type; he was obnoxious in the club, a show-off, and he hassled the showgirls. He was also known to pick up drag queens and frequent gay bars. Garrison did his best to talk his way into her apartment, but Suzanne was firm in her refusal. He finally gave up, saying, "You won't forget this."

Over on Conti Street, Norma was wondering what Garrison was doing for his fee on behalf of Elmo. Her brother's eighteen-month sentence was passing, and he was getting sicker. The charges against her girl Faye had been dropped, no thanks to Garrison, but Faye's Cadillac remained city property.

Garrison had been busy, but not with what Norma had hired him to do. In 1961 he decided to run for district attorney. He was given no chance to win, but—dubbed the Giant by the media—he made quite an impression as he campaigned for a cleanup of the French Quarter. He was especially effective on television, and people remembered him. His victory took the city by surprise, and Garrison became the newest political darling of Uptown New Orleans.

During the campaign Garrison's old army buddy Pershing Gervais had collected contributions from the nightclubs along Bourbon Street. The Poodle's Patio, where Pershing's wife, Beverly, worked as a bartender, gave ten thousand dollars each to Garrison and to Richard Dowling, the incumbent. When Garrison was elected, he appointed Gervais as his chief investigator, even though Gervais had left the police department under a cloud of suspicion. Garrison made a point that he and Gervais had been in the military together, but the Giant was too smart to hire a chief investigator for sentimental reasons. He publicly stated that he liked the idea that Gervais had ties to the underworld, followed by a reminder that Gervais had cooperated with the Metropolitan Crime Commission and Aaron Kohn. Polished and convincing, Garrison swayed public opinion and the press, and the matter was dropped. The only person who might have made a difference in what followed was Gaspar Gulotta, the Little Mayor of Bourbon Street, but he had died in 1957.

There had always been seedy bars run by rough characters and B-drinking establishments along and right off the strip. Gervais was part owner of at least one, the Dungeon, a gay hangout, but papers were destroyed and altered to hide his ownership. Most clubs, though, like the Poodle's Patio, were well managed and the showgirls were never allowed to consort with the patrons. Gervais told his wife that there was nothing he was going to be able to do to help them, and the first raid took place at the Poodle's Patio.

Suzanne ruefully remembered Garrison's threat as she was taken from her dressing room and hauled off in a paddy wagon. She was shaking so badly by the time they reached the station that a lieutenant she knew gave her a stiff drink before sending her back to the Quarter. She was in shock, but she pulled herself together and tried to get on with the show.

A few weeks later Suzanne was onstage, fully clothed in a gold lamé outfit with a cape. The audience was large that night—a good crowd of local people swelled with a tour group, ladies in cocktail dresses and gentlemen in suits and ties. Suzanne was just getting into her act when a man in khakis, his shirttails out, jumped up onstage.

Suzanne stopped the act. "Excuse me, sir," she said, "but you'll have to get off my stage."

"You're under arrest," he replied. He handcuffed her and took her away in front of a club full of people.

This time Suzanne was not only shocked, she was humiliated. She was shoved into a van, where she sat until showgirls from other clubs were jammed inside with her. They were taken to Central Lockup. Suzanne and a dancer named Linda Bridges clung to each other, crying. They were thrown into a cell so filthy that they couldn't sit down.

Court was even worse. As they walked up the steps to the courthouse in their modest dresses and white gloves, newspaper photographers and television cameras dogged them. They were put in the same category as B-drinkers and strippers. Suzanne's case was dismissed, but what became clear to her (and to many of the dancers) was that Garrison was out to make a name for himself and he wouldn't stop there. The same places that Pershing Gervais had shaken down for contributions to Big Jim Garrison's campaign he was now padlocking. If a dancer was onstage and moved even her hands in what could be considered a suggestive way, she was arrested for committing "a lewd and indecent act," and the club could be padlocked for a year, which meant the end for most places.

The local people, made nervous, stopped coming. The girls stopped dancing, many giving up their careers. The smart owners bailed out before they lost everything. Then, after Garrison became distracted by his investigation into the Kennedy assassination in 1963 and his subsequent trial of the New Orleans businessman Clay Shaw for the murder, the sleazy strip joints moved in and took over. Instead of getting cleaned up, Bourbon Street became what it is today; Garrison turned the French Quarter into the very thing he said he despised.

The newspaper headlines in 1962 were full of the results of Garrison's activities: QUARTER CRIME EMERGENCY DECLARED BY POLICE, DA; QUARTER B-DRINK RAIDS SNARE 15; MORE THAN 30 ARRESTED IN NEW QUARTER SWEEP; GARRISON BACK, VOWS VICE DRIVE TO CONTINUE [after he'd served two weeks in the National Guard reserve]; 14 ARRESTED; ARREST 2 WOMEN ON VICE CHARGES [prostitution]; 12 MORE NABBED IN QUARTER RAIDS.

Joe Giarrusso watched Garrison and Gervais's performance in the French Quarter. They were arresting a lot of people. Some were strippers, some might have been prostitutes, but many of the cases were being dismissed. The way Giarrusso saw it, if they weren't doing anything, what was the problem? It was what the superintendent called the Big Razoo, and he knew that notoriety was likely to follow.

Next Garrison charged the police with being apathetic about the crackdown on vice. "The same old beat men are there," he stated in the *States-Item*. "I'd say that the First District [the French Quarter], given word from the top, could stop B-drinking in a few weeks. It's obvious that the word is not being given and we are going to have to proceed on our own to eliminate B-drinking."

Giarrusso immediately challenged Garrison "to file charges against any police officer who had been derelict in the crackdown on vice in the French Quarter."

Resentment built as Garrison continued his splashy raids and arrests. Giarrusso came out with figures indicating that his men had made over three hundred arrests, while Garrison's were responsible for only sixty. He said, "Let's not forget that he is the district attorney and I am the superintendent of police. Don't forget that distinction." He would not elaborate on his statement, but it reflected his growing resentment "that the DA is trying to run the police department."

Nevertheless, many Vieux Carré property owners backed Garrison, and through 1962 he commanded the headlines, with Giarrusso lashing back lamely as Garrison and Gervais investigated allegations of police brutality.

Giarrusso understood Gervais's motivation—a vendetta against the police department. Garrison's motivations were murkier, perhaps only the machinations of an egotist and headline grabber.

In any case, from nearly the first day in early 1962 that he occupied the district attorney's office, Garrison's actions turned Giarrusso into an adversary rather than an ally, thus setting the stage for the last act in the last house of prostitution of its kind in the French Quarter, run by the last madam. An era was at its end, and a legend was about to fall.

CHAPTER FOURTEEN

Out-tricked

Joe Giarrusso went over the arrest reports and decided that the commander of the vice squad wasn't producing. It was time for some fresh blood, and Giarrusso knew just the man to tap, Frederick Soulé, one of his top men when he'd been head of narcotics. Freddy was a smallish man with a black mustache who defined the word *dapper.* Because he always wore a colorful bow tie, the men called him Jellybean. He was easygoing and well liked, but Giarrusso also knew him to be shrewd, a schemer who thought fast on his feet, like the time he simply unscrewed a fuse to give the narcotics squad a few critical extra seconds to enter a building before the drugs were flushed. Beautiful.

As the new commander of vice, Soulé would be going head-to-head with Pershing Gervais, who had been his partner as a motorcycle cop when they joined the police department back in the forties.

Giarrusso told Soulé what his priorities were, and one of them was Norma Wallace. They discussed the fact that Norma had been operating for at least forty years and so far no one had ever gotten enough evidence to close her down. "She knows what it takes to stay in business," Giarrusso commented.

One of the things it took was to have the goods on some very important people. Big shots liked to talk, especially after sex, over a cigarette and a snifter of brandy. Rumors about her black book were going to make busting Norma touchy; some big people were going to be very nervous.

Soulé told Giarrusso that he wanted a free hand to take Norma Wallace down. Giarrusso said, "Handle it any way you want, Freddy. I've got confidence in you. And if you need money, we can get it from City Hall." He added that what they were really going to need were a few new tricks.

Soulé smiled under his trim, black mustache. "With the prostitutes," he said, "what we need is to *out*-trick 'em."

Giarrusso laughed, then told Soulé, "Just get her before Garrison does."

When Soulé took over the vice squad, he kept three men from the previous command because they were supposed to be good, trustworthy, and experienced. One of them was Donald Pryce.

One day Soulé was in the office where the desk sergeant typed up applications for warrant. Pryce was also there. Soulé couldn't have said what made him think so, but he got the feeling—one of those cop intuitions—that Pryce was hovering, waiting for something.

Soulé said to the desk sergeant, "Type me up an application for tomorrow night. I'm gonna go get Norma." He gave the sergeant all the information he needed, then gestured toward Pryce. "Let Pryce here go get the judge to sign it. I got some things to take care of."

Soulé found a place where he could watch. A few minutes later Pryce came out of the office and went to a pay phone at the end of the hall. Soulé was too far away to hear what he said, but he'd have put a bet on where Pryce called. He knew then that he'd better come up with a gimmick, and a slick gimmick at that, if he was going to get Norma Wallace.

A week later, on a balmy Friday night in June, Donald Pryce, with his neat crew cut and frat-boy good looks, arrived at Norma's house dressed in a tuxedo and carrying a corsage. He was graduating from college and had come to pick up Terry, who was going to the big dance with him. Norma liked Pryce, though she felt somewhat sorry for him, because he loved Terry and probably wanted to marry her but Terry was just a chippie at heart. She wouldn't even sleep with him without pay; true, she had a kid to support, but she also knew that Pryce had money from his extracurricular activities over on Bourbon Street. While Terry finished dressing, Norma asked Pryce if he'd heard anything more about that Soulé bastard's shenanigans, since the raid the previous Saturday night had never materialized, but Pryce said that the only warrant Soulé had was for the Old French Opera House over on Bourbon. Norma gave him his envelope, and, as a graduation present, she gave him a buyout—an entire evening with one girl—so he could spend the night with Terry.

Earlier that Friday, just before class was over, Freddy Soulé had gone to the police academy. He looked over the thirty to forty cadets and picked six of the youngest looking men in the class. He told them to meet him there, at the academy, at eleven the following night for an undercover operation. He gave them no details but instructed them to rent white tuxedo jackets and wear boutonnieres.

Late Saturday night Soulé told the cadets that they were to pose as college students out celebrating their graduation. First they were to go to the Jung Hotel on Canal Street, park their cars, and meet in the lobby. Then they were to taxi over to Dan's International for a couple of drinks, and after that walk across the street to the Old French Opera House bar and attempt to make B-drinking cases and possibly an obscenity case—there had been reports of a girl taking off her clothes after midnight, as Saturday night became Sunday morning. Soulé gave each man about twenty-five dollars in different denominations, bills whose serial numbers he had recorded. He remembered that Norma had an eye for dark, good-looking young men like John Datri, so he selected Paul Nazar as the spokesman for the group. Nazar, a handsome Mediterranean type with deep brown hair combed back in a perfect wave, was egotistical and glib, a sweet talker if Soulé had ever seen one—his classmates called him the Silver Tongue. But Soulé said absolutely nothing to his rascals, as he liked to call his men, about Norma Wallace's house.

The six tuxedoed cadets hit Bourbon Street in high spirits—they were on their first big case, not even out of the academy yet. They went to Dan's, where they bragged about graduating from college and acted drunk after two drinks. (Nazar, taking his role as spokesman with utmost seriousness, had only 7-Up.) Then Soulé's rambunctious rascals went to the Old French Opera House to continue their revelry.

Midnight came and went, as did waitresses with regularly priced drinks. Close to two o'clock Nazar found a pay phone and called Soulé at the Morning Call coffee stand about five blocks away. Soulé wasn't surprised to hear that no girls had offered his boys three-dollar bottles of champagne for a hundred. He told Nazar to round up the rascals and meet him at the Central Fire Station on Decatur Street. There he gave them more money, all prerecorded bills, after which he detailed Operation A.

What a dull Saturday night, not lucrative in the least, but Norma expected things to go that way in the summer, when most of the Good Men took their families to their beach houses on the coast. At two-thirty, four or five of the girls had asked if they could leave early, and Norma had told them to go. Six girls were left, along with Jackie—Rose Mary was out for the night—and a bartender from over on Chartres Street, who was having a couple of drinks in the second parlor. Norma looked at the clock. Almost three. She thought that if business didn't pick up in the next few minutes, she'd get Terry to go over to Dan's with her for a drink.

The troupe of six college types in white jackets reached 1026 Conti just then. They'd all heard about Norma Wallace, and they were a little jittery; if they succeeded tonight, it would be a real feather in their caps.

They knocked on the front door. A female voice from the side startled them. "Come around," she said, and when they reached the shuttered window she admonished them sharply: "Don't you know better than to go to the front?"

Five pairs of eyes turned to Paul Nazar. "Yes, ma'am," he said.

"Go to the back," the woman told them.

As they went up the driveway, each cadet removed his boutonniere from his lapel and let it fall to the ground. If they failed to gain entrance, they were to retrieve the carnations, the flowers indicating their position to the backup officers.

Norma gave them the once-over through the little window. "I don't know you," she said.

Nazar was afraid she was going to close up on them before he had a chance to work his charm on her. "Sure you do, Norma. I'm Paul. Don't you remember me?"

"Why should I?"

"I was here last year with a couple of my college buddies."

"What school?"

"Southwestern, in Lafayette."

"I have no idea who you are."

"Gee," Nazar said, sounding hurt. "I thought you'd never forget, the way we laughed."

"Do you have any ID?"

All six cadets started digging for their wallets. Norma opened the door. They held out their driver's licenses.

"Do you have any school ID?" Norma asked.

"Oh, no," Nazar said without missing a beat, "we had to turn all that stuff in when we graduated, the library cards, everything. Look, Miss Norma, we're out celebrating tonight. We just graduated!"

Nazar's performance had loosened the tongues on the others, and they chimed in with "Yeah, we're celebrating," and "We need some women to celebrate with."

"You better go away," Norma told them.

Nazar slapped his hand to his forehead. "I can't believe you don't remember," he said dramatically.

Bobby Frey, a roughly handsome fellow who would head up the vice squad one day, thought Nazar could use some help. "Some of us are going to law school," he told Norma, his hand on his chest; then he gestured toward Billy McGaha and Jerry Lankford. "Tulane," he said proudly.

Norma tipped her head back to look at the six foot eight Lankford. "You're a tall one," she remarked.

They all started talking at once about how they might go to law school, they weren't sure, but wouldn't she need a few good lawyers someday? Norma waited for the melee to settle. "I already have a few good lawyers," she said coolly. "I think you boys better go on now."

But Nazar wasn't about to give up. He let out a loud burp. "Gee, Miss Norma," he said, "I'm really kind of sick from drinking. Do you think you could get me something?" She looked at him hard. He swallowed another burp, his hand rolling as if he was about to say something and, just as he opened his mouth, let go another whopper. "Sorry," he muttered, clutching his stomach.

Norma laughed. "Oh, come on," she said. "I'll see what I can find for you." And she let them into her parlor.

The six cadets looked around at the finery—the Tiffany lamps, the red-velvet drapes, the elaborate scrolled furniture, the crystal chandelier—just like an old-time whorehouse out of a movie, except for the jukebox over in the corner. Ronald Vega put a quarter in the slot. They were into the act now, punching at each other, wowing and wondering aloud where the ladies were. They were actually *in*. But they had only thirty minutes before Freddy Soulé busted down the doors.

Norma returned with an Alka-Seltzer and a glass of water. Paul drank it down, belching softly. "Much better," he said and put his soft brown bedroom eyes—irresistible to most women—on Norma. "Oh, please, Miss Norma, we're in *dire* need of some ladies!"

What the hell, Norma thought, and she called the six girls who were still in the house.

Nazar's eyes popped for a beautiful honey blonde named Betty. He followed her up to a second-floor bedroom right off the balcony. First thing, Betty whipped out his penis and checked it for venereal disease. Then they began negotiating a price.

Vega couldn't believe his luck getting Terry. Too bad all they were going to do was arrest these girls! He went into a room with her, and as soon as she had the door closed, she grabbed his penis. As she milked it, she said jokingly, "Give me some money." Vega took out a twenty-dollar bill. Terry asked coyly, "Do you have a dollar for the maid?"

Bobby Frey picked a girl named Diana. Diana's boyfriend was a third-generation pimp called BeBe Anselmo. (When Norma heard who Diana was going with, she exclaimed, "Oh my God, lightning has struck *three* times!" One of her girls had had a baby with BeBe's grandfather; another of her girls had knifed BeBe the second.) BeBe the third was a heroin addict who wasn't going to be happy with Diana's paltry earnings that slow Saturday night. So the first thing she said to Frey was "Let's talk business. Just what do you want to do?"

"Anything, baby," he said with feeling. "What do you want to do?"

"A little bit of everything," Diana said coquettishly, and he handed over every dollar he had.

Joe Liemann got his penis grabbed by a cute little number named Linda and gave her every bit of his money too.

Jerry Lankford folded his six foot eight frame onto the stairway to the third floor, where he and his girl, Julie, waited for a room. As they sat there, Julie asked, "What do you want tonight?"

Lankford said, "All I can get."

"Okay," Julie replied and took twenty-five dollars off him. She left briefly to give the money to Norma before they went to their room.

Billy McGaha never made it out of the parlor. His girl told him to wait there for her, but she didn't get back before there was something of a disturbance upstairs.

All the girls turned the money over to Norma before they got down to business. Paul Nazar, though, had been charged by Soulé to follow the path of the money, since it would be their best evidence in court. It was time to get moving, because Soulé had said thirty minutes tops, then he was busting in. Nazar hurried the negotiations, and when Betty took his money, he followed her out to the balcony, talking as he went. "Do you mind if I go out to the veranda with you?" She hesitated but finally nodded. "Need a little fresh air," he went on. He looked out over the courtyard, his eyes sweeping right and left, and said, "This is a beautiful house! I like the motif."

"Uh-huh," Betty replied. She called out to Norma and dropped the money down to her.

Nazar leaned on the rail to the balcony. "What a great courtyard!" he gushed. "All those plants . . . do I hear water? A fountain? Wow, this is really something." All the time he talked he was watching

Norma. He saw her go into the glassed sunroom, where he had a partial view of her desk to the right of the door and, behind that, another door that led to a bathroom.

He went back into the bedroom with Betty. He talked incessantly, asking her questions such as how she came to work at Norma's, making comments about the bed with the canopy and the pretty little chairs in the room.

Finally Betty said, "Man, you're a talker, aren't you? Don't you want to get undressed and go to bed?"

But Nazar didn't want to take off even his socks because he had his police ID stuck down inside them. He stalled, sitting on the edge of the bed and talking ferociously as he waited for Betty to disrobe. As soon as she was naked, he reached into his sock and said to her, "Look, darlin, the reason I can't go to bed with you is because I'm a police officer and you're under arrest." Just as he said this, Julie, on the third floor, shrieked, "Norma, it's the cops!"

Betty, stark naked, ran out to the balcony and screamed, "Norma, Norma, it's the police!" Nazar was right behind her, his hand on her elbow.

Norma went into action before Betty finished screaming. Without panicking or even seeming to hurry, she eased the bartender and the sixth girl, the one who'd told Billy McGaha to wait in the parlor, out the side door, and she told Jackie to go out the front. Jackie's nerves weren't good enough anymore to go through this. Bobby Frey had come downstairs and was using the phone. Norma came back to the desk and said, "I knew you bastards were coppers." She knew it in hindsight: She should have realized that college boys wouldn't have that much money on them; she just hadn't given it the right thought. But who were these guys? She didn't recognize any of them, nor did she have pictures of them; she bought the badge ID photos from one of her contacts in the department. She said to Frey, "You must be new." He offered no information.

Down the street, Freddy Soulé checked his watch. Another two minutes and he was going in. He saw a woman rush out the front door and run down Conti Street toward Bourbon. He was about to instruct one of his officers to pursue her, but just then the radio dispatcher called with a message from Bobby Frey to proceed with Operation A, and Soulé told the officers to break down the side door of Norma's house.

Chaos had erupted in the house, with naked girls screaming and crying, cops crawling all over the place, and doors coming down, but Norma continued her smooth preparations. As soon as Frey turned away from the desk, she pulled her nightly record from the drawer. This she kept on tissue paper. She also took about a hundred and twenty-five dollars she'd collected from these supposed college boys and handed the money to Marie. Then she held the tissue paper over the toilet and put a match to it. She flushed it away.

No one seemed to notice the maid go out the back door. Marie put the marked money in a garbage can and moved it into Mike Persia's car lot next door. Then she slipped back into the house. As far as she could tell, she was invisible.

But Soulé had seen Norma pass something to the maid, and he assumed it was the marked money. His attention had been diverted, but now he told Norma he wanted the money the officers had given her.

"You'll never find it," she told him. She'd felt no nerves at all as she'd hidden as much evidence as possible, but now she could feel herself getting angry. "I was supposed to be notified of this," she snapped.

Soulé asked her what she meant, but she refused to answer. He told her she might as well give up the money.

She opened her desk drawer. "Help yourself," she said, and waved her hand over the night's take. Soulé picked up the money, about five hundred dollars, but his marked bills weren't there. Something else in the drawer caught his eye, though. Photographs—of himself! He shuffled through them and pictures of a number of other officers. He had no idea where she could have gotten those pictures, and she wouldn't tell him.

He said, "I'm not leaving until I get the money."

"Suit yourself," Norma replied. She sat in her chair behind the desk.

The white tuxedos and the girls, dressed again, started coming downstairs. Terry caught Soulé's eye. "Can I talk to you a minute?"

"Sure," he said.

She cut her eyes toward the second parlor. He followed her in, and she closed the door. "I'm friends, good friends, with one of your officers."

"Who's that?" Soulé asked.

"Donald Pryce. Do you know him?"

"Sure. I know him."

"We're more than friends; we're lovers," Terry said. "It's serious." Soulé lifted his eyebrows; he nodded. "Do you think you could just let me out the back door?" Terry asked.

Soulé smoothed his mustache with his thumb and index finger, then shook his head. "No, I'm gonna arrest you. Unless you want to be a witness for us. Then I'll let you go."

"No way."

"Then I'm sorry," Soulé told her, and he laughed, a rather wicked laugh for the Jellybean.

In the sunroom he and Norma got into it about the money. "You'll never see it again," Norma insisted. She sat with her arms folded and refused to say another word about it.

"Then I'm gonna tell my officers here to start bustin up the place, punch holes in the walls, whatever they have to do," Soulé told her.

"Where's your warrant?" Norma wanted to know.

That *was* a problem. Soulé worked over his mustache. Given the hour, it would be impractical to try to get one. He was thinking too that the woman he'd seen running from the building could have taken the money with her.

Norma was thinking about Jackie as well. She was glad that she and not Jackie had let these scoundrels in; otherwise, she knew she would have gone the rest of her life blaming Jackie. But she'd done it herself, and she had no excuse for letting down her guard. Thinking about it was making her very tired. She watched Soulé as he thought, his thumb and index finger running repeatedly over his mustache.

Soulé decided to let the money go. As they were all leaving the house, Nazar sidled up to Norma, cupping her elbow with his hand. "No hard feelings?" He looked at her with his beautiful, sleepy eyes.

"You're a little son of a bitch," Norma told him. She moved her elbow away. He was the touchy-feely kind; she could even feel his eyes on her. She asked his name. "Good theatrics, Nazar." He laughed. Nice teeth too. She lowered her voice. "Why don't you have dinner with me one night? I'll take you to the Black Orchid." Nazar agreed immediately. "Give me a call," Norma said, and off she went to Central Lockup.

On June 10, 1962, Norma Wallace was arrested on three serious charges—prostitution, pandering, and letting the premises for prostitution. When they booked her, she lied about her age. The newspaper reported that she was forty-nine. She was sixty-one.

The article about the bust was on page 12 of the front section of *The Times-Picayune*. It was at the bottom of the page and was four paragraphs long. Norma had called in a favor.

"A good piece of work, Freddy," Giarrusso said. He drummed his fingers on the folded newspaper. "Jail will be a bitter dose for her."

"If she goes," Soulé said. Not one of the girls had given a statement. The girlfriend of that pimp BeBe Anselmo—her mother had been so upset that Soulé had thought sure the girl would rat on Anselmo. Instead, she married him. No statements, no marked money, just naked women and his cadets. He wouldn't want to call it.

Giarrusso shrugged. "True." Suddenly he laughed. "Don't you know there're some *big* people praying right now. She's upset; if they play it right in the DA's office . . ."

Soulé sat across from the Chief. They looked at each other, then Soulé watched as Giarrusso threw the newspaper into the trash can next to his desk. He had more disappointing news: He told the Chief he thought Donald Pryce was tipping people off. Giarrusso flipped his hand. "He's gonna deny it, then it's gonna be his word against a prostitute's."

But with Garrison and Gervais raking through the city, the last thing Giarrusso needed was a policeman like Donald Pryce. They had a way of dealing with his kind. At the end of June, Giarrusso transferred Pryce from the First District, the French Quarter, to the Fifth, out toward the Industrial Canal, a rough and dangerous district riddled with shoot-outs and murders, a far cry from the razzle-dazzle of Bourbon Street. And they watched him. Closely. Pryce turned in his resignation effective July 31, 1962, only a year and three months after he'd joined the NOPD.

Freddy Soulé had been on the force for nearly twenty years, and he'd seen it happen too many times before. Bourbon Street had been the ruin of many a young cop. They had a name for it; they called it the Policeman's Graveyard.

CHAPTER FIFTEEN

Jailbird

At seven o'clock Norma got the familiar rush that came every night when the house on Conti Street opened for business. This particular night she was in Waggaman, and she was alone—no husband, no phones, no girls, no dates. Since the June 10 bust McCoy had been miserable, saying he knew it would come to this, and now she might go to jail. He was drinking more than ever. Last week he'd stopped at a barroom and all the linens for the house had been stolen out of the car. They'd had a terrible fight over it, and Norma had told him to go away and let her have some peace and quiet.

She put on a tight red cocktail dress with deep décolletage to highlight her greatest assets. She meant to get his attention, and she remembered where it had been riveted. The straight skirt fell just below her knees and showed off her shapely calves. She took her time with her hair and makeup. When she was ready, she slipped her feet into matching red high-heeled pumps and slid behind the wheel of her Cadillac.

Over the years Norma had kept up with Wayne Bernard through his aunt and her best friend, Elise Rolling. She knew Wayne still worked at Avondale Shipyards six days a week, that by the time he was twenty-one he'd been married, had a child, and divorced. That had been a year ago; he was twenty-two now—and legal. She did not need to play coy with Elise, so she had asked her where Wayne would most likely be found on a Saturday night. Elise gave her the names of several lounges over on Fourth Street. And the Mist, right there in Waggaman, was also a possibility.

Norma guided the Cadillac around the long gravel horseshoe drive in front of her Waggaman property, under the low-limbed, moss-hung oaks, and turned right on River Road. She took the long way, following River Road until she could intersect with Fourth Street where it began in Westwego then ran through Marrero and Harvey to Gretna.

The Fourth Street "strip" was studded with nightspots—restaurants, lounges, nightclubs, and dives. Norma drove slowly past the Keyhole, the Gay Paree, Scorpio's, and the Moulin Rouge. It was barely eight o'clock, and she could tell from the numbers of cars in the parking lots that she'd found the Saturday night action. But she turned the Cadillac around and drove back to Waggaman. She parked in front of the Mist, a low cinder-block building with an off-center, V-shaped roof—1950s-modern, Elvis architecture—fronted with four aqua lightning bolts that zigzagged from the roofline to the ground. She decided to try the Mist first.

Wayne and a few of his friends sat in a booth in the bar inside. They usually met for drinks there to decide where they were going for the evening, and sometimes, after barhopping over on Fourth Street, they'd wind up back at the Mist for a late-night breakfast.

Whenever the door opened everybody turned an eyeball to see who was coming in. When Norma walked in that night, their eyeballs popped. "Who the hell is *that*?" one of the guys asked.

But Wayne knew who it was—there was no mistaking Mrs. Patterson, with that hair like Marilyn Monroe and those dark sunglasses. She walked up to the bar, a fire red hourglass on high heels, and he pushed his way out of the booth, all those guys pulling on him, creating quite a ruckus, but Wayne didn't say a word. He just slid on up to the bar right next to Mrs. Patterson. They had a drink, and then they left together, while Wayne's friends gawked from the booth.

They drank and danced their way through the hot spots along Fourth Street, until at two or three in the morning, on the dance floor at Scorpio's, Mrs. Patterson put both her arms around Wayne and said, "Come on over to the house with me."

"But Mr. Mac's going to be there," Wayne said.

Mrs. Patterson told him no, Mac wouldn't be there. She said they were separated, she'd put him out.

She had locked herself out of the house, but the bedroom window was open, so Wayne muscled himself up and over the sill, checking to see if Mr. Mac was in the bed. He wasn't. Wayne dropped to the floor, went around the front to let Mrs. Patterson in, and then they finished what they had started all those years ago under the oak tree before Snapbean almost stepped on them.

The next morning Mrs. Patterson served Wayne breakfast in bed—coffee and French toast, eggs and bacon—on a big silver tray. She had on a negligee, and he could see that she was wearing nothing underneath. She watched him as he ate; then he pushed the big silver tray to the side and pulled her down on top of him. What Mrs. Patterson served up he'd never had a taste of before, and he wasn't sure he could ever get enough of it.

But it wasn't heaven quite yet. Wayne and Mrs. Patterson would go out one night, then he wouldn't see her for a few days. The next evening, she'd show up at the Mist. Sometimes he went home with her; sometimes she would vanish into the night.

Suddenly Mrs. Patterson stopped dropping in at the Mist. She just disappeared. Wayne regarded the situation with his usual imperturbability, figuring that he wasn't what she fancied, that she didn't want anything more to do with this old country boy.

Norma disappeared from Wayne's life because she decided to go to jail.

One consideration was the publicity a trial would bring. After her arrest she had managed to subdue the newspaper publicity, and she had hidden out from the TV cameras, but a trial would mean a big blast, and then everyone in Waggaman would know who she was.

Ed Baldwin, the lawyer Norma used for certain underworld activities, including any criminal charges, was ready to go to court and fight. Before the trial, though, Norma decided to talk to the judge, Bernard Cocke, a customer and, Norma thought, a friend. Behind closed doors, without her lawyer present, Norma and the judge came to an agreement.

The morning of the trial Norma told Baldwin that the judge had said if she went to trial with a jury and was found guilty, he'd give her a year and a day; if she pled guilty, three months, and she could do it in six weeks.

In the hallway outside the courtroom, Norma said, "I'm going to plead guilty."

"You're *what?*" Baldwin demanded to know if she knew what she was doing.

"I have a good reason, Baldwin." He could see her mind was set.

The way Norma figured it, for six weeks Wayne was probably safe in Waggaman—but to leave him for a year, so dangerously close to all those good-looking young women who swooned over him in the West Bank lounges, could only be folly.

Norma knew she'd been off her game because she had been considering quitting the business. She and McCoy were at such odds that she was on edge all the time, so she'd said she would give it up. She sat in the courtroom wishing she'd done it sooner so she could have quit clean. If she had, she would have been the only big-time landlady who'd never gone to jail.

Some of the vice cops from the bust sat in the back, waiting to see what would happen. For a fleeting moment Norma wished she had listened to Baldwin and tried to beat the charges just to show them.

Judge Cocke sentenced Norma, banged his gavel, and called for the next case. She was handcuffed and led from the back of the courtroom through connecting corridors into Parish Prison. She felt stripped, laid bare in some indefinable way. For the first time since she'd been a teenager in Memphis, she was utterly powerless.

They led her to the third floor. The place was filthy, unsanitary. McCoy asked to see her. Norma was already exhausted, and seeing Mac was almost unbearable. He seemed so hurt to see her in such sordid conditions, yet he wouldn't stop harping that he'd known it would come to this. His visit only compounded their estrangement.

Her next visitor was Arthur Carroll, a man she had known all her life, who had once been a policeman in the red-light district. When he left Norma was so tired that she curled up on a cot with a bare, filthy mattress, covered herself with the blanket the matrons had given her, turned her face to the wall, and silently cried. Tired as she was, only the consolation of Carroll's promise that he'd see to it she got a cell to herself allowed her to sleep.

During the night Norma dreamed that mice were jumping in bed with her, only to wake up and realize that it was no dream. She was scared to death of mice, so there wasn't much sleeping after that.

When she got up the next morning, it was only to another nightmare. The toilets didn't have any doors, not even curtains, they just sat out in the open. All the girls sat around smirking and snickering, watching to see what she would do. She couldn't go to the bathroom in front of an audience! She waited until the matrons brought in breakfast, some kind of pale mystery goop that made oatmeal look gourmet, and picked the one she thought would be most sympathetic. Her instincts were good; the woman, Mrs. Nix, let her use the toilet in solitary.

The showers, the whole place, crawled with roaches. "If you want to eat something in this hellhole," Norma told Mac dramatically, "you have to knock the roaches off first—they try to take the food away from you." Roaches, mice, and bedbugs too, as Norma discovered when little red bumps began popping up on her milky white skin. If she got lice, she was just going to roll over and die.

But fear of the wildlife was nothing compared with fear of a group of dirty, unkempt girls who called themselves the Gang of Six. The word was they'd whipped up on a couple of landladies, and two or three women who owned honky-tonks had been given a good going-over as well.

The first night these girls said to her, "Get the dish rag, it's your turn. Every newcomer has to do the dishes."

Norma got up, but Mrs. Nix heard what was going on and said, "Don't do that to her. She's tired, she's had an ordeal. Let somebody else do it."

But Norma was too smart to let someone take up for her. "I'm game," she said and started toward the sink.

Behind her she heard a little voice say, "Wait, I'll do it for you."

Norma turned. The girl was as small as a child. Her brown hair was thin, unhealthy looking; her eyes were large, doelike.

"Who are you?" Norma asked.

"I'm Nell," the girl said with an exaggerated drawl that gave her name two syllables. She was from rural Mississippi, in for shoplifting and forging checks. Nell said humbly, "I'll be your maid."

"And what do you get?" Norma wanted to know. Nell wanted Norma to buy her cigarettes. Done, Norma told her, and Nell went off to do the dishes.

Already Norma felt better: She was making deals; she had her own maid. That evening Carroll came through with a private cell, and he brought seeds for the mice. Mac arrived with dinner from the Black Orchid.

But now Norma had to deal with the Gang. Not only did she not want these girls to beat her up, she wanted them to like her. She didn't want them to think of her as someone who had people on her side and got favors. So she bought them cigarettes too, all of them, every day. Nell didn't object—she knew that jailhouses weren't democracies. And when the wagon came around on Saturdays, Norma bought ice cream, sodas, whatever they wanted. She talked to them and told them stories about what went on at her whorehouse. She was careful never to act superior, or as if she was unique, that they were a bunch of dope fiends—since most of them were in on drug charges—and she was a big-time landlady. "But it turned out I *was* unique, no question about that," Norma said. "They all swore they were innocent; I was the only dame in the place who was guilty."

Some of the girls had been in for two or three years, waiting for appeals. In all that time they'd had no yard privileges, and so no sunshine. Since the food was so terrible—what was served over spaghetti could have been chopped squirrel or the warden's mother-in-law, for all they knew—a few of them ate only from the wagon. One of them, Linda, had terrible tooth problems because she ate nothing but sweets.

No matter what they did, Norma never ratted on them, even when a couple of them set a fire one night. She knew that would be a quick way to get killed. They got into trouble because they had nothing else to do, not even a radio to listen to, only television at certain hours. So they found other ways to have fun.

Behind the toilets the floor didn't meet the wall because the building was literally falling down. On the second floor, directly underneath the girls' cellblock, were the black men. (The jails in Louisiana were still officially segregated.) The girls would hang over the toilets and send kites down to the men, notes on strings that they would drop through the crack, then, after the men wrote back, they'd pull them up. When they went down to the yard for garbage detail, they'd write the men notes and stick them on the insides of the can covers with chewing gum.

The matrons knew what was going on. Mrs. Nix told Norma, "You know, I sit here with fear in my heart. All those men have to do is just push the walls down and come up here and there wouldn't be a thing we could do about it."

Mrs. Nix was a lovely woman, very pretty, Norma thought, and totally out of place at Parish Prison. For one thing, she was in her late seventies. She'd try to be tough, but it wasn't easy handling a bunch of hookers and streetwalkers and counterfeiters—even a murderer, but the poor girl was only sixteen years old. She and her boyfriend had killed her mother. Norma felt sorry for her because there were a number of lesbians up there who were having their fun with the girl.

The only diversion the jail provided was in the form of a Saturday-night revivalist, a woman who sang "Amazing Grace" in a voice as deep as a man's and worked up a sweat thumping on the Bible. Did they really think they were going to rehabilitate a bunch of hookers, shoplifters, and dopers by reading to them out of the Bible?

The way they treated the inmates was a crime worse than most that those poor disadvantaged girls had committed as far as Norma was concerned. She got a taste of it when she asked permission to use her blood pressure medicine and had to see the jail doctor. Right away he got nasty and started calling her the housemother. When she told him what she wanted, he acted as if she were a dope fiend because she'd asked to use her prescription. Norma got nasty back, told him to forget it, that the medicine wouldn't do her a lick of good in that place anyway.

Of all the women who were in jail, for all their different crimes, the alcoholics disturbed Norma the most. She watched them come back over and over again. These women—some of them had children—would get drunk, get picked up; they'd be given ten days, but they'd get out in five. The next evening they'd be right back. The alcoholics roused Norma's childhood memories from their place of rest far away from the life she had made for herself.

As her personal crusade she adopted one of them. The girl had three children, and Norma nagged the life out of her, telling her what it was like for her children, illustrated with stories and feelings from her own childhood. Even after they were both out of jail, Norma stayed on that girl for three years. "Like gravy on rice," Norma said. "She wound up on a farm in Bogalusa, back with her family. I believe she was rehabilitated.

"But if anyone was to be rehabilitated, it wouldn't be in that fleabag joint. If those women libbers are looking for a place to start, there it is. I'd help, but they have this rule that once you've been in, you can't go back to visit. It's too bad. I would have liked to talk to the girls, because I've seen too many of them, beautiful girls too, go down the drain. There's a way to get through to them, but it's not with bad food and preachers."

Norma did her six weeks playing counselor, den mother, and raconteur. When her time was up, she decided not to go back to the business. "I'd told myself many times, the day I do time in jail, unless it's at the Roosevelt Hotel with bars on the door to a suite, I'm out of the business. Anybody is entitled to one fall, but you can't fall twice. If I'd been stupid enough to go to Parish Prison twice, I would have been a bum. Three times, you're a tramp.

"I did my six weeks—an eternity in that hellhole—and it made me see the light. I was rehabilitated. Hell, I was converted."

CHAPTER SIXTEEN

Endgame

 Norma's conversion—her decision to get out of the business—lasted long enough for her to put 1026 Conti Street on the market in the summer of 1962. She listed it, including most of the furniture and a three-thousand-dollar rug in the living room of her apartment, with the real estate agent Frosty Blackshear for fifty thousand dollars. She wanted nothing except out. The agent advertised the house, and many people came to see it, but no one made an offer.

While prospective buyers wandered through the house, tour guides brought sightseers by the busload. From her apartment Norma could hear the guides telling the tourists all about her—over a microphone! She all but ran to Waggaman, moving her official residence to her house across the river. She stayed away from Conti Street. But she didn't stay away from the business altogether. She worked some of the girls out of motels and hotels in New Orleans, others from two or three apartments. Jackie still answered the phones at 1026, and Norma stayed there occasionally or had Marie stay on the premises. She didn't like leaving the place unattended. She'd done that once a couple of years earlier, and linens, light fixtures, even some furniture had been stolen.

While Norma was in jail, Mac had started driving a taxi. He had hoped that during her six weeks Norma would really see the light and quit prostitution. But her intentions were clear enough to him now. He got together with a few other drivers, and they started the A Service Cab Company. He told Norma he was leaving her.

Norma's emotions ran the gamut as Mac prepared to go. She loved him, and she was hurt that he was leaving her. She was also angry at the way he was looting the Waggaman house, taking furnishings as well as his belongings. When Norma did the leaving, she left everything intact, but her pride was such that, even though she was stung badly by Mac's actions, she wouldn't let him know for hell and be damned. She hated being the one left, yet she couldn't see going on with Mac. They had been married for nearly eighteen years, and for many of those years they had battled over desires to live completely different lifestyles. For quite some time Norma had been restless, casting about for something to ease her, and always she had looked for that something in the form of a man. She found that she couldn't stop thinking about Wayne Bernard. She hadn't contacted him since she'd been out of jail, but before Mac left he told her, "I know what you've been doing, Norma. I know you've been fooling around with that young boy."

During the time in 1962 that Norma disappeared from Wayne's life, he began spending his time with Betty, a blonde from Marrero, and Betty started to toy with a few ideas about her future. Her plans, however, were abruptly foiled when Mrs. Patterson appeared at the Mist one night. She and Wayne picked up as if they'd just seen each other the night before, and Betty was history.

Norma and Wayne made the rounds of the West Bank honky-tonks, then, for the first time, Norma took Wayne to her favorite haunts in the French Quarter. They had dinner at Dan's and drinks at Lafitte's Blacksmith Shop. Sometimes they brought Carmen Miranda with them; Wayne would walk behind Norma, carrying the poodle on a royal blue velvet pillow with gold tassels. In Jefferson Parish they stopped in at the Town and Country Motel, where Mrs. Patterson would tip the piano player twenty dollars. Wayne watched, fascinated, as Mrs. Patterson slipped the maître d' ten bucks, another ten for the bartenders, never calculated a tip for the waiters, just left a pile of money on the table. Wayne was making thirty-five dollars a week at the shipyards.

Mrs. Patterson started giving him a couple of hundred dollars before they went out, telling him how to spend it. They ate at the Black Orchid and Masson's Beach House out by the lake, Antoine's and Arnaud's in the Quarter. Wherever they went, they got the best seats; they were ushered in like royalty. Wayne watched Mrs. Patterson closely at the big fancy restaurants so he'd know which fork to use. Sometimes after a meal at those places, he'd still be hungry and he'd say, "Let's stop and get a hamburger." Mrs. Patterson would laugh, and he'd pull in at the first fast-food drive-up. Then they'd hit the West Bank and dance at Scorpio's or the Gay Paree until they couldn't keep their hands off each other any longer.

Wayne was having too much fun to notice that wherever they went Mrs. Patterson always sat facing out, her eye on the crowd, and she always put Wayne with his back to the room. He was too amazed—here he was, just an old country boy, and suddenly the whole world had opened up to him.

Norma generally stayed on Conti Street after a wild night with Wayne. Once she didn't get up until almost seven o'clock in the evening. Jackie and Rose Mary were in the office.

"Look at her," Rose Mary said. "She's still drunk or she wouldn't be walking like that."

Norma, in her nightgown, fussed around in the office. "I hear you talking, don't think I don't hear you," she said.

"We're talking about you," Jackie told her.

"Who else would you be talking about?" Norma demanded.

During the next few months, Paul Nazar called her a couple of times. He was friendly, very chatty, but he always refused Norma's dinner invitation. Freddy Soulé had told him to be careful, that it might not be a good idea to take Norma up on her offer. Nazar knew that someday he'd wish he'd had the chance to really talk to her, though, a woman of her stature and notoriety. He was officially part of the vice squad now, but he didn't know how it could get any better than the night they busted Norma. It was his best case; other cops were jealous.

Assuming that Nazar's calls meant the police were still interested in the house, Norma kept the action off the premises. So it was surprising when one winter evening Rose Mary saw two men in topcoats and hats coming up the alley. She knew they were cops. She threw the buzzer and flew to the back of the house, calling for Norma and getting no response. It irritated her the way Norma ignored the buzzer.

The parlor door was wide open. Rose Mary stepped outside. Nothing. She cautiously peered around the side of the building just in time to see Norma turn the hose on the two detectives. They yelled, "Wait, Norma, wait!" One of them got out of the stream and reached in his pocket. "We have a warrant," he told Norma, holding out the document. She blasted it right out of his hand.

Sometimes the temptation was just too much. The bell would ring, and Norma began to make exceptions here and there until, by spring of 1963, 1026 Conti was somewhat back in play.

On a warm night in late April, she was at the house with a sick hangover after a night out with Wayne. She called a friend who gave her a quick cure—fresh salted tomatoes to settle her stomach. She told Leon, the porter, to go out and get her a can of tomato juice. She didn't want to wait for him to try to find a fresh tomato in the French Quarter on a Friday night. "I'm absolutely dying," she told him so he'd hurry.

The front doorbell rang. She looked out and saw a man by himself. She called to him to go around the side. Through the shuttered window he told her he was from out of town and gave a local reference.

Norma made a quick assessment. She had four girls in the house at the time. She told the man to go to the corner and she'd send one of her girls to pick him up and take him to a motel. She told her girl not to go anywhere with him unless he could produce a plane or train ticket.

She couldn't wait to get her girdle off and lie down. But just as she started to undress, a car pulled into the alley. She thought it was someone taking advantage of her parking lot in the back, which annoyed her, but she was too tired to deal with it. Three men, however, got out of the car and rang the bell. They were Hispanic, very polite, speaking in broken English. Norma invited them in and called the three girls down. Rose Mary was going to have a fit when Norma told her to go with one of these Latins. She would help out in a pinch, but she didn't like Latin men, because they always wanted to kiss and they sometimes got angry when they were told they couldn't.

Sandy, Barbara, and Rose Mary took the men upstairs—Rose Mary shooting Norma a look to kill. They sent down the money, and Norma put it in the desk. Leon arrived with the tomato juice, and Norma took it to her apartment. Before she did anything, though, she wanted to change her clothes. She threw her girdle over a chair and stripped down to her bra and step-ins.

With no warning at all, Norma heard what sounded like sledgehammers on the front and side doors. She threw the buzzer, but the girls upstairs had heard the noise and already grabbed the men, running down to the courtyard and into the hideout. The cops had a hole in the side door by that time. Looking through it, Freddy Soulé saw a flash of red—Rose Mary was wearing a red kimono—and heard the clatter on the stairway. He already knew the men were in the house because he'd been staking the place out for several hours.

Norma handed Rose Mary the black book and watched as Leon, the Latins, Sandy, and Barbara disappeared into the hideout. Rose Mary followed. At the last minute Maggie, one of the poodles, bolted in behind Rose Mary. "Maggie!" Norma called, but it was too late. The door closed. She heard the bolt slide. She rolled two plant boxes in front of the entrance; then she assumed her stance, arms folded, facing the side door. She completely forgot that she wasn't dressed. She also forgot that she had a hangover. All she could think about was that the men's car was in her lot and that they were foreigners. In her experience foreigners were hard to handle if they panicked. They might want out of the hideout regardless of the consequences.

Norma heard the front door crash to the floor. Carmen Miranda, who was standing next to her, jumped and let out a yelp. She scurried into the sunroom. Then the side door came down only a couple of feet from where Norma stood. Not just the door but the iron gate and the entire door frame. Freddy Soulé, with his bow tie and natty little mustache, stepped dapperly through the hole. Norma nearly snorted with disgust. From the front hallway and from behind him enough cops swarmed into the house to start a new precinct, including that good-looking little bastard from the last time. He raked her with his eyes.

Soulé held out a search warrant; when Norma put her hands on her hips, she realized she wasn't dressed. Nevertheless, arms akimbo, she said coolly, "I understand you're supposed to try to give me the warrant *before* you knock down the doors."

He smiled at her, hitching his pants up with his thumbs. "We asked you to open the door, Norma."

"I never denied you entrance," she said heatedly. "I never even heard you until you crashed down my doors. What were you doing out there? Whispering?" Soulé stood smiling like a goon. She said to him, "If you don't mind I'll put my clothes on." He pushed the warrant toward her. She snatched it out of his hand and went into her bedroom.

He followed her, staying so close as she stood in front of the closet that she finally said, "Do you mind?" He stepped back, and she pulled out one of her long, loose, flowy numbers. Then Soulé reached into the closet, pushing back the clothes as if he expected to find bodies in there.

But that was merely the beginning of the search. On and on it went because Soulé and the rest of the goons knew people were hiding, but they couldn't find them. Soulé kept saying, "I saw a red dress on those stairs."

Some of the cops went upstairs, where they discovered Terry's letters from Donald Pryce, salacious enough to keep them enthralled. Norma could hear them reading passages aloud and repeating phrases as they tapped on the walls, looking for the hideout. Not much bound by sentiment or possessions, she considered it silly of Terry to have saved those letters.

She and Soulé stood by her desk. A huge black man entered the office from the courtyard.

"Who's that?" Norma asked.

"That's our informer. He was on the corner watching. He saw the car park in the back."

"People park back there all the time," Norma said. "They go down to those little honky-tonks around the corner."

One of the young cops was going through the desk drawers, fooling with everything in a most irritating manner. Norma had taken the phones off the hook; he put them back. He read her personal mail. As a rule she didn't leave any records or anything that could be considered evidence in her desk. But that night a letter from a woman named Honey Day was in the stack. Norma didn't know her, but she'd heard of her, an abortionist in the Quarter. She'd written from jail, asking for a job when she was released.

The young cop showed Soulé the letter, making a big deal over it, saying it could be used as evidence against Norma. She said to him, "I don't even know that broad, and she says in the letter she doesn't know me. You stick that letter."

In the hideout Rose Mary heard Soulé talking about the red dress, telling one of his officers to check upstairs, and she heard a different voice ask where the black book was. She could feel sweat dripping down her sides. The three Hispanics thought all this was kicks, part of the program. Maybe they were going to get into a little group sex, three for the price of one. *"Tres muchachas,"* they said, licking their lips and trying to find the girls' mouths in the dark. The girls poked at them and told them to be quiet, and the boys poked them back and groped whatever their hands found. Maggie the poodle didn't like the boys, and she was getting nervous. With one hand the girls slapped away the boys, with the other they petted Maggie, whispering, "Quiet, puppy, please be quiet, good puppy." Rose Mary heard the tapping getting closer, louder. "Ssh, ssh, pleeeze," she hissed. The taps were right behind her; she thought she could feel them in her spine. She held her breath. They moved on, stopped, and started on the front wall of the hideout. One of the boys giggled; Maggie let out a low growl. "Leon," Rose Mary whispered, "this dog is going to bite them. Tell them to be still."

"I can't tell them anything," Leon whispered back. "They don't speak English."

"Well, do *something!*"

"*Do* something?" Leon repeated. "What you want me to do?"

The night was wearing thin and, as the search went on, so were Norma's nerves. The incessant tapping on the walls was like Chinese water torture; it sounded eerie coming from upstairs, like the beating of that dead man's heart in the Edgar Allan Poe story. Norma was worried about the people trapped in the hideout. It must be sweltering in there, with the water heaters in the very back. She was afraid that the boys would start hollering any time. She needed to get Soulé and his cops out soon. She argued with him; she claimed harassment; she finally told him she was so tired she thought she was going to drop dead if he didn't leave, and that gave her an idea. In the top drawer of the desk was an EKG she'd had made the week before. She was convinced that Soulé wasn't as smart as he thought he was—he'd have found the hideout by now if he had any brains at all. She pulled out the EKG and showed it to him.

"Can you read this?" she asked. He gave no sign that he had a clue. "If you can't, you'd better learn quick, because if I drop dead right now, you're in plenty of trouble."

He perused the graph of her heartbeats. She went on. "You can raid me and put me in jail, whatever, but let's get this over with. There's nobody here but me and my dog, and I've had it. I'm ready to call the newspapers and tell them to come down here and see what harassment is all about. You've been here almost five hours now!"

Soulé stared at the EKG, smoothing his mustache, not saying a word. Norma remembered something else in her desk, an agreement to renew her real estate contract for another three months with Frosty Blackshear.

She put it in front of Soulé, over the EKG. "Mrs. Blackshear just dropped this off today," she said. "I told her that I'm very anxious to sell, that I'm being harassed by the police, and I know I'll never have a minute's peace. Does that look like I want to stay here and conduct a business?"

"Doesn't *look* like it," he said and laughed. He asked Norma a few personal questions, like where her husband was and if he had anything to do with running the operation. When he sat on the edge of the desk and started counting up the months he and Norma had known each other, she thought she'd blow.

"That's it," she said, "I'm going to call the carpenter."

"Go ahead," Soulé told her, "but I want to be here."

Daylight was creeping over the Quarter rooftops, and Norma felt frantic about the seven people still in the hideout. But she said slowly and calmly, "Sure, honey, it's all right with me if you want to stay. We can board up the place together." With her eyebrows coyly arched, Norma looked at Soulé until he looked away, then she called her carpenter and got him out of bed.

Paul Nazar was back on the third floor. Normally long on stamina and good humor, he was now feeling frustrated. His knuckles had started bleeding from tapping the walls. He stood in the middle of Terry's room and took a few deep breaths. They'd heard the people, Soulé had seen one of them—they *had* to be here. Where? *Think,* he told himself furiously.

Rose Mary had no idea what time it was, but she thought if she had to stay in this pitch black armpit one more minute she was going to start screaming. "Leon," she said, "isn't there a flashlight in here?"

"I don't know. I ain't never been in here before."

"I think there is, up on one of the shelves, toward the back." She didn't want to get up because Maggie was sitting calmly in her lap, possibly sleeping. Beside her, Leon uncurled himself and stood. He stretched. As he started moving toward the back of the hideout, he bent over and put his hand on Rose Mary's head for balance, trying not to step on anyone, especially that mean little dog. He got past Rose Mary and started to stand upright, but his shoulder hit the bottom shelf. Something fell off it. Sandy let out a sharp cry of pain, which she immediately muffled. The noxious, suffocating odor of paint spread through the hideout.

"What the shit, Leon!" Rose Mary said.

"Christ!" Leon moaned. "My shoulder."

Sandy started to weep. The three Hispanics began talking to each other in rapid, under-the-breath Spanish. Maggie barked, and everybody fell silent. Over the paint fumes came the smell of fear.

But by that time Charley the carpenter was there, nailing up the doorways. Once Soulé saw him lay out his tools, he said to Norma, "Okay, we're leaving."

Norma watched him and his little bastards walk out into the alley and get in their car. "Can you believe this idiot?" Norma said to Charley. "He must think I'm as stupid as he is." She went to the bottom of the stairs. "You can come on down, Nazar, and whoever else is up there," she called.

Soulé had left two goons besides Nazar—one last effort to catch her. Nazar, though, didn't realize he'd been left. The other two came down grinning. Nazar had recovered his goodwill toward man—and woman. He swaggered up to Norma.

"Don't come sweet-talkin me now, Nazar," she said.

"Aw, come on, Norma. It's just my job."

"I know that, honey, and I still love you, but hit the road, will you?" She watched them go out the back parlor door. "Better luck next time," she called out and threw the door closed behind them. It was six o'clock in the morning.

Rose Mary and the gang in the hideout could hear the pounding of a hammer. Were the police gone? Why wasn't Norma coming to get them out? Rose Mary wanted to kick at the door, bellow, tear out her paint-covered hair. But she decided it was her job to keep the others calm.

Norma knew she couldn't afford to make a mistake now. She called down to Pete's and asked Poke Chop, the emcee, to get in his car in about half an hour and case the neighborhood. It was the longest hour in eternity for the people in the hideout, but Poke Chop reported back that the coast was clear.

The sun was up when Norma opened the hideout door. Sandy was covered in Cherries Jubilee, the red paint Norma had used in one of the parlors. It was in Rose Mary's hair and speckled across Leon, Barbara, the black book, and the Latin boys. Maggie looked as if her toenails had been dipped.

Norma tried not to laugh. She busied herself getting the boys' money. "Boys," she said, "I can't thank you enough, you know, *muchas gracias,* and all that. We're all nailed in now. If you want to go upstairs"—

she pointed up the stairs and at the girls—"it's on the house. *No dinero.*"

Sandy started crying again. Rose Mary let out a string of curses that would have set the parrots off if their cages hadn't been covered. But the boys were ready to leave.

"You left us in there all night," Rose Mary said as soon as they'd gone. "You forgot us in there!"

"You want to come out and get us all arrested, fine," Norma said.

"Admit it, you forgot us. You think you had it bad in jail? You had *luxury* in jail compared to what we just went through!" Norma started to speak. "Stop, don't even say it," Rose Mary said, waving her off. "I'm firing myself," and she flounced off, up to the third floor.

"Garrison wants to padlock the building," Pershing Gervais told Norma.

"Rose Mary!" Norma yelled. "Have you been bringing Garrison his envelope?" Rose Mary yelled something unintelligible from another part of the house. "What have I been paying for, Pershing? Every week, like clockwork, Rose Mary puts the goddamn envelope in his hand. Talk to him—tell him the building's up for sale. What the hell am I paying *you* for?"

Gervais laughed. "You know me, Norma. I ain't never done nothin for nobody for nothin." His big shoulders rolled forward in a shrug. "Yeah, sure, I'll talk to him. It's prob'ly worth it. You think it's worth it?"

Norma went to get her purse.

Norma offered the house to Mr. Holzer, who owned the sheet-metal works next door. He acted as if fifty thousand was far too much. Frosty Blackshear kept bringing people in, many of whom knew what a hot spot the place was. It was a landmark; it would be a prank to have it. But those people never made an offer to buy it. On the street one day Norma ran into Pete Ricca, who had a demolition business and owned several pieces of property on Rampart Street. She asked him if he'd like to buy it. He offered her forty-five thousand, and Norma walked away.

She never turned another trick at 1026 Conti Street.

CHAPTER SEVENTEEN

The Discreet Mrs. Patterson

Norma hadn't had an orgasm in five or six years until she was with Wayne a few times. Then she only had to look at him—that muscular, bronze body, his wavy black hair, his deep brown eyes—and she was ready. And Wayne had been with a number of women in his nearly twenty-three years, but none of them had the know-how of this woman, the one he still thought was Mrs. Patterson. He didn't think of her as being older; he thought of her as being experienced. She knew how to touch, how to moan and groan, how to make a man feel as if he was the greatest son-of-a-bitchin lover in the world. She knew all the moves. With the younger girls, he had to make the moves, do all the work. With this woman, he sat there like a king. There was no comparison.

She moved a big, red-velvet, curved couch into her bedroom, and some days Wayne would just lie around on it, and she would stroke him, kiss him, make love to him any which way anyone could mention, name, think about, or imagine. It was nothing for him to have two or three orgasms a day. Sometimes all she had to do was touch him. He was impressed, and then some. The sex he'd been having with those other girls? The only way he knew to express it—it had been like riding a bicycle, then jumping into a Lincoln Continental.

. . .

Wayne drove a pink Nash Rambler. Every evening when he got off work at the shipyards, he drove the Rambler to Mrs. Patterson's. Then they'd go out to dinner and hit a few clubs.

One weekend night they were at Scorpio's, dancing a slow dance. Mrs. Patterson liked the slow dances; she had to be at least on the way to being drunk to do anything like the jitterbug. As they were coming off the floor, the band struck up a fast number, and a girl Wayne knew grabbed him, pulling him to the middle of the floor, where she jumped and jittered and he slid her through his legs and rolled her across his back, for which they got a loud ovation. After a few drinks Wayne got very friendly, so, as the crowd hooted and clapped, he put his arm around the girl, gave her a squeeze and, into the act, a quick kiss on the lips before he eased off the dance floor and sat at the table with Mrs. Patterson.

"That dog won't hunt, Wayne," she said.

Wayne, taking a long pull at his drink, put his glass down and said, "What does that mean?"

Mrs. Patterson leaned toward him and put her chin in her palm. "Did I ever tell you how I like to play baseball?" she asked. Wayne shook his head. "Well, I like to play ball, but when I play, I'm the pitcher, the catcher, the batter, the first base, the second base . . ."

Wayne began to laugh. "Okay, I got you, but where the hell do I come in?"

"Oh, honey," Mrs. Patterson told him, "you've got the balls."

This was true, which gave Wayne a certain amount of power with Mrs. Patterson, though he never seemed to be exercising it. Wayne would simply get caught up in whatever he was doing and let the rules of baseball slide every now and then. This would cause little ruckuses, as Wayne called them, like the night Mrs. Patterson got angry with him and chased him around the Cadillac in the parking lot at Scorpio's. She had taken her high heels off, and in her stockings she ran across the shells that covered the lot. The next morning the bottoms of her feet were cut and knotted. "It's amazing what a little Bacardi and Coke will make you do," she told Wayne as he rubbed her feet and doctored her bruises.

In those days even the fights were romantic. They made up, walked hand in hand on the levee, and rolled down its grassy slope as if they were young lovers; they made love in the backseat of the pink Rambler—the pink vagina, Mrs. Patterson called it—as if they were teenagers again. Wayne was at Mrs. Patterson's every day, and he usually spent the night so they could play a little ball. One night she said, "Why don't you just bring your clothes over and move in?" Wayne was having the time of his life, so the next day he moved in with Mrs. Patterson and her nieces, which is how Wayne had heard her introduce the girls to her neighbors. The woman who ran the neighborhood grocery store had said, rather sarcastically, "Gee, what a big family you have," and "My goodness, so many nieces—no nephews?"

There were strange goings-on, with four or five girls in the big house some nights and more over in the little house. But live and let live was the way Wayne thought. He didn't wander far from Mrs. Patterson's bedroom. She'd get up now and again, confer with the nieces, but she wasn't explaining anything, so he didn't ask any questions, and before he knew it she'd be back, setting a mood with some music and a few candles, and then his mind would be somewhere else altogether.

One night, though, Wayne went down the hall to the bathroom. He passed a room with curtained French doors. One door was slightly ajar. He heard a low moan and looked in. Illuminated by a single candle, a man and one of the nieces were going at it. Wayne tiptoed to the bathroom, and when he returned to Mrs. Patterson's room, he closed the door and said to her, "Okay, what exactly is going on around here?"

Mrs. Patterson put her finger to her lips and motioned for Wayne to go with her to a small screened porch off her bedroom. They sat in the dark and listened for a moment to the country sounds, frogs croaking, cicadas scratching, until Mrs. Patterson's near whisper came to him on the balmy breeze. "I'm not Mrs. Patterson," she said.

"Okay," Wayne said laughing, "I'll bite: Who are you?"

"I'm Norma Wallace."

Wayne's hands hung over the arms of the rocking chair he sat in. He lifted them, holding them open for a second, fingers splayed, and let them fall. "Whatever you say." He laughed again.

Norma took one of his hands. "Wayne, do you remember, a long time ago, Bubba took you to a house in the French Quarter?" Wayne's eyes were wide open, the whites nearly glowing in the dark. "A lot of pretty girls?"

"I remember."

"I ran that house." She paused, to let it sink in. "Now I'm running it here."

"Son of a gun," Wayne said calmly. And that was the beginning of a little bit of excitement, as Wayne liked to say in his understated way.

Norma kept the fact that she was running a whorehouse from the people in Waggaman as long as she could, but a few things happened that blew the lid right off the action. First the washing machine broke down. This was a critical piece of machinery in the operation, because Norma was not about to use a commercial laundry and risk the IRS counting her towels as they had Marie Bernard's. To expedite matters, Norma called Sears and charged a new washing machine to Wayne's mother's account. When Helen Bernard saw the bill, she hit the roof. Wayne tried to explain, giving her cash to pay it, but Helen demanded to know what Wayne was doing at Mrs. Patterson's. So Norma had a long visit with Helen one afternoon, after which everything calmed down. Then, when Wayne went to his parents' house, Helen would ask, "How is Mrs. Patterson?"

Finally one day Wayne said, "She's not Mrs. Patterson, Mother."

"That's all right," Helen said. "I just love Mrs. Patterson."

"Mother, she's Norma Wallace."

"Well then," Helen responded cheerfully, "I just love Norma Wallace." Wayne realized that if she even knew who Norma Wallace was, by that time she didn't care.

Once Wayne's family knew that he was living with Norma, the situation became a little looser. Wayne stopped hiding the Rambler in the back and began driving Norma's Cadillac around. But he made the mistake of driving it to work. All the men in the yard stopped working and watched as Wayne got out of the car. Then they started riding him. He told them, "I just borrowed the lady's car." They said, "You borrowed your ass!" They'd seen his pink car at Mrs. Patterson's house. They'd seen those nieces too. They got wise to the nieces, and the next thing, they wanted Wayne to make a connection for them. They bought him beers; it wouldn't cost them nothin, would it? At Norma's suggestion Wayne retired from the shipyards.

Not long after that a girl named Betty called the house and said she was Wayne's friend. She told Jackie she wanted to go to work for Norma Wallace. "That slut," Norma said and suggested that the girl was looking for trouble.

Trouble, though, was much closer to home. Wayne was feeding the horses in the stable behind the big house one afternoon when one of the girls, Cindy, a cute blonde, joined him. She didn't waste much time, only giving the time of day before she ran her hand up Wayne's thigh and said, "Norma's not home. Wanna get together?"

Wayne had no time to react, which he later considered lucky. He heard a noise at the other end of the barn, where the washing machines were. Marie, the maid, stood there looking at them. Wayne didn't know what to make of Marie. She was a pretty, light-skinned black woman with reddish hair who was very quiet. Norma had told him that men offered large sums of money to sleep with Marie but she always refused. Marie was mysterious, somewhat intimidating because of her silence. Apparently Cindy thought so too. "Maybe later," she said to Wayne and hurried back to the house. She never approached him again.

But even bigger trouble was on the horizon. Word had spread about Norma's presence in Jefferson Parish, and it had reached Sheriff Alwynn Cronvich. Bubba Rolling, who was Cronvich's chief of detectives at the time, gave Norma as much protection as he could. But one evening, just as a date's car parked at the top of the horseshoe drive, Norma spotted the men on the levee across River Road. The date was ringing the bell as Norma rounded up the girls and told Wayne to take them across the field and hide them.

"Where?" Wayne asked.

"I don't care," Norma answered, "Just go *now!*"

So off they went, streaking across the field, then through the woods toward the railroad tracks. The girls weren't exactly dressed for hiking. As they went he heard a series of staccato female tones. "Shit!" "Oh, hell!" "Damn!"

"Keep it down," Wayne told them. It only got worse.

The woods were so thick in the back that when Wayne reached the tracks, he thought it would be prudent to walk them, unless a train happened to come along.

"Please don't let a train come through here now," he repeated over and over. He turned in the direction of his parents' house and told the girls to hurry. He headed for their barn. When they got there Wayne saw that the girls were bleeding from the thorns and barbed wire. Some had shredded stockings hanging around their ankles and blood running down their legs. One girl was in shorts, and her legs looked as if Bubba's fighting cocks had been working out on them. Another girl was missing a shoe and trying to pick the burrs out of her foot.

They looked at each other, huddled in the barn, and they began to laugh. Wayne's father, joined by Snapbean, came out to see what was going on. He looked at them, scanned the girls' legs, and left without a word, never said a word to Wayne about it either. He just thought the world of Mrs. Patterson or Norma Wallace or whatever she wanted to call herself.

"Where's Mrs. Patterson?" Snapbean wanted to know. He'd called her that for so long that he was having trouble remembering her name was Norma. He loved her too. Wayne's father came back and had to drag Snapbean off with him. For a minute Snapbean thought it was his lucky day.

After that first brush with Alwynn Cronvich's deputies, in early fall of 1963, Norma shut things down for a while and decided that she and Wayne should take a trip to Mexico.

When Norma's hairdressers, Francis Davis and Janice Roussel, first heard that Norma had been seen running around with someone in blue jeans, they were astounded. "Not Norma!" they said. McCoy had always been so well dressed, nothing but the best—raw-silk suits, custom-made shirts, Italian loafers of snakeskin and alligator.

"Oh no," Norma told them, "I spent my money dressing the others, but I'm not dressing this baby."

She may have meant what she said, but her good intentions fell by the wayside early on—the first outfit she bought Wayne was a red jumpsuit made out of a stretchy material that fit him like a second skin. But Wayne wasn't a jumpsuit sort of guy. He put it on, took it off immediately, and was back in his blue jeans.

The trip to Mexico called for another shopping excursion. Norma bought Wayne several suits and herself a wardrobe of dresses, nothing casual—they were going to be dressed to kill the entire trip. One of the dresses was sequined, a long, tight tube of a dress that looked as if it were made of thousands of tiny opals and must have weighed ten pounds. Wayne thought Norma looked quite sharp in that dress.

Their first stop was Mexico City. Norma wore her sequined gown, Wayne a classy continental-cut suit, and they went to dinner at the restaurant of the hotel where they were staying. They were shown to a table near the mariachi band. Norma, as usual, sat so she was facing out, with a view of the room. Wayne faced her; the only view he had was the scenery outside the windows. She had on dark glasses, which she wore all the time now, day and night.

Wayne studied the menu, looking for the biggest steak on it. He looked up to see Norma with a seductive smile on her face, her head tilted, flirting—not with him but with someone behind him. He looked over his shoulder. The castanet player winked at Norma.

"What the hell is going on?" Wayne asked her. Norma's face broke into a big smile. "You ought to be ashamed of yourself," he said, but she wasn't. She'd wanted to see how he would react, and she liked his reaction. Wayne went back to reading the menu.

After Mexico City they went to Acapulco, where they stayed at the Hilton Hotel, famous for its cliff divers. Their first night they dressed up again, Norma ultraglamorous in her opalescent gown and dark glasses, Wayne sharp in an Italian suit, and went out to have drinks by the pool. It was getting late and people started going in for dinner, but Norma and Wayne stayed to watch the stars come out. Hand in hand they walked to where they had a view of the cliffs in the moonlight. As they were coming around the pool, Wayne stepped in front of Norma, dropping her hand. He heard a splash behind him. Norma had walked right into the deep end of the pool!

Wayne knew she hated water and couldn't swim. And he figured she sure as hell couldn't swim with that dress on. He was ready to jump in after her when she shot to the surface like a geyser, her dress sparkling in the underwater lights. He lifted her out, and she didn't have her feet on the ground before she was laughing. Then Wayne laughed. They got hysterical. Two waiters on the other side of the pool stopped gawking and started laughing. Norma called them over. "Get my purse out of there, will you?" She pointed to a little beaded bag at the bottom. The waiters scooped it up in a net. Norma opened it to give them a tip, and Wayne saw rolls of hundred-dollar bills. Norma had five thousand wet dollars in her purse.

The next day they went shopping again and bought all casual clothes. They stayed in Acapulco, eating, drinking, walking, and making love on the beach until the money dried out, whereupon they spent every dollar of it.

Back in Waggaman, the dates started coming up the horseshoe drive again, and Sheriff Cronvich's men spied from the levee. One evening Norma saw them coming down the slope onto her property. Wayne wasn't home, so she led the girls herself out to the railroad tracks. Again their clothes caught and ripped, thorns flayed their skin. Rose Mary said, "Goddamn, Norma, there went the heel of my shoe."

"Shut up and keep running," Norma told her.

"Oh, this is great, just great. Then what? I'll spend the rest of the night opening the door with twigs in my hair?"

"Would you rather be in jail?"

"I would. I'd rather be in jail than out here getting run down by a train. As long as you and I are in different cells."

"You'd have made a great actress, Rose Mary."

"Yeah, I'd be right up there with you. You have more faces than Eve. Where the hell are we going, anyway?"

"To Bubba's."

"Oh great. That's just great, a bunch of whores hiding out at the chief of detectives' house."

"What the hell, Rose Mary? Who'd think of looking there?"

In April 1964 Bubba Rolling had an automobile accident that blinded him in one eye, left him with a limp, and forced his retirement from the sheriff's office. He told Norma that he wouldn't be able to give her protection anymore. He told her to shut it down tight.

Norma listened to her friend. It seemed that times had changed, that the tolerance of the last four decades was at an end, not so much because corruption was on the wane but because busting prostitutes was an easy way to get headlines, concrete proof that a sheriff or DA was doing his job.

Norma needed to find a way to square up for good. She decided to turn her house into a restaurant, and Norma Wallace, maven of the demimonde, went legit.

CHAPTER EIGHTEEN

Tchoupitoulas

Norma chose Tchoupitoulas Plantation Restaurant as the name for her new establishment. It was of no consequence to her that the original name of her property was Cedar Grove Plantation and that the original Tchoupitoulas Plantation was on the other side of the river. She loved the sound of the Indian word, loved that it meant "big water." She also believed people would remember it by the name and be sure to come again.

She and Wayne moved to the smaller house on the property, and Norma began to plan her menu and amass collectibles—copper pots and kettles to hang around the brick fireplace, lanterns for the bar, crystal and silver objects for the mantels. She bought comfortable captain's chairs and, for the first time, retained a linen service. She spent a small fortune on salt and pepper shakers that looked like cut crystal and cost thirty dollars a pair. Wayne planted more azaleas and camellias, a wisteria vine at one corner of the front porch, and painted the buildings. He erected a rustic cypress sign with the name of the restaurant branded into the wood, along with "Built 1812" and hung it in a black iron wagon wheel. Norma bought a flock of peacocks to roam the property.

Norma had in mind a small operation: hire a good chef, serve just one thing—great steaks—and come up with a signature drink. She and

Wayne concocted what Norma called the Southern Belle—gin, rum, brandy, lemon juice, orange juice, and passion fruit. After their experiments to get the perfect mix, they could attest to the fact that the Southern Belle was every bit as potent as Pat O'Brien's Hurricanes.

But when her friends found out what she was up to they said, "Norma, do you think men will risk taking their wives or girlfriends to your restaurant? You'll take an awful beating."

Norma didn't want her notoriety to hurt the place's chance for success, so she hired Ray Dulude, veteran restaurateur, and put him in charge. Then she decided it would be his restaurant; she would collect rent. She was thinking that she and Wayne had had such a wonderful time in Mexico, why not Europe? She made no plans, though, waiting to make sure that Ray was off to a good start.

But a month went by, and he wasn't making it very well at all. Norma's friends from her former life—like Dolores, one of her girls who'd married a state trooper, and Duke Dugas, a fence and the only man Norma had ever allowed her girls to roll—came to support her. Pershing Gervais arrived, larger than life, with his big appetite, but he wanted a free meal. Mac sent Norma a check for twenty-four hundred dollars along with a note, "The Marines have landed," but she was going to lose her entire twenty-thousand-dollar investment if she didn't do something soon.

Elmo came up with an advertising scheme. Over the years he'd had some big ideas to promote his lounges. Once he advertised free gumbo at the Gold Room, but just as the promotion was drawing people in, the cook failed to show. Panicked, he ran to the corner and asked the newspaper lady if she could fill in. She was glad to do it, and the gumbo acquired a new ingredient—the rubber bands from her newspapers. After that Elmo decided to stay clear of food altogether. When he needed to attract customers at the Moulin Rouge on Bourbon Street, he came up with quite a gimmick. Everyone else had gorgeous showgirls dancing at their bars; Elmo hired obese women. The only problem was that he hadn't considered that three- and four-hundred-pound women would need a lot to eat to keep up their energy.

Norma was skeptical, but Elmo insisted, so she ran a newspaper ad. But it only attracted one couple, a Singer sewing machine salesman and his wife. Norma gave them a free meal.

Norma thought good food and word of mouth were the best ways to get people in. She went to a nearby golf club and told a few men there, "Come on out to Tchoupitoulas. It's beautiful." And then she found herself saying, "It's my place." The next Saturday night they came in droves.

Norma's small operation turned into a large operation fast, and after only a couple of months she invested another thirty thousand dollars to rebuild the kitchen. The first three months, though, she could have been serving greasy-spoon hash. She'd hired an experienced steak chef, and the food was delicious, but her patrons were coming for an entirely different reason. The women wanted to see what a real madam looked like; they wanted to know about her life, the kind of place she'd kept. And the men, many of them former customers at Conti Street, brought their wives to introduce them to Norma. She, of course, continued in the tradition of discretion, though she decided to hang the paintings of the nudes that she'd kept from Conti Street. She put them all in one room, her former bedroom, which she painted Chinese red and called the Art Room. As she'd expected, it became the most popular room in the house.

One night a lady whose picture appeared frequently on the society page came with her husband, one of the Good Men, and another couple. The man called Norma over to introduce her to his wife. The woman began to drink Southern Belles, and after she'd been hitting them for a while, she started asking Norma what was going on upstairs. When Norma went into the restaurant business, she'd told her girls to stay away, to forget her and she'd forget them, but she couldn't convince this woman that no whores were upstairs screwing the customers between courses. Finally, she took the woman on a tour, showing her the upstairs rooms, which she used to store linens and tableware. Miss High Society was terribly disappointed. She said, "Ah, Norma, you've taken away all the glamour." Norma was insulted; she thought that Tchoupitoulas was very glamorous. Later one of the waiters told her he'd seen the woman pocket of pair of salt and pepper shakers on her way out. Norma sent her a bill for sixty dollars, twice what they cost. She received a check and a note of apology, as well as the woman's gratitude that Norma hadn't embarrassed her in front of her friends. When a lawyer, a former client who had always been slow to pay, stole a pair of the shakers, Norma got so angry that she decided to give them away to her friends as souvenirs rather than have them lifted.

Norma had changed the telephone number and, to avoid suspicion, she hired no waitresses, only black waiters, but people continued to ask her if she was turning tricks at Tchoupitoulas. "I'll take a lie detector test," she told them.

But no one, including Sheriff Cronvich, seemed convinced that only food and drink were on the menu at Tchoupitoulas. One night the sheriff's men stormed the restaurant just before closing, all wearing black turtlenecks and packing guns. Wayne was at the front cash register. Under the counter he had a .357 Magnum, which he nearly used on what he thought was a band of robbers. A few weeks later Norma heard from a woman that Cronvich had propositioned a relative of hers to try to get Norma. "Honey," Norma told her, "I was propositioned straight to Parish Prison. Joe Giarrusso took care of that. When he was made superintendent of police, he saw to it that was the end of me."

One night another of the Good Men came in. He put a hundred-dollar bill on the bar and asked Norma to get him a girl. The old temptation rose in her like a fever, but she forced herself to say, "No, darlin, I'm sorry, I'm finished in that business," and she walked away.

But Norma couldn't turn down an old friend, a judge, when he asked if he could use the little house. He was meeting his young girlfriend. Norma reluctantly gave him the keys and told him to use the guest room. When he tried to leave a couple of hours later, his Cadillac wouldn't start. Norma asked Wayne to give him a push. Wayne pulled his pickup truck behind the Cadillac and pushed the judge out to River Road. Then he put the pedal to the metal. The judge was frantically waving out the window for Wayne to slow down, but not for long—he had to keep both hands on the wheel. Wayne laughed all the way to the gas station, and the judge never asked Norma for a favor again.

Within the next month business exploded at the restaurant. The new kitchen wasn't quite finished, and one night the orders got so backed up that Norma had to go out to the dining room and apologize for the long wait. She told everyone that drinks and dinner were on the house that night. It cost her a couple of thousand dollars, but almost everyone there became a regular customer. Norma started booking reservations, three and four hundred people for lunch alone. She hired Elise Rolling to keep her books and fill in as bartender. She immediately began expanding the kitchen, and Wayne, with the help of his handyman, Dutz Stouffert, built a new bar. In another six months they needed more tables. Wayne and Dutz enclosed the front porch.

The hours were long and the work relentless. Wayne dug out the old septic tanks and put in bigger ones. He laid a larger patio and made a fountain out of an old iron sugarcane pot. In the middle of the patio and in front of the fountain he also laid two small brass plaques that read, NORMA BADON, 10-24-64. He maintained the ten acres, kept the buildings repaired and painted, came in to work the lunch crowd, and went on into the night, everything from bartending and cashiering to parking cars.

Norma handled the money, did all of the ordering, and took care of the personnel. She told Wayne, "The only bad thing about the restaurant business is you have to buy the stuff and have it here. The whorehouse business, you don't have to have anything but a few tail towels around."

The personnel were always calling to say they couldn't come in, and Norma would have to get on the phone for substitutes. And she knew the help stole things too. One time she saw her day chef, who was also a preacher, coming out of the kitchen looking as if he'd gained thirty-five or forty pounds. She put her arm around him; he'd packed steaks all over his body. Norma's anger became legend after that. She cursed him in front of all the help. "Lawrence Jacobs," she yelled at him, "I pay you well and you treat me like this? All you had to say is you wanted some steaks, I'd have given them to you. A god-damn preacher," she said with disgust. "I never did like that you were a preacher." Jacobs was on his knees begging. Norma didn't fire him; she made him go home and pray over it for a week while the night chef took double shifts.

The help's stealing wasn't new to Norma. She'd once told Wayne, "I know Jackie slips a little extra in her pocket, but here are you and me, we're out on the town, and I know everything's going all right. So if she takes an extra fifty or a hundred, what the hell?"

Norma was easygoing unless things weren't going her way, and Wayne was hardly immune from her rages. She bawled him out after he mixed a gallon of Southern Belles one morning and spilled it all over the electrical panel, shorting out the entire restaurant. She got angry with him one day while they were still at the little house and threw a huge brass ashtray at him so hard it stuck in the side of a French door.

Norma was too busy for anyone to contest the orders she gave. But her young lover just let her rages slide off him. He didn't protest when he signed his paychecks over to Norma or that he didn't have his own checking account. He just went along with the flow, doing his work, doing whatever came naturally. And that, as it turned out, was the rub.

When people found out who Norma was, they'd stay at the bar and drink with her until as late as three in the morning. Even if they knew her, they'd stick around to hear her stories. People were drawn to her; Norma never met a stranger. Wayne, admiring Norma and giving her all the credit for making the restaurant what it was, watched her dress up every night and welcome people—every night in a different fabulous outfit, with her diamond rings and her stories. She was the center of attention, and she loved it.

But what she couldn't abide was the attention Wayne got from other women. When she saw a woman talking to him at the bar, it would drive her into a frenzy. Wayne would ask, "What am I supposed to do, Norma? Turn my head on a customer? Not talk? We can't run a business like that."

Norma considered this reasonable, but it didn't help. She decided that she and Wayne should get married. She told him that her lawyer suggested it would ease their tax situation. But she needed no excuse; Wayne was happy to marry Norma.

They applied for the marriage license, and the next time Norma went to the Davis Beauty Salon, she announced that she was going to take the leap again. She glibly told Franky, "I've married so many. It can't be all of them; it must be me." She took the responsibility for her marriages, then tossed it off. This time, of course, things would be different.

Norma and Wayne were married on February 18, 1965. The honeymoon lasted a few months. Big Mo came to dinner at Tchoupitoulas often. Bubba and Elise joined in, and they would reminisce late into the night. Phil Harris heard about Norma's venture and arrived with Alice Faye, his daughter, Alice, and his mother. As always when Phil Harris was around, there was a lot of laughter. Alice Faye and Norma found they had a love of animals in common. And Norma was proud to show off her handsome young husband.

It was always a memorable evening when Norma's former lovers, male friends, and ex-husbands came to Tchoupitoulas. But it was a different matter when the visitors were women who'd known Wayne before Norma.

The Hamiltons had once lived in the house that was now a well-known restaurant. Elise knew them and was delighted they'd stopped by. She introduced them to Norma and told her, to their daughter's embarrassment, that Wayne and Jeanie had once had a little puppy love—they couldn't have been more than twelve—they were so cute, holding hands and gazing at each other.

Jeanie was all grown up now and quite a dish at that. Norma excused herself to find Wayne. She flew to the back, where he was behind the bar, and threw him the keys to the car. "Hurry, Wayne. We're running out of French bread. Get five or six loaves. I don't care where you have to go to get them." She hustled him out the back door.

Later his aunt asked him if he'd seen the Hamiltons. I'll be damned, he thought. He would have loved to have seen the Hamiltons, but he didn't like to rock the boat, so he never said a word.

Norma and Wayne started looking for a getaway place in Mississippi. They found some beautiful land near Poplarville—rolling hills, pines and hardwoods, good pastureland too. Norma bought seventy-five acres, all in her name. When the property next door went up for sale, she bought another hundred and five acres. Wayne began building a house, moving a trailer onto the land so they had a place to stay. Whenever they could, they took a couple of days off from the restaurant and went to Mississippi.

Progress on their Poplarville house was slow and stopped for a while when Elmo got sick—complications from the tuberculosis. He stayed at the little house with Wayne and Norma for several months. His wife, Sarah, faithfully came every day with food she'd cooked especially for Elmo, and she continued to maintain his downtown lounge, though Elmo had hired a manager by that time. He stayed at Tchoupitoulas to recuperate so he could see both his wife and his mistress, telling Sarah that he didn't want to contaminate their house. Sarah, naïve or happy to be on her own or averse to confrontation, never questioned any of Elmo's actions. Elmo's mistresses came and went, but he stayed married to Sarah. As long as he did, Norma considered Sarah family, and she was generous with her sister-in-law, giving her jewelry and other gifts. Eventually Elmo went home, his illness continuing its progress until he was too weak to care about mistresses.

Norma wore the diamond rings that Andy Wallace and Golfbag Sam had given her every night in the restaurant. If a waiter dropped a tray or anything crashed in the kitchen, she'd go out to the dining room and tell her patrons, "That was one of my diamond rings. It fell off my finger."

The patrons loved it, but Bubba Rolling, a cop to his core, told Norma she shouldn't wear those rings. "One night," he said, "somebody's going to be waiting for you, girl."

"I don't have these rings so they can sit in a box, Bubba." Norma was used to putting on seventy thousand dollars' worth of jewelry and walking over to Bourbon Street to have a drink at Dan's International.

One evening in 1967 she donned an apron and rubber gloves and performed the ritual she ended every evening with—cleaning the stoves and wiping down the hoods, making sure her establishment was spotless. When she finished she walked over to the little house. She could see Wayne walking to the front to close the gates.

When Norma entered the little house, her dog Rusty greeted her, along with two men wearing ski masks and holding guns. They demanded the diamond rings. A gun aimed at her nose, Norma began twisting first one ring then the other, but she hadn't removed them for so long that she couldn't get them off. She told the robbers that.

"Take them off or we'll cut off your fingers," one of them responded.

Norma frantically worked the rings, but not quickly enough. The robber who'd done all the talking produced a pair of metal snips. Norma was horrified. "Please," she said, weak with horror as he grabbed her hand roughly. He cut both rings off, and Norma felt her fingers to make sure they were still there.

She heard the screen door to the house opening and wheeled around, but Wayne had seen the bandits before Norma could open her mouth. Quick as a gazelle, he jumped the fence and ran to Bubba's house.

It sounded to Bubba as if someone was trying to beat his door down. He limped to it as fast as he could. One word from Wayne and Bubba threw him a huge Magnum shotgun, scooping up another for himself, and the two men went back to the little house.

The robbers were gone, but Bubba went out front and ducked behind some bushes. He saw a car make four passes in front of the property, and he knew that the robbers were still on it. He looked over at the thick canes growing on the property line and he waited.

Three cars and six deputies arrived within minutes. Bubba told them that if they searched in the canes, they'd find the men. But no one took any initiative; Bubba watched them looking at each other until in exasperation he said, "I'll go in the canes. You cover me."

He entered the thick growth, breaking through it, steeled for a gun blast, at a serious disadvantage because of all the noise he was making. He looked out for his backup. Hell and be damned if they weren't all walking, the six of them, over to the restaurant! He couldn't yell out to them; he couldn't run because of his leg; all he could do was abandon the canes and go after the deputies at his snail's pace and risk losing the robbers.

Bubba was so angry that he lay in bed that night nearly crying with frustration and rage. "Going to get coffee! I'd fire every last one of 'em if they worked for me," he told Elise. The next morning he told Wayne to look in the canes and see what he could find. Wayne found parts to his guns, Confederate money they'd taken from the house, more than enough to indicate that Bubba had been right and the bandits had probably spent three or four hours in the canes before they could come out. They'd also been in the little house for quite some time before Norma walked in on them, because all of Wayne's guns had been taken apart and everything had been rifled. But apparently it was only Norma's rings they were interested in; they left other pieces of jewelry untouched and didn't take any of the guns.

Wayne could see that some of the fire had gone out of Norma, that the robbery had knocked off some of her spunk; she simply wasn't her same brazen little self any longer.

CHAPTER NINETEEN

Striking Out

After the robbery Wayne and Norma began spending more time in Poplarville as Wayne continued working on their house. The cypress he used came from Pershing Gervais's house near the Fair Grounds in New Orleans after a hurricane hit the city.

Gervais had bought the house because it had a view of the racetrack from the upstairs windows. Through his binoculars he watched the races and made book. In a test of nerves and timing, he waited to see which horse won, then took bets from New York and California before the results were official.

The hurricane blew the roof off Gervais's house and landed it on his neighbor's, closing down another of his scams. The damage was extensive enough that he decided to tear the house down instead of repair it. Wayne, Snapbean, and Dutz Stouffert signed on for the job, and Norma paid Gervais for the lumber they hauled away.

Norma wanted a huge fireplace in the country. So on one trip Wayne loaded their station wagon with bricks, and he and Norma set off for Poplarville after a busy weekend at the restaurant. On the way they had three flat tires. After the third, as they waited for help, Norma said, "If people could only see me now." She had not yet abandoned her role as proprietor of a famous restaurant, but already she was uncomfortable with country life.

Nevertheless, as she had once before, Norma gave up her working life for a move to the country. In 1968 her brother Elmo died, which removed the last obstacle to a decision to sell Tchoupitoulas and move to Mississippi. The restaurant sold quickly. Norma and Wayne moved into their nearly finished country house, and Marie, Norma's faithful maid of many years, moved into the trailer.

The land was incredibly isolated, much deeper in the woods than Norma's Pearl River farm had been. This property was two and a half miles off the main highway, the road to it a long twist of gravel that took a good fifteen minutes to negotiate. And it was more isolated from family and friends, nearly a three-hour drive to New Orleans.

At the beginning, though, isolation was an ideal, not an issue. Wayne loved the land and took his time finishing the house, then building four barns and fencing part of the property. He liked the slower pace and gave little thought to the lucrative business he and Norma had left behind. Norma named the place Waynewood and, relieved of the long hours at the restaurant, and of having to keep an eye on the impression her handsome young husband made on other women, she decorated the house and catered to him and their occasional guests. She gave up thoughts of travel; she had everything she wanted right at home. At night she and the man she called the greatest love of her life would sip wine in front of the fire, and, at one word from Wayne, Norma would reminisce about her scandalous past. They made love on the contour sofa and the big bearskin rug in front of the fireplace.

The green-eyed monster was not dead, though. One afternoon Mr. Ard, who had taken care of the property when Norma and Wayne traveled between New Orleans and Poplarville, arrived in his pickup truck filled with his numerous daughters, all leggy, long-haired beauties wearing short shorts and halters. Norma had Wayne in the car before he knew what was happening. She waved to Mr. Ard, calling from the car window that they had an appointment and were late, and she took Wayne to lunch at a popular Poplarville eatery, where she sat him with his back to the restaurant.

Other small incidents began to erode the good life in Poplarville. One night the woman in the ticket booth at the movie theater told Norma she had a good-looking son. Furious, Norma informed the "hussy" that Wayne was her husband. They left without buying tickets. But the locals became curious about this older woman with the young man, and Norma's reputation followed her into the woods. The Poplarville constabulary made a surprise visit on a weekend evening, apparently expecting to find a prostitution operation in full swing.

Norma thought it would be fun to spend a little more time in New Orleans. But the French Quarter was no longer the same, and she had been away for several years, too long to have changed with it. She felt somewhat an outsider as she and Wayne sat in Jackson Square surrounded by long-haired hippies or walked down Bourbon Street, which was full of cheap dives instead of the nightclubs she remembered. So many of the old places were gone—Dan's International, Gaspar's—and Pete's had already changed hands a couple of times (it was a gay bar one day, a screaming rock 'n' roll club the next). Instead of the Chinese café across the street from Pete's or the tailor, there was now a tourist attraction, the Wax Museum. Otherwise, the whole neighborhood seemed rotten with age, terra-cotta and pastel stucco falling away to reveal crumbling red brick underneath. Time, heat, and humidity had touched many of the buildings with decay, not the prototypical elegant decay of New Orleans but the result of neglect. The house on Conti Street was no exception. The third-floor gallery was gone, the side wall was beginning to bow, the marble steps to the entrance were chipped and covered with a film of urban grime. The fluted columns flanking the door were rotting, and, between the columns, the fancy scrolled ironwork of the gate was all rust and peeling paint. The house had the sad and weary look of an aging courtesan.

Bubba and Elise Rolling visited Norma and Wayne for the weekend as often as they could—Bubba liked to get in some deer hunting.

Bubba was always joking about something, but on one visit he told Norma (in all seriousness) that she shouldn't let Pershing Gervais come around—he'd heard there was a contract out on him. Norma laughed it off, so later Bubba told Wayne, "If Pershing's here and you hear a car on the road to the house, hit the woods running and don't stop—they'll kill everyone in sight."

It seemed that the volatile Gervais, with his appetites for money, women, lies, and vengeance, had been "playing results," as he liked to call his system of operating, and gotten himself into big trouble.

Gervais had quit as the district attorney's chief investigator when Jim Garrison started his probe into the Kennedy assassination. He went around telling people that Garrison had "gone off half-crocked over the Kennedy thing," and the old army buddies had an irreparable falling out.

Several years later Gervais found he was in trouble with the Internal Revenue Service, and to bail himself out he told the feds that Garrison had been taking bribes from the amusement company operators for years to protect illegal pinball gambling. As a result Garrison was indicted for bribery and the pinball operators for bribery conspiracy, illegal gambling, and obstruction of justice. Since Gervais was the chief witness for the government, Bubba reasoned that any number of people would have been glad to take him out.

But Gervais never visited Poplarville again. Instead he called one day; Norma and Wayne left immediately for New Orleans. They drove directly to a seedy motel in East New Orleans, where Norma and Gervais had a private confab. That was the last time Wayne saw Pershing Gervais.

On the way back to Poplarville, Wayne asked Norma what was going on. She said, "It's better that you know nothing about this business. I don't want you to be involved." She told him she was protecting him by keeping him in the dark.

It may have sounded romantic to Norma when Golfbag Sam told her that thirty years earlier, but for Wayne it was old news: Norma didn't want him involved in her business, legitimate or illegitimate. Pershing Gervais disappeared—into a witness protection program, as it turned out. And Wayne began to feel that he had been put away too. But the closer Norma tried to keep him, the further he slipped away.

.　　.　　.

In 1972 the journalist Clint Bolton went to Poplarville to write a story on Norma for *New Orleans* magazine. The two got along famously, Norma saying that Bolton was "her kind of man," one who liked to laugh and tell stories late into the night as he knocked back a few drinks. Norma told her stories to Bolton—about her early life, her loves, her houses, and her restaurant. She told him about the raids on Conti Street and Freddy Soulé's big moment that sent her to jail; she could hardly disguise her glee that he was now in trouble himself. Soulé had been arrested as part of the pinball conspiracy, for bringing payoffs to Gervais intended for Garrison, taking his cut—a bagman, Norma called him. Sixty-three thousand dollars was found buried in his backyard in a pickle jar, a detail that Norma relished. Now it looked as if he would go to jail. Norma and Clint Bolton laughed about the ironies of life, and as the profile took shape, the idea came about quite naturally that it should be turned into a book. At the end of the article, in a brazen "Epilogue," Norma promised that "if the truth will make you clean, I'll come clean . . . all the way." She added, "I don't want to be bothered with judges, juries, lawsuits, and all that. But if that does happen, I won't take the Fifth, and a lot of people had better stand back."

The article itself prompted letters to the editor, some irate, condemning its reportage of immoral practices as inappropriate subject matter for a magazine of high caliber. Yet when Norma was invited to the Press Club on August 12, 1972, to speak and be presented with a key to the city, people flocked for the ex-madam's autograph.

In line to see Norma were many of her former clients. One of them, a lawyer who had gone to her house when he was a Tulane student, brought his new wife to see Norma, never thinking for a minute that this infamous woman would remember him. He stepped up to the table with a copy of *New Orleans* for her signature. He didn't see her eyes meet his from behind her dark glasses. "Hello, Waterproof," she said, taking the magazine and scrawling her name across her photograph on the cover. The lawyer was astonished. "Oh, I remember you," she went on, as if to say, "I remember everybody." Rumors spread about her black book; the whole city enjoyed speculation about who would be named in Norma's autobiography.

At seventy-one years of age, Norma was still powerful, a woman to be reckoned with. It was an exciting time for her. Because of the magazine profile, she heard from people she hadn't talked to in years, and she got in touch with old associates from out of town. She mailed a copy of the magazine to J.G. and Helen Badon, her half brother and his wife, and she decided to send one to their son, Johnny, and his wife, Pat. It was clear from the letter she wrote to the young couple that she was afraid the life she'd led might cause them embarrassment. After so many years she was still worried about what people, especially the progeny of her father's respectable family, thought of her.

Respectability be damned, though; she attacked her memoirs with energy. She began to tape her stories, but a peculiar thing happened: Norma found that her habit of reticence was too deeply ingrained; she couldn't name the names she'd promised in Clint Bolton's article. Her soul, as she'd told Joe Giarrusso so many years ago, was the soul of discretion. She had a code—a code of honor, a moral code—and she could not violate it.

Nevertheless, Norma continued taping her life story, talking into the recorder as she sat on the contour sofa in her living room in Poplarville; Bolton, in his French Quarter apartment, listened to the tapes and started writing the book. Tantalizing references to Norma's autobiography appeared in the newspapers' gossip and society columns. But only three chapters into the book, Bolton had a serious heart attack. He returned Norma's papers to her in Poplarville.

Norma stopped taping for a while and searched for a new writer. After interviewing two from New York, she decided she wanted a New Orleanian to write her story and chose a young woman who wrote for *The Times-Picayune*, Patsy Sims. She gave Patsy a copy of the New York madam Polly Adler's best-seller, *A House Is Not a Home*, and told her that was the kind of book she wanted Patsy to help her write. But Patsy was offered a job in Pennsylvania and decided to take it. Norma began to be frustrated.

Wayne had watched Norma put her lipstick on hundreds of times. She carefully applied it outside her lip line to make her lips appear fuller. Teasing her one night as they prepared to go out, Wayne said, "You missed your lips." Norma lit into him with the ferocity of a trapped viper. The making-up part, which she had always said made the fight worth it, often got eliminated these days: Their sex life, after ten years, had slowed markedly.

Yet Norma's jealousy remained unabated. Her sister-in-law, Sarah Huff, who had remarried after Elmo's death, visited Poplarville one weekend with her pretty young niece, Linda. Wayne and Linda made eye contact once too often, and Norma berated Sarah for having the nerve to bring Linda with her, not caring that Wayne and Linda could both hear her.

Wayne let it all slide off him, as was his habit, but he wasn't quite as imperturbable as he'd once been. He too was without work, having finished the fence and the barns. He would be out in the pasture or tending to the animals, all this beautiful country around him, the rolling hills and far-reaching vistas, a place he loved, yet in all this open air he felt as if he was suffocating.

Wayne decided to take a job. Eddie, a contractor friend of his, needed help with some construction on the Gulf Coast. The site was close enough that Wayne could drive from Poplarville and be home at a reasonable hour. Norma didn't want him to take the job, but Wayne overrode her, for the first time. "I need something, Norma," he told her. "I need something to do."

At first Wayne came home, extremely tired, watched a little TV, and went to bed. Then one night Eddie suggested that they stop for a drink on the way home. Eddie was about Wayne's age. They sat at a bar and talked. It was the first time Wayne had talked about football in he didn't know how long; Norma had no idea what a football game was. Another night they went to a juke joint, and Wayne realized he'd never heard some of the great music from the sixties and seventies. Eddie couldn't believe it; he had to tell Wayne about the Beatles and the Rolling Stones.

Wayne began to get the feeling that his life was passing him by. All he was doing was reliving Norma's life with her. He kept going to the bars and juke joints with Eddie. He started noticing the younger girls. He looked around and saw what other young people were doing, going to the races, dances, football games—the things young people do. All he did when he got home was watch TV and go to bed. Norma was there, but he'd already started asking himself where that was going to get him. He was tired of sitting with his back to the restaurant. He was tired of Norma's anger if he wanted to go out alone or if he as much as looked at someone female. He was tired of being left out of the big decisions. Norma hadn't bothered to ask him if he wanted to give up the restaurant. Or if he wanted his paychecks, five hundred and sixty dollars a week, which he'd turned right back over to her. But he had his own money now, and there was nothing Norma could do about it. He knew he was making her very unhappy, but there was nothing *he* could do about *that*. He needed something, all right; he needed something besides Norma.

That year, 1973, Norma and Wayne went to Bubba and Nan Ease's house for Thanksgiving dinner. Bubba's limp had become more pronounced because of the arthritis he'd developed. Norma said to Nan Ease, "Look at him."

"Don't worry, girl," Bubba said, "one of these days, you'll be limping too."

"Oh no, Bubba," Norma told him, "you'll never see this old whore limp." Then she added darkly, "You'll never see this whore get old."

At first Wayne thought that he had no sexual feelings for other women. He was so used to Norma's touch that he could hardly get aroused with anyone else. But women kept finding Wayne, and he started going to bed with them. And some nights he didn't make it back to Poplarville.

Norma cried. "Why, Wayne? What went wrong?"

Wayne didn't know how to articulate what had gone wrong. He felt terrible that he was hurting Norma so badly, but something pulled at him, something that made the guilt seem small and inconsequential, maybe even necessary if he was to move on with his life. He told Norma he didn't know what had gone wrong, but she demanded an answer. Finally he said, "We're just not compatible, that's all."

That was when she told him that if he married a younger woman and had a bunch of kids, he'd have to work like a dog until he was sixty. He just shrugged. "You always knew this couldn't last forever, Norma."

He couldn't look at the pain on her face. But in a clear voice she said, "I told you if you weren't happy and you wanted to leave, there'd be no hard feelings. I meant that, Wayne."

He held her and they made love that night and Wayne wasn't so sure he wanted to leave at all.

Wayne was working a construction job near Franklinton, Louisiana. At noon he stopped at a convenience store in town to get some lunch. He got in line to buy his sandwich but found himself fumbling with his money when he got up to the counter. The girl holding her hand out for his change was a good-looking petite blonde with very short hair that gave her a gamine look. She had on a halter and a pair of cutoffs. She hardly gave him a glance as she took his money. Wayne was intrigued.

Thereafter he stopped at the store as often as possible, trying not to go until the breakfast crowd had dwindled or the noon rush was over. Her name was Jean. They spent a few weeks talking to each other in the store. He liked her voice, a little throaty—sexy. He liked her coolness; she wasn't all over him. She was seven years younger than he was, recently divorced, and had two little boys. He thought that was fine too.

It wasn't easy telling Jean about his marriage and how unhappy he was. He explained that Norma was older, that she'd told him if he wanted to leave there would be no hard feelings. Jean seemed to be able to deal with it. She and Wayne started going out together.

Early 1974 found Norma in a downward spiral. Her health was good, but she was surviving many of her friends. Elmo had been gone six years now; Pete Herman had died in 1973; in May 1974, J.G. died. Wayne went to the funeral with Norma, but his mood was dark and edgy. He sat out in a waiting room by himself, not even attending the service. Helen asked Norma where he was. Norma told her and added, "I need to get rid of Wayne. He's too young for me."

She'd said that cavalierly enough; she went a step further with Sarah: "Wayne needs to find himself someone younger."

"Oh, Norma," Sarah replied, "Wayne would find someone young if he wanted to. He wants to be with you."

They went back to Poplarville—Wayne going off to work; Norma, waiting, remembering, afraid. About the time Wayne met Jean in April, Marie had decided to return to New Orleans. So Norma was alone in the woods, without her confidante and companion of many years. Her closest friends, Bubba and Elise Rolling, knew little about the demise of her marriage. Elise was Wayne's aunt, and Norma, with strong feelings for family herself, did not want to put her friend in a position that might force her, if the marriage totally disintegrated, to choose.

Norma put a couple of steaks out to thaw so she could cook if Wayne came home. She got dressed in her red pantsuit that she knew he liked. She went out the back door with Rusty, her Irish setter, for their last walk of the day. They went down the path, past the barns and into the woods. Rusty, running ahead of her, began to bark fiercely. When Norma got to him she saw the diamondback rattler coiled, ready to spring.

She told Rusty to come with her, and she went back to the house. She got her .410 shotgun and took the path again, past the barns and into the woods. The snake was still there. Norma was a crack shot, and it took only one round. The snake lay headless.

But she was shaking after she killed the snake. The long night stretched ahead of her. She sat on the red-velvet sofa, listening for a car, hoping for a phone call. The twilight faded.

Norma decided to finish taping her memoirs. She pulled out the recorder with something like determination. She told the story of the suicide of Mr. McCann; then she spent the rest of the evening telling about the deaths and death scares that had happened at her houses, beginning with the man who died in flagrante at Louise Jackson's house over a half a century ago. Then she told about a wealthy man from the North who'd stayed on the third floor on Dauphine Street, his ticker so bad that he could hardly make it up the stairs, drinking himself into a stupor every night until Norma telegraphed his family and put him on a train home. She remembered another man who was under doctor's orders not to screw because his heart was so bad. He was a trick all right—he'd tricked her into letting Terry give him a blow job. When she heard a few days later that he'd died, she wondered what she would have done had he died there on Conti Street—rolled him out into the alley and waited for someone to discover him?

All she could think about was death. She put the machine away. She needed to face reality: She had no love and she had no work. She couldn't stand this any longer, not knowing when he would come home. She couldn't bear to be in the woods, so afraid, one more day. It was time to make a move.

Wayne was furious when she told him. They'd had a bitter argument about his staying out all night again, and Norma had said, "You're not leaving me alone in these damned woods." Then she told him she was going to sell the place.

"I've put my heart and soul into it, Norma," he said angrily. He loved the property, and he was hurt.

They fought some more. Norma told him how she'd followed him since he'd started working with Eddie and come home with beer on his breath. She'd disguised herself and sat in a bar in Biloxi; she'd followed him once to New Orleans and questioned the barmaids.

"Those motherfucking barmaids," she said.

Norma didn't understand how Wayne could love the property and not want to leave it when he was hardly there anymore.

"You always said I could go, Norma."

Norma didn't seem to hear him. "We'll find another piece of property that you can love. We've just got to get rid of this property. I'm telling you, Wayne," she said miserably, "I can't be out here alone."

She was just getting back at him; she knew how much he loved this land and the house he'd built. But Mississippi isn't a community property state. The property was in Norma's name, like everything else, and he'd let her do it that way. He had no one to blame but himself.

Nevertheless, he told her he wouldn't agree to sell the place unless they could make a killing, knowing full well he wouldn't get a dime out of it if she didn't want him to. But she agreed. They sat together in silence after that. To Norma selling the property was another way to control him if he dared to run around on her. She could do it to Mac, but even now no one ran around on Norma Wallace.

CHAPTER TWENTY

Obsession

These days Rose Mary Miorana ran an operation out of Kenner, a suburb of New Orleans, calling girls to meet men at a swank apartment on St. Charles Avenue. She made a living, but she had no ambition to run a large call-girl operation or have a house or be in the life in any way. She wanted, more than any-thing, to have a baby and live quietly in the suburbs. But it wasn't easy. Problems with pernicious anemia had prevented her from getting pregnant for years during her first marriage. When she met Sidney Scallan, who became her second husband, she had been praying in earnest for a child, boy or girl, ill or insane or crippled—none of that mattered. She would take care of it and devote her life to her child. God answered her prayers and delivered her a test of their sincerity: Rose Mary's baby was born with cerebral palsy.

Rose Mary, Sidney, and Sidney Jr., the baby, lived on Georgetown Drive in Kenner. Rose Mary stayed home with her baby while Sidney worked as a butcher at a nearby grocery store. They became friends with their next-door neighbors, Bill and Elaine Newton, who had four children. During the day Rose Mary and Elaine would get together and talk babies. Both brunettes, they dyed their hair blond. On weekends Bill and Sidney barbecued.

Rose Mary kept her promise to be a devoted mother. She took little Sidney to the best doctors and learned from physical therapists how to work with him; she went to her church for help raising money when he needed surgery. She knew she would spend the rest of her life caring for her son, because he would never be able to care for himself. And that was all right with Rose Mary.

But Sidney was not at ease in suburbia. He liked life in the fast lane, not the daily grind of working in the meat department and then going home to a squawling baby. Growing up, he had learned the lessons of life from the underworld characters in a rough section of Carrollton. He knew how to make money other ways than the eight-to-five shift. He had been a player in the drug world since his teens, breaking and entering when he needed money for the heroin habit he was acquiring. By the time little Sidney was born, his father had already served time in Angola for burglary.

Sidney knew he was going to let Rose Mary down one day. So when he heard through the underworld grapevine that Norma was living in Mississippi, he thought he'd surprise Rose Mary, do something nice for her. She talked about Norma a lot, about how much she missed her. He called Norma, and the following Sunday he took Rose Mary and little Sidney to the Poplarville woods.

The reunion came at a time when Norma truly needed a friend and confidante. She fell in love with little Sidney. He was bright, cheerful in spite of his painfully twisted body, and although still an infant, he already showed signs of a good sense of humor. Norma put him on the big bear rug in front of the fireplace and talked to him. The two women reminisced about Conti Street, and Norma gave Rose Mary her big black book, which she'd kept all those years, a ledger with everything—the men's names, their body marks, and the money they spent—written in code. But she told Rose Mary she was glad she was out of the business and living the life she was clearly meant to live: Norma thought motherhood had made Rose Mary more beautiful than ever.

Wayne, Rose couldn't help but notice, had hardly a word to say. He stayed outside the entire time the Scallans were there and the next time they visited as well. Rose Mary had no idea what was wrong until Norma broke down and told her everything.

Wayne came through for Norma, though, when Howard Jacobs of *The Times-Picayune* went to Poplarville to interview her in June 1974. He posed for pictures with her, playing the adoring young husband. Norma repeated some of what she had taped for her autobiography, and the two-part profile ran that summer—a provocative, thoughtful, and amusing portrait of a shrewd, powerful woman. But it held none of the excitement for Norma that the *New Orleans* magazine article had. She was moving on.

The Poplarville property sold almost immediately to a New Yorker for eight hundred dollars an acre, eight times what Norma had paid for it. Ida May Ard, the caretaker's wife, told Norma about a piece of property in the town of Bush. Norma went to see it, an acre on Dad Penton Road, a slithering cut through the woods, but not nearly as isolated as the Poplarville place. A covered patio stretched the width of the house in back and looked out on a large, fenced pasture beyond. Norma thought Wayne would like it and decided to buy it. She wrote to Wayne's mother, telling her about the house, how much it reminded her of Tchoupitoulas with its dormer windows, the banks of azalea bushes, and the oak, wild cherry, and pine trees around it. She never mentioned the shambles their marriage was in. She packed up the Poplarville house, and in September she and Wayne moved, along with the dogs, the cats, a couple of horses, and the foulmouthed parrots, to Bush, Louisiana.

Wayne moved his possessions into the house and, with Dutz Stouffert, set to work on the property. Norma wrote to Rose Mary, "Wayne will never be the same, he asked a big price for the Mississippi place but he really didn't want to sell. He is pouting with me."

She tried talking to Wayne, asking him why he thought they were so incompatible all of a sudden. And he tried to explain, telling her that he wanted to be able to go to football games, do normal things like that. Norma told him she could go to football games, he was just going to have to tell her what was going on for a while. They went to a game in Bogalusa the next weekend, and Wayne called the plays for her halfheartedly. He was moody, silent. She understood that the problem was more than incompatibility.

Norma did not know it at the time, but the move to Bush had put Wayne closer to Jean. He started staying out all night again, though he had agreed to go with Norma to the Phil Harris roast, taking place on October 17. Norma tried to keep busy. She asked Rose Mary to come see her. She called Pershing Gervais, who had returned from Canada and the witness protection program, where he'd been very unhappy, in time to recant at the pinball trial, which ensured that Jim Garrison was acquitted while the other defendants (including Freddy Soulé) went to jail. Norma was too overwrought to get any joy out of Soulé's fate. Gervais told her he would get to Bush as soon as possible. Meanwhile, Norma began to take Valium so she could sleep.

On the night of October 17, Norma dressed in a new black suit—flowing silk pants with a camisole top and a jacket. She put on her red cashmere coat with mink collar and cuffs, and she and Wayne drove into New Orleans to the Roosevelt Hotel for the testimonial dinner in honor of Phil Harris. In *The Times-Picayune* Norma had been listed as one of the celebrities attending the event, along with Bing Crosby, Louisiana Governor Edwin Edwards, and Mayor Moon Landrieu. Phil had arranged for Norma and Wayne to have a room close to his and Alice Faye's and to be seated at his table, along with the governor.

It was quite a gala affair, and everyone complimented Norma on how good she looked. After a five-course dinner the notables mounted the rostrum to roast their friend Phil Harris—but not Norma.

Then there was dancing. Norma and Wayne got out on the floor for a few numbers, but a couple of hours into that part of the evening, Phil still had not asked Norma to dance. He'd hardly looked her way the entire evening. All of a sudden Norma turned to Wayne and said, "Let's go."

Wayne thought they'd been having a good time. He asked Norma why. She wouldn't answer him. Her mouth was set in that way that told him there was no point in arguing. She did not speak to Phil before leaving but passed by the table to tell Bubba and Elise goodbye. When Bubba heard they were going home, he told them they shouldn't drive the Causeway, the twenty-four-mile bridge across Lake Pontchartrain, because the fog was so thick that night. Norma refused to hear his protests. She and Wayne left.

In the car she said, "Who the hell does he think he is?" Even though Wayne tried to get her to talk about why she was so upset, she didn't say another word all the way to Bush. But Wayne knew what the problem was: Norma liked everything with a big bang, and with Phil Harris the bang just wasn't there anymore; here was her old compadre, and he wasn't giving her a high note, and here was her young lover, her husband, slowly slipping away.

Wayne moved the trailer from Poplarville to Jean's mother's place in Franklinton, where Jean lived with her two young boys, taking only his clothes from the Bush house. He had told Jean that once he and Norma sold the place in Poplarville and he got her settled in Bush he would leave. Jean relaxed into the relationship after Wayne moved, but not for long. Norma started calling her mother's for Wayne, and every time she did Wayne was off like a shot, back to Bush. Jean noticed that he never, ever said anything against Norma. She was jealous; Wayne was telling Jean he was with her, yet he was still married to that woman, running whenever she needed him.

Then one day she and Wayne were driving in Bogalusa when Wayne blatantly began giving the eye to some girls standing on a corner. It wasn't the first time she'd caught his roving eye. Jean had a quick temper; she elbowed him hard in the stomach. "What's wrong with you?" he shouted at her.

"You son of a bitch," she told him, "you better keep your eyes on the road." From being jealous of Norma and angry with her for calling Wayne, she began to feel some sympathy.

Another night in Bogalusa, they went to a restaurant. "You sit here," Wayne said, and held a chair out for Jean. She was reading the menu when she noticed him flirting with someone at a table behind her, a very young woman sitting with two older women—her mother and aunt, Wayne told Jean later. "She can't be more than sixteen," Jean yelled. "What do you want—to get brought up on statutory?" She never let him seat her with her back to the restaurant again.

Wayne and Jean were on again, off again. When Wayne put his wandering eye on another woman once too often, Jean told him to get the trailer off her mother's property. Wayne moved it to Bogalusa, and he and Jean didn't speak for a couple of months.

Norma wrote to Rose Mary, "In our eleven years, Wayne always was a model husband but if he wants to go, go, just don't do me this way. I would have bought a house in or near New Orleans had I known this. Being here alone is rough."

In another letter she wrote Rose Mary, "If I didn't have these dogs I would take off and get an apartment in the Quarter but I can't desert them." Rose Mary came to Bush the following weekend, and Norma tried to get her to take home all the boxes still stacked in the living room. Rose Mary refused. "I want you to move to New Orleans, Norma. If I take those boxes, I'll never get you out of here." The state Norma was in, though, made another move seem impossible.

Norma didn't know that Wayne and Jean had split up. When Wayne finally told her he'd moved the trailer to Bogalusa, he let her think it was because of a job he'd taken there. But he refused to put a phone in the trailer. Norma continued to call him occasionally at Jean's mother's house, which meant she had to wait until someone could track him down and give him the message, but for once Wayne was coming and going as he pleased.

At last Norma decided to call Jean. She wanted to know if these were at least nice people; perhaps if she could talk to the young girl, it would make her feel better. But the day she called she got Marsha, Jean's younger sister, who told her Jean was at work. She got in her car and drove to the convenience store in Franklinton.

The girl Norma saw behind the counter was a nondescript blonde with her hair chopped off, in cutoff blue jeans and a tank top. How could Wayne leave her for this cheap little tart? What could this young girl possibly have that she didn't? Ah, but there was the answer—youth. Norma went home and took a Valium.

Pershing Gervais tried to be with Norma as much as he could during the week, but it was difficult for him, he told her—all the driving. And if he stayed in the house with her, they argued—two older people set in their ways. She gave him money, and he bought a small place in Sun, next to Bush, so he was nearby. Then he went into New Orleans on the weekends, when Rose Mary and Sidney came to Bush with the baby.

Wayne showed up at the house the next week, after Norma hadn't seen him for several days. She tried to talk to him, but he only said hurtful things to her. He said he wanted someone young to run through the fields with; he fabricated wild tales of group sex, three women at a time. He wanted her to shove him away. Instead she cried. For the first time since Wayne had known her, Norma looked old.

When Rose Mary arrived the next weekend and saw how many bottles of Valium were in the house, she was frightened. But Norma told her it was the only way she could sleep, repeating Wayne's nightmarish sexual adventures. Rose Mary began to hate Wayne. She tried to convince Norma to leave him behind, to move to New Orleans with her.

"I'll take care of you," Rose Mary said.

"I know you would, honey," Norma replied, "but why should you have to?"

"Because I love you. Because we're friends."

"You're an angel, you'll go straight to heaven," Norma told her, "but you have this baby to take care of. Anyway," she added, "I don't want to get too old; I don't want to be bedridden or handicapped. I want to look at least decent when I die."

Then she laughed and told Rose Mary that Wayne was styling his hair in an Afro now, which Rose got to see for herself when he stopped to pick up some more of his belongings that Saturday. Norma made fun of Wayne's hair, to his face, in front of Rose Mary and Sidney; she too could be cruel. But if it got to Wayne, she couldn't tell—he just shrugged everything off. The frustration of trying to get to him was more than she could bear. She began to feel that she would have to either kill him or die.

From one weekend to the next, Rose Mary didn't know how she would find Norma, desperate or immobile or rampaging. Sometimes she'd try to get Norma out, and Norma would despondently tell her that going out wasn't the answer. She confided that her marriage wasn't in such good shape either. Norma immediately took her to a dealer and tried to buy her a new car, so she could be independent of Sidney, but Rose Mary refused. She told Norma to keep her money for the move to New Orleans. Norma became incensed and took off in her Gran Torino with little Sidney, leaving Rose Mary stranded at the lot.

In late November a letter arrived that gave Rose Mary some hope. Norma wrote, "I hope before long I can adjust and that Afro hair bastard will be not even a memory."

Norma had been writing in a diary; now she wrote inside the front cover, "The joy of love is only for the moment, but the pain of love is forever." She cut out inspirational columns about aging and pasted them in the diary. One, an Ann Landers column called "Advice to the Unsure," read in part: "Take kindly the counsel of the years, gracefully surrendering the things of youth."

Norma tried God too, quoting Matthew's Gospel: "Again, when you pray, do not be like the hypocrites, they love to say their prayers standing up in a synagogue and at the street corners for everyone to see them. I tell you this, they have their reward already. But when you pray, go into a room by yourself, shut the door and pray to your Father who is there in a secret place, and your Father who sees what is secret will reward you."

Norma gave Rose Mary a diamond cross with a ruby at each end and wrote to her, "There is a place in heaven for you, but I worry about that as I know I won't be able to get there."

Now she wrote in her diary, "Virtue consists not in abstaining from vice, but in not desiring it."

She pasted a poem called "Saints and Sinners" in her book, and she pressed four-leaf clovers between its pages. But no advice or superstition, regret or prayer could calm the obsession that consumed Norma, body and soul.

CHAPTER TWENTY ONE

The Gun

In the early fall of 1974, Sidney Scallan stopped at a methadone clinic in New Orleans to check the action. He was taking methadone himself, but he also had a couple of bags of heroin in his pocket. A young character approached him outside the clinic and asked Sidney if he would trade a bag of heroin for a .38 caliber pistol that belonged to his father. He had the pistol on him. Sidney looked at it, liked its heft, and the exchange was made.

About a month later Pershing Gervais called—he had some new results to play. He asked Sidney to meet him at a restaurant off Veterans Highway in Metairie. Gervais ordered a couple of steaks. As they ate he told Sidney that he had a friend who wanted someone eliminated, an out-of-state job, and was willing to pay five thousand dollars.

"That could be done," Sidney said, "but it would cost ten, not five."

"I'll have to talk to my friend," Gervais said.

"Fair enough," Sidney replied.

Five days later Gervais called for another meeting, same place. "My friend will be with me," he informed Sidney.

"No way," Sidney said. "I don't want to know who he is, and I don't want him to know who I am."

"I can deal with that," Gervais said. They agreed on a time to meet.

At the restaurant Gervais told Sidney, "Five. That's the offer."

Sidney, his ice blue eyes flecked with black, gave Gervais a flinty look. "Can't be done for five."

Gervais returned Sidney's stare. Sidney wasn't going to budge on this. Gervais excused himself to call the friend. Five minutes later he eased into his chair across the table from Sidney. "Seven's as high as he'll go."

Sidney smiled. "Only made yourself three on that one, huh, Pershing?"

Gervais ordered rib eyes and got down to business—a photo of the subject, the location, and four grand up front. Gervais started to say something about a bad gambling debt, but Sidney held up his hand. "I got what I need," he said. The way Sidney felt, you played the game and you knew the odds, but he didn't want to know about any particular game. The two men closed the deal with a cup of coffee and went their separate ways.

Sidney filed the serial number off the gun the young character had traded for heroin. Then he called a friend. He gave this friend part of the money, and the job was done. Afterward Sidney buried the pistol in the woods behind the New Orleans airport, not far from where he and Rose Mary lived. He had no intention of digging it up again.

Norma's habit was to hide cash all over the house. Sometimes she put it in the pots and pans. If it wasn't a lot, she put it in an early American–style lamp, in a little well on one end of the lamp's arm that held metal rounds for balance. She took out some of the rounds and stuffed money down in the well. Another place was a huge vase in the hallway, underneath the bouquet of artificial flowers. She'd hid three thousand dollars in the vase, she thought, but now she couldn't find it. She called Jean's mother's, looking for Wayne.

When he called her back, she demanded, "Did you take the money that was in the vase?"

"Lord no, Norma, I didn't take your money," Wayne told her.

"It's gone. Unless I don't remember where I put it." Wayne told her he'd come help her look for it as soon as he got off work.

They tore up the house. Norma wondered if she wasn't losing her mind. Pulling at her hair, she told Wayne how bad she felt—physically, mentally, every way. She told him if she didn't start feeling better, she was just going to shoot herself.

The following weekend Rose Mary and Sidney arrived in a new car, secondhand but in good shape, a car that could easily have cost three thousand dollars. Sidney had told Rose Mary he bought it with the money he'd made from a little job on the side. She assumed he'd been selling drugs again.

When Wayne came to the house four or five days later, Norma said, "Well, I think I know where my three thousand dollars went. I don't like that guy. He's an ex-con and a thief. He hasn't been out of Angola long. I'm afraid of him."

She complained again about not feeling well. Wayne listened with half an ear, and Norma could tell. She said he'd be more sympathetic if he only knew how rough it was for her; she told him she'd been to the doctor and she had a blood clot in her leg. She really didn't know how much longer she could go on. She told Wayne again that she wanted to kill herself.

Wayne didn't believe her. It wasn't that she didn't have the guts—he didn't believe Norma was the type of person to kill herself. She was strong, and suicide was for weaklings. Besides, Norma had always loved life too much. Nevertheless, he didn't like the sound of it. He left the house and called Dutz Stouffert, who still worked for Norma, and told him next time he was there to be on the lookout for a gun.

Rose Mary and Sidney drove up the following Saturday, and Rose Mary immediately took little Sidney in to the bathroom. One of the parrots saw her and shrieked an obscenity. Rose Mary called, "Norma, you've got to get rid of those parrots!"

But Norma was outside, standing at the side of the car as Sidney peered under its hood. "Sidney," she said, "do you think you could get me a gun?" Her question surprised him. Not more than a month before he'd seen a real pretty gun, a brand-new pistol, in a box under her bed. But maybe that gun belonged to the young dude, her husband. Then Norma said, "I want one without a serial number."

Sidney wondered if Norma wanted to off her husband, the way she cried and carried on about him to Rose Mary. He didn't know Wayne, but the way he figured it, the dude was nothing but a stupid redneck, didn't know how to handle a good thing. When Norma bought him a Corvette, he traded it in for a pickup truck. Dumb. The kind of guy who would get eaten up in the fast lane. In Sidney's estimation Norma was one cool lady. It was nothing to him if she wanted to get rid of the guy. He'd even do it for her if she asked. For free. But she wasn't asking; she just wanted a gun.

"Sure," Sidney told her, "I can get one for you."

Later that week Sidney went out to the woods behind the airport.

That Thursday, Wayne decided to check on Norma after work. Dutz Stouffert had told him he'd looked through the house and found no handgun. Wayne couldn't have said why, but he didn't think Norma would kill herself with one of his guns, the shotguns and rifles on the rack in the living room. She was probably just talking anyway.

They spent a quiet evening together, and for once Wayne was in no hurry to leave. At one point Norma told him she'd changed her will, leaving her money and her half of the house to her nephew Johnny Badon. "Do whatever you want with your money, Norma," Wayne told her. His indifference was genuine and complete.

But he stayed with Norma that night. He fell asleep with his head in her lap. He woke up several times, surprised to find her wide awake, just looking at him. She smoothed his hair, stroked his forehead, and he went back to sleep. When he woke up in the morning, he told Norma he'd see her later and left.

The next day, Saturday, as he and Rose Mary got ready to go over to Bush, Sidney stuck the pistol down in the waistband of his pants. He knew Rose Mary wouldn't think anything of it; he usually carried a gun, a nine-millimeter automatic. She wouldn't notice that this was a different gun.

Little Sidney was fussy, running a low fever. Rose Mary decided to leave him with her mother. Sidney drove to his mother-in-law's first, then over to Bush. Norma seemed particularly upset that little Sidney wasn't with them that day.

As he walked in, Sidney laid the pistol on a small table to the right of the door. He caught Norma's eye when Rose Mary wasn't looking and nodded toward it. When he went into the kitchen, Norma slipped three hundred-dollar bills into the pocket of his shirt.

"The gun didn't cost me nothin, Norma," Sidney said.

"Go on," she told him, "keep it."

But Norma was in a mood that day—running around frantic, upset and crying about the young dude, pulling at her hair. Like a bitch in heat, Sidney thought. Hard into shooting heroin at the time, he told the women he was going over to Bogalusa to visit some friends. He was gone for a couple of hours.

After Sidney left Norma calmed down for a while. She used the phone a couple of times, then she and Rose Mary sat in the living room, Rose Mary in a chair, crocheting an afghan, Norma on the sofa, writing, taking care of some business.

"Where's your purse, Rose?" Norma asked after a while. Rose told her, and Norma got up to get it. "I'm putting this jewelry and some money in it." Rose Mary looked up to see her put her pearl brooch and some other pieces along with a wad of cash down in the purse. She wanted Rose Mary to put it all in her safe-deposit box on Monday. Rose Mary told her she would, and they fell silent again, Norma writing and Rose Mary hearing her tear a page from her tablet every so often.

Norma was writing several letters. One began, "Rose and Sidney, forgive me for giving you this trouble." It went on to ask them to contact Wayne at the trailer park in Bogalusa, followed by Jean's mother's Franklinton phone number.

Another letter was to Elise Rolling, a short note saying that she had tried to call, she just wanted to say goodbye.

The longest letter was to Wayne:

Wayne, I am so sorry to bring all this trouble on you and these people but I just cant go on any longer, when you walked out

that door Friday morning and said in such a cold voice see you
later Norma, I died you could have at least kissed me on my
forehead, I know you were fooling with Jean for some time
but had hoped you would come home, I was right the way it
turned out, you left me lying here with 101 fever and a blood
clot, I couldn't do that to a dog, the ten years didn't mean a
thing. Stay here in this house and take care of Rusty for my
sake and if you cant, put him to sleep, put all my cats and dogs
to sleep, give Rose Tippy as she loves her—you wanted your
freedom now you have it, all my friends have done everything
for me but I just cant go on, alone so much and carrying in
wood and I am sick, oh such a lone feeling only God knows,
Rusty and I could have gone on if you had moved me back to
N.O. you knew when I moved here you had met that girl, and
all you wanted was to leave me, you are entitled to your own
life and I hope it will be a happy one, you cant find a happy life
in bar rooms—

Now, please stay here and take care of Rusty.

In our old hiding place is some money for Rusty's food.

That day Norma had reconsidered her will and decided that she
wanted Wayne instead of her nephew to have her half of the house,
and that Rose Mary's and Sidney's signatures would witness this last
wish. She also wrote to Wayne that she wanted to be cremated.

Business taken care of, Norma's letter became thoughtful:

The last thing in my mind is I love you and your mothers last
words, dont be mean to Norma, remember me as the one person that wanted only the best for you.

But you seemed happy this last months with trash, you were a
wonderful husband to me for ten yrs. I am grateful for that,
Something just came in my mind,

Mourn not for what you have lost but be thankful instead for
what you have had

Norma

About the time that Norma finished her letters, Sidney returned from Bogalusa, still flying, but he knew he'd nod soon. He told Norma and Rose Mary that he thought he'd take a nap, but first Norma asked him and Rose Mary to witness something for her. She turned first one sheet, then another over, and he and Rose Mary signed their names twice. Then Sidney went off to the guest room.

Norma put the letters in envelopes, one marked "Rose," another "Elise Rolling." On a third envelope she wrote, "Wayne Bernard, Strictly personal." She thought a minute, then wrote the address of the trailer park above Wayne's name. She sealed the envelopes and, holding them up, said to Rose Mary, "Give these to Arthur de la Houssaye." She put them with Rose Mary's purse.

Rose Mary was used to signing things for Norma and taking papers to the lawyer's. She thought nothing of it. For the moment, at least, Norma seemed calm, saying she was going to call Pershing Gervais, she had a few things to talk to him about. Rose Mary continued working on her afghan. She saw Norma pick up a small pillow from the sofa and walk over toward the door. Norma stood by the little table a moment, then she turned and went into the kitchen, closing the door behind her. After a minute or two, Rose Mary heard her on the phone, crying.

Norma had called Elise and Bubba Rolling's number. She let it ring and ring, but there was no answer. That Saturday afternoon Elise had gone to work to catch up on a few things. Bubba was outside with his roosters. He didn't hear the phone.

Next Norma called Pershing Gervais. He answered, and when he heard her crying, he asked her if Rose Mary was there. She said yes, she was, and he told Norma to go talk to her and Sidney.

Norma, in despair, called one more number. It belonged to her sister-in-law, Sarah Huff. Sarah and her second husband, Gus, were at home that afternoon, doing a few domestic chores. Sarah had put an Engelbert Humperdinck record on the stereo, a record Norma had given her. Gus was up in the attic. When Sarah answered the phone, Norma told her without preamble that she was going to kill herself.

"Oh, no, Norma, don't do that," Sarah said. "Look, I'm coming over right now. Gus and I are coming over."

"I told you I'm gonna do it and I am," Norma said, and then she fired the gun, getting off two shots—one entered her head, another went up into the kitchen ceiling.

Sarah heard the gun go off, then she heard the phone hit the counter, and she started screaming for her husband.

Rose Mary heard the shots and was on her feet, tripping over the afghan to get to the kitchen. She pushed open the door and couldn't take in what she saw. Norma was on the floor. There was a lot of blood. She rushed to her. She started to cross over her to get to Sidney.

But Sidney heard the shots and leapt out of bed. He came through the hall into the kitchen, and as soon as Rose Mary saw him, she took off running, through the front yard and out to the road.

Norma still had the pistol in her hand. Sidney didn't touch it, but he saw the small sofa pillow, and he put it under Norma's head. The gun fell from her hand. She was still alive, wheezing hard, one arm waving, the other side apparently paralyzed, because she was looking at him with only her right eye. He looked back at her long enough for that image to be imprinted on him forever before he turned away to call the ambulance.

When Rose Mary saw the car on Dad Penton Road, she started screaming that her aunt had been shot. The Sun sheriff's deputies brought her back to the house. Rose Mary gave the deputies the letters, and when the ambulance arrived she got in it with Norma.

Norma opened her right eye, and Rose Mary cried, telling her, "I'll take care of you, Norma." But Norma, groaning as if to tell Rose Mary to help her, kept trying to rip the oxygen mask from her face. The ambulance made a sharp turn, and Norma rolled toward Rose Mary. Rose Mary thought the whole side of her head had been blown off.

At the hospital Rose Mary passed out for a while. When she awoke she was clutching a bag with Norma's bloody clothes in it— the beautiful red pantsuit they'd cut off her body and the shoes with Rusty's hair all over the soles. Rose Mary's purse with Norma's jewelry and money in it was gone.

CHAPTER TWENTY TWO

The Last Word

A knock on the trailer door interrupted Wayne's quiet Saturday afternoon. He was surprised to see Jean's sister. Marsha had driven over to tell him that the police had called and wanted Wayne to come to the house of his estranged wife. She didn't know why.

Wayne drove the fifteen miles from Bogalusa to Bush in a state of dread, trying to keep a rein on his imagination. Once he was on Dad Penton Road, he slowed enough to navigate the sharp turns, then bumped his yellow El Camino across the cattle guard onto the property.

Norma's two-tone blue Gran Torino was pulled up in the gravel driveway, no police or police cars in sight. Wayne parked a couple of car lengths behind the Torino. He stood with the door to his truck open and listened to the ominous silence. Then a blur of dark red caught his eye on the other side of the front yard. Rusty, their Irish setter, bounded from the honeysuckle and azaleas and raced toward him, twigs flying and leaves fluttering in the whirlwind. Norma didn't usually let Rusty roam without her.

With the dog Wayne walked around the house. The side door was wide open, strange because of the chill in the air, strange because Norma didn't use that door much. He went around back and crossed the patio to the kitchen door. It too was open.

Wayne went into the kitchen and practically walked into a pool of blood. He didn't think; he mechanically skirted it to the bathroom, got a couple of large bath towels, and wiped it up. He called Rusty in, closed up the house, and drove to the St. Tammany Hospital. There he was told that his wife had been transported by ambulance across Lake Pontchartrain to the Ochsner Foundation Hospital in New Orleans, with a gunshot wound to the head. When Wayne arrived at Ochsner, Norma was in surgery. She died less than an hour later—at 5:07 p.m., December 14, 1974.

When Wayne arrived at Ochsner and saw Sarah, he fell to his knees and buried his head in her lap, holding her so tightly that she was finally forced to tell him he was hurting her. He went home that night with Sarah and Gus.

When Norma's ashes were returned from the crematorium two days later, Sarah took on the task of disposing of them. Norma had told her that she wanted to be cremated and her ashes spread along the streets of the French Quarter. But Sarah hated the French Quarter after having worked Elmo's clubs for so many years. She told Wayne she wouldn't put Norma's ashes downtown. Wayne gave Sarah no argument when she suggested that they take the ashes to Lake Pontchartrain, even though he knew Norma hated water.

Sarah turned the urn over and let Norma's ashes fall into the choppy water. As she did so, she thought to herself, Poor thing, she don't know, but the fishes will be eating her pretty soon.

Upstairs in the house in Bush is a room filled with Norma's things. Her four-poster bed from Waggaman is there, along with her mahogany dresser and its matching mirror, a boudoir chair left over from Conti Street, a small antique drop-leaf table from her family, and a sliding-door rattan cabinet. Some of the dresser drawers are still lined with the flowered paper Norma put in them. In one is a heavy gold-tone metal belt, part of the costume she wore to a gay Mardi Gras ball; in another is a hairbrush, strands of Norma's white hair still tangled in its bristles.

A couple of years ago some of Jean's relatives came to spend Halloween weekend with the Bernards. One of the women spent the night in Norma's bed upstairs. It was an unseasonably warm Halloween night, but in the middle of it, the woman woke up shivering and aware of a most unpleasant odor. She slept fitfully for the next few hours, huddling beneath the light blanket on the bed, covering her nose with it to block the smell. In the morning she told Wayne and Jean about her strange night.

Wayne laughed. "Well," he said, "you were sleeping with your head just a few inches from the urn that Norma's ashes were in." Not knowing what else to do with the urn and unable to part with it, he had sealed it in the wall behind the bed.

A couple of months after Norma's death, Wayne and Jean got back together, and Jean went to live in the house in Bush with her two sons, Jim and Darby; that was when Wayne decided he needed to do something with the urn.

Even with Norma gone, Wayne and Jean's relationship was rocky, and Jean returned more than once to Franklinton, thinking she should end things with him. But Wayne and her older son, Jim, who had never known his father, had formed an attachment by then. "I was doing what a man my age should have been doing," Wayne said of that time. "I had a son." Jean and her sons had helped get Wayne back into ordinary life. When Wayne and Jean married a couple of months later, he adopted Jim.

But even for a while after they were married, Jean wasn't sure that they would make it. She began to get superstitious. In their bedroom she thought she could see Norma's face where two knotholes formed eyes, and other markings in the blond paneling created an oval face and waves of hair, like Norma's. She tried hanging pictures over the spot, but she always felt weirdly compelled to take them down. She thought Norma had put a jinx on her and Wayne, to keep them from staying together.

Not only that, Norma's old dog, Rusty, had an overwhelming dislike of Jean. He wouldn't go near her, and he snapped at her a couple of times; at night when she and Wayne tried to go to bed, Rusty would sit in the middle of the bed and growl. Jean thought Norma's spirit had taken over the animal.

But it wasn't Jean that Rusty finally went after; it was her younger son. Rusty bit Darby in the face, an unforgivable act in Wayne's eyes. He shot the dog.

Norma's rival hadn't been just a younger woman; it had been children. Norma had never wanted children; she'd always said her animals were her children.

When Wayne first left Norma, he wanted to go wild. He wondered if Norma had felt as smothered in her marriage to Charles McCoy as he'd come to feel in his marriage to her. But as strong as his need had been to break free, when Snapbean, whose heart was broken over Norma's death, cried and wouldn't speak to Wayne for some time, it brought Wayne's guilt into sharp focus. Bubba saw what his nephew was going through and told him he was lucky Norma hadn't killed him that Thursday night he'd spent on the sofa with her. "It's the kind of thing people do," Bubba said, having seen it enough times during his years as a cop.

But Wayne felt completely responsible. He had returned to the Bush house to find Rusty curled up on Norma's robe at the foot of her bed. He mourned with the dog. He thought that if he had only done things differently, if he'd really believed her when she said she was going to kill herself, if they'd never gone to Mississippi in the first place, none of this would have happened. He blamed himself for being nothing but an old country boy who couldn't see that he should have taken more of a role at the restaurant, gotten into the business end of it so that all Norma would have had to do was get dressed up in her fabulous dresses every night and tell her stories. He blamed himself for not moving her to New Orleans, getting her back to friends, to a life of her own to grow old. He blamed his own passive nature, going back in time as if to will it away and make room for other possibilities.

In the end, though, character is destiny. Wayne's passive nature was perfect for Norma's need to be dominant and in control, and his indifference both frustrated Norma and made him more desirable to her—a deadly combination.

When Norma told her sister-in-law that she needed to get rid of Wayne, that he was too young, part of her was speaking to self-preservation. But the matter was far too complicated, because from the start she'd wanted Wayne in her life for exactly that—self-preservation. Wayne had enhanced her image; his presence had kept her from facing up to the fact that she was aging.

Norma came of age in the 1920s, when for the first time in American history youth-oriented culture prevailed. She was a woman ahead of her times in many ways and one in a profession that capitalized on youth, beauty, and sensuality. Norma wanted to remain young and sexy at any cost. When she married Wayne, a man young enough to be her grandson, she was proud of her achievement. What she didn't see was that this pride would overcome her.

When Norma was a girl, Mr. McCann, her parents' tenant, committed suicide by drinking carbolic acid; her own mother had tried to kill herself many times. But in the underworld, to which Norma escaped, you never waited until you were cornered. "You jump the gun," she told Wayne. "Do it to them first, never lay back and wait. That's kept me rolling for many years. It cost me here and there, but I'm still going, and I'm the last one that had a big, open house, girls actually living in it."

That was a good philosophy for life in the underworld, and Norma carried it into her marriages as well. She borrowed money, put it in Wayne's name, and gave him no access to it; she wrote him a paycheck that she put back into her business. She was always covering herself.

Norma denied that she was suited for marriage at all, yet she married five times. Her husbands, by and large, were respectable men; Pete Herman was the only one with ties to the underworld, but, because of his boxing titles, the establishment and law enforcement looked the other way. Norma wanted the respectability marriage gave her, and she needed a man to love her, but she didn't want the traditional roles that marriage forced upon women, domesticity and motherhood. With one foot in the world of respectability and one in the underworld, Norma was in the same conflict between love and work that, at the time of her death, more and more women were having to face.

Norma identified strongly with her masculine side. She knew how to make money, vast sums of it, both legitimately and illegitimately, during a time when most women were not concerned with making money and very few had any real moneymaking capabilities. She wanted the kind of power a man had with his associates. Her associates were policemen and underworld figures, and she wielded considerable power with them.

But the most intriguing aspect of Norma's desire for power revolved around sexual power. She wanted total control over her marriages as well as the freedom to have affairs. "I want to be free," she said, "like a man." She cheated on her husbands, left one for another, liked to go to bed with young men, wanted a young man to take her arm. She had said of Charles McCoy, "He was young and beautiful, of course; I was susceptible to young and beautiful people." In the end, though, the one man she never cheated on, the youngest of them all, left her for another woman. The one time she should have jumped the gun and been the first to leave, she found herself powerless.

When Norma opened the Tchoupitoulas Plantation Restaurant to crowds and acclaim, she turned infamy into fame. When she was honored at the Press Club after making the cover of *New Orleans* magazine, her notoriety became celebrity. When she accepted the key to the city, she seemed like any other legitimate businesswoman, beloved and respected for her achievements.

New Orleans, with its European heritage and sensibility, has always had a large tolerance for sins of the flesh. More than just a predominantly French or Spanish ancestry, though, came to bear on this tolerant attitude: The mostly male populace of the old colony was concerned with a much more practical consideration—the shortage of women. While prostitution undoubtedly ruined many poor girls, it provided opportunity for others, as it did for Norma, a way to make more money than in any other occupation open to women, or a path to a more traditional way of life, either marriage or legitimate enterprise. So many women wanted to avail themselves of this opportunity that, by the late nineteenth century, no thought was given to eradicating prostitution, the effort was only to contain it, and thus Storyville came into existence.

Storyville's fame and the enduring romance associated with it make it easy to forget that the area had a very short life, less than twenty years, in the history of one of the oldest cities in the country. The openness of the red-light district obscures the fact that unpopular, repressive laws also existed and were in part responsible for the city's developing certain salient characteristics that earned it the name Sin City and gave it its reputation for corruption.

While New Orleans was still a colony with a shortage of women, white women specifically, free women of color were legally prohibited from engaging in sexual relations with white men. This led the Creole men to institute a custom of their own, the secret system of *plaçage,* in which they kept free women of color as their mistresses or actually set up second households with them in close proximity to their legitimate families. This custom was practiced clandestinely, but it was a "public secret," getting a nod from the clergy while the law looked the other way.

Because of such laws and the customs that rose from them, New Orleanians developed an exotic, secretive way of life and a romance with the underworld, much as what happened during Prohibition, when bootleggers and gangsters were seen as romantic individualists.

Early on in the city's history, American visitors found the way of life in New Orleans foreign and some of the residents, with their European habits, like keeping taverns open on Sundays, shocking. They viewed the city as rife with sin and corruption. New Orleanians liked the reputation, and they liked to tell stories about themselves. After all, New Orleans is a river city that was the last stop on many hard journeys. It was always (and still is) a place to disembark, get a drink, find a card game, have a good fight, and go off with a woman. Even as businessmen and politicians were trying to drag New Orleans out of the Old World and turn it into a progressive American city, the wide open aspect of the city throughout the first half of the twentieth century acquired mythic proportions, and legends about loose women, strong drink, and corrupt politicians proliferated.

New Orleanians like nothing better than exploiting their own myths and legends, though the times have changed and the city is not as open as it once was. In an uneasy alliance with the media, politicians and city administrators clamor for its attention and, at the same time, accuse it of sensationalism and invasion of privacy. A house like Norma's could never be the "public secret" it once was. Now the news broadcasts incidents of policemen taking payoffs from operations masked as massage parlors and escort services, and New Orleans vice becomes the subject of national television newsmagazine shows.

With the scrutiny comes a feeling of loss, perhaps a loss of innocence, when cheap operations promote sex and pornography, and call girls, alone and vulnerable, work the streets, and houses like Norma's—opulent and protected places to conduct rites of passage—are gone. It's as if only the outsider, the tourist, can see the city as it once was: read or hear the myths and legends; wander the streets to see where the stories happened; witness Sin City on six blocks of Bourbon Street. If you come to town and expect it, you will find it. Because even with New Orleans as shut down as it has ever been, the residents are still more tolerant than in most places, and they revel in the past; they have a boastful attitude about New Orleans and a belief that it is, indeed, a wicked city.

"I look back on it all and wonder how I ever did it," Norma said, "but in those days there was so much going on, so much excitement, things happened and you lived with it. Running a house was always a strain, always trouble. But it was never dull. I used to wake up around noon and have my coffee and wonder what this night will bring.

"Things are so different now in the French Quarter. I don't like the idea of the hippies lying around on the sidewalk. I saw one the other day exposing everything. I remember the time a man peed in my alley and they took him down and fined him fifty dollars. The other day, they were peeing right in front of us in Jackson Square. I don't like that. But I don't actually object to the hippies, because I understand their way of life. They don't want to wind up with a two-car garage and struggling for thirty years with the mortgage on the house. I understand how they feel.

"And girls were more beautiful then than they are now. Maybe it was because they knew how to wear clothes. Girls have typed themselves now, with long hair, miniskirts, and blue jeans. In those days girls all had individuality, because they wore their hair differently, dressed differently, and they loved to dress.

"As for abolishing prostitution—what's better, to have a nice, clean, sanitary house, or what is going on in the Quarter today, fornicating in the square, parks, everywhere for everybody to see? And don't think for a minute that every man who visited a house was only interested in a quick screw. Many of them desperately craved companionship. In some cases, houses took the strain off marriages. I know for a fact that some women were glad to be let off sexual obligations. Just because a man goes discreetly to a house doesn't mean the marriage is shattered.

"But the women libbers are all running around saying women are prostituting themselves keeping house, having babies. And here's the deal—women get married for one thing, security. They sell it to one man for the rent, food, clothes. When you look at it that way, hookers get more for what they sell. If I was still in the business, though, I'd probably be sending one of those lady liberation groups a check every month. Any landlady will tell you bossy broads will sure send her a lot of customers.

"And as dirty, crummy as the French Quarter is today, I still love it. I loved it then because it was good to me; it represented a life I enjoyed. I was very happy there all those years. Yes, it's dirty and people knock it, and when people knock it, it hurts me.

"The Quarter, you don't know what it does to me. When I'm there and I have to leave it, I feel a lump comes here . . .

"Maybe I shouldn't say this, but every now and then around about seven in the evening, that bell rings in my head. I still miss the action.

"You know, in another life, under other circumstances, I might have been a captain of industry. What the hell—maybe I was."

Bibliographical Note

The most important source for the writing of *The Last Madam* was Norma Wallace's memoirs, which she taped during the last two years of her life. Being able to hear her voice, her laugh, her inflections, and her accent gave me a sense of the woman that added aspects of her personality and emotional depth that otherwise would have been missing from my story of her life.

The profiles of Norma Wallace by Clint Bolton (*New Orleans,* June 1972) and Howard Jacobs (*The Times-Picayune,* June 30 and July 1, 1974) were invaluable addenda to the memoirs. Bolton's article gave a telling glimpse of Wallace's early life, and the original draft of his interview with her provided additional material. Jacobs, in his inimitable style, covered Wallace's working life and love life concisely and comically, and he elicited some of her most colorful quotes.

Louis Andrew Vyhanck's dissertation, *The Seamier Side of Life: Criminal Activity in New Orleans During the 1920s* (Ann Arbor, Mich.: University Microfilms, 1979), animated the era and the street life of the city during Norma Wallace's first working decade, and enhanced her descriptions enormously.

Other vivid writing about that era was done by John Magill, a curator at the Historic New Orleans Collection, in two essays, "Welcome

Old Man Gloom," about Prohibition in old New Orleans, which was legend for its consumption of alcohol, and "The Dance Craze," about the city's obsession with the dance that named the infamous Tango Belt. Both essays appeared in *The Historic New Orleans Collection Quarterly* (vol. 6, no. 3, Summer 1988; and vol. 10, no. 4, Fall 1992, respectively).

Rosemary James's articles about Pershing Gervais and Jim Garrison, which appeared in *New Orleans* magazine during the 1970s, and *Figaro,* a New Orleans weekly published in the seventies, brought to life two New Orleans characters who acted on the city and changed it, as well as the course of Norma Wallace's life.

J. A. Walker's nostalgic story, "Gaspar Gulotta—The Little Mayor of Bourbon Street" (*New Orleans,* May 1971), gave a lively look at the nightclub proprietor and cigar-smoking brother of prizefighter Pete Herman, and offered a tantalizing excerpt from the Special Citizens Investigating Committee report. The fourth volume of the report, *Prostitution* (April 1954), the transcriptions of the testimony linking police to prostitution, showed the close connections between the law and "the life" and was filled with vivid details and events.

Political works that informed the writing of this book were Edward Haas's important book, *DeLesseps S. Morrison and the Image of Reform: New Orleans Politics, 1946–1961* (Baton Rouge: Louisiana State University Press, 1974), a compelling and highly readable portrait of the man and his times; *Silk Stockings and Ballot Boxes: Women and Politics in New Orleans, 1920–1963* by Pamela Tyler (Athens: University of Georgia Press, 1996), which shows the influence and power of women—in politics, in New Orleans, in the world; and Garry Boulard's *Huey Long Invades New Orleans: The Siege of a City, 1934–36* (Gretna, La.: Pelican Publishing, 1998), a superb look at the Kingfish, both the man and the politician, and an evocative portrait of the city in the thirties.

Other essential reading included Al Rose's indispensable and classic work, *Storyville, New Orleans* (Tuscaloosa: University of Alabama Press, 1974); Herbert Asbury's *The French Quarter: An Informal History of the New Orleans Underworld* (New York: Alfred A. Knopf, 1936), an imaginative rendering of crime and street life in New Orleans before Storyville; Robert Tallant's descriptive look at life and people in this unique city, *The Romantic New Orleanians* (New York: E. P. Dutton, 1950); and Mel Leavitt's *A Short History of New Orleans* (San Francisco: Lexikos, 1982), a deft and delightful chronicle of the city.

To these writers and their masterful works, I am deeply indebted.

Acknowledgments

Many people gave freely of their time and memories while I was writing this book. Wayne Bernard's account of his life with Norma Wallace was essential, as was the belief of his wife, Jean, that Norma's story should be told. I thank them and the following people, who told their stories about Norma and her times: Sam Adams, Johnny and Pat Badon, Frank Bertucci, Major Albert Cromp, John H. Datri, Francis Davis, Marie Delouise, Richard "Jack" Dempsey, Pete Fountain, Robert Norman Frey, Charles Gennaro, Joseph I. Giarrusso, Sarah Huff, Rosemary James, Captain J. D. Jarrell, Edgar McGeehee, Nick Macheca, Sandy Margiotta, Rose Mary Miorana (who generously lent me the letters Norma wrote to her as well), Helen Moran, Paul Nazar, Barbara Price, Alice Regan, J. Cornelius Rathborne III, Suzanne Robbins, Earl and Elise Rolling, Janice Roussel, Sidney Scallan, Earl Scramuzza, Patsy Sims, Frederick Soulé, and Kathryn Swartwood.

Many thanks to Elaine Newton, who was a skip tracer in a former life and located many people who had been friends and associates of Norma. Her role as detective played a large part in uncovering and demystifying the story of Norma Wallace.

Thanks, also, to Marion Tanner, Nancy Gore, and Noah Robert, who helped find the writer.

Others whose help with finding secondary sources, locating information, and making connections was invaluable are Allain C. Andry III, Phil Anselmo, Joe Arrigo, Bob Bass, Jason Berry, Tony Buonagura, Chris Bynum, Nancy Dibelka, Susan Finch, Frank Gagnard, Beverly Gianna (Director of Public Relations, The New Orleans Metropolitan Convention and Visitors Bureau), Betty Guillaud, Leonard Gurvich, Rudolph Holzer, Hillary Irvin, Scott Jefferson, Allen Johnson, Mary Allen Johnson, Regina Kramer (curator of the Phil Harris–Alice Faye Collection in Linton, Indiana), Steve Lacy, Susan Larson, Melanie McKay, Valerie Martin, Chief Jimmy Miller, Randy Moses, Lester Otillio, Earl Perry, Diana Pinckley, John Pope, Joann Price, Lee Pryor, Bryce Reveley, Gail Ruddock, Tom Rushing, Julie Smith, Jack Stewart, Ronnie Virgets, Charles Watson, Lanier Watson, and Helen Wisdom.

I would also like to thank the Historic New Orleans Collection, especially curator John Magill and reference librarian Pamela Arceneaux; the New Orleans Public Library, especially Wayne Everard and Irene Wainwright in the Louisiana Division, and the librarians at the Nix branch; and the Tulane University Library, especially Joan G. Caldwell, head of the Louisiana Collection.

A very special thanks to my researcher extraordinaire, Noel A. Ponthieux, who also acted as a detective and got the goods on the elusive madam, her associates, and her adversaries.

Others to whom I am indebted for seeing this book through are my editor, Paul Elie, who set me free; Dan Weaver, who took a chance; and my agent, Jonathan Dolger, who knew.

I am very appreciative of the cheering section, otherwise known as my daughter, Marigny Pecot, and most of all, I thank my husband, Joe Pecot, who listened.